LIBRARY OF HEBREW BIBLE/
OLD TESTAMENT STUDIES

706

Formerly Journal for the Study of the Old Testament Supplement Series

Editors
Claudia V. Camp, Texas Christian University, USA
Andrew Mein, Durham University, UK

Founding Editors
David J. A. Clines, Philip R. Davies and David M. Gunn

Editorial Board
Alan Cooper, Susan Gillingham, John Goldingay,
Norman K. Gottwald, James E. Harding, John Jarick, Carol Meyers,
Daniel L. Smith-Christopher, Francesca Stavrakopoulou,
James W. Watts

SOCIAL IDENTITY AND THE BOOK OF AMOS

Andrew M. King

t&tclark
LONDON • NEW YORK • OXFORD • NEW DELHI • SYDNEY

T&T CLARK

Bloomsbury Publishing Plc

50 Bedford Square, London, WC1B 3DP, UK
1385 Broadway, New York, NY 10018, USA
29 Earlsfort Terrace, Dublin 2, Ireland

BLOOMSBURY, T&T CLARK and the T&T Clark logo
are trademarks of Bloomsbury Publishing Plc

First published in Great Britain 2021
This paperback edition published in 2022

Copyright © Andrew M. King, 2021

Andrew M. King has asserted his right under the Copyright, Designs and Patents Act, 1988, to be identified as Author of this work.

Cover design: Charlotte James
Cover image © Vince Cavataio/Getty Images

For legal purposes the Acknowledgements on p. ix constitute an extension of this copyright page.

All rights reserved. No part of this publication may be reproduced or transmitted in any form or by any means, electronic or mechanical, including photocopying, recording, or any information storage or retrieval system, without prior permission in writing from the publishers.

Bloomsbury Publishing Plc does not have any control over, or responsibility for, any third-party websites referred to or in this book. All internet addresses given in this book were correct at the time of going to press. The author and publisher regret any inconvenience caused if addresses have changed or sites have ceased to exist, but can accept no responsibility for any such changes.

A catalogue record for this book is available from the British Library.

Library of Congress Control Number: 2019956638.

ISBN: HB: 978-0-5676-9529-1
PB: 978-0-5676-9841-4
ePDF: 978-0-5676-9530-7

Series: Library of Hebrew Bible/Old Testament Studies, ISSN 2513-8758, volume 706

Typeset by: Trans.form.ed SAS

To find out more about our authors and books visit www.bloomsbury.com
and sign up for our newsletters.

For Lauren, Naomi, Ben, Ezra, and Judah

Contents

Acknowledgments	ix
Abbreviations	xi

Chapter 1
INTRODUCTION 1

Chapter 2
THE SOCIAL IDENTITY APPROACH 8
  Social Identity 8
  An Outline of the Social Identity Approach 10
    Beginnings of the Social Identity Approach 10
    Social Identity Theory 12
    Self-Categorization Theory 17
    Texts and Identity 23
    Application in Hebrew Bible Studies 25
  Conclusion 30

Chapter 3
THE PEOPLE OF GOD IN AMOS:
THE PROPHET AND PROTOTYPICALITY 31
  Intergroup Conflict from a Social Identity Perspective 31
  Oracles Against the Nations (Amos 1:3–2:16) 35
  The Confrontation at Bethel (Amos 7:10-17) 45
    Amaziah's Complaint (7:10-11) 47
    Amaziah's Address (7:12-13) 49
    Amos's Response (7:14-17) 54
  Conclusion 65

Chapter 4
HISTORY AND SOCIAL IDENTITY IN AMOS 66
  Social Memory 68
  The Past in Amos 71
    2:9-12 73
    3:1-2 74
    4:6-11 79

5:25-26	86
9:7	94
Conclusion	100

Chapter 5
ESCHATOLOGY AND SOCIAL IDENTITY IN AMOS 101
    The Day of YHWH Motif 102
    The Remnant Motif 109
    The Restoration of Israel 117
    The Future and Identity-Formation 119
    Conclusion 121

Chapter 6
CONCLUSION 123

Bibliography 128
Index of References 149
Index of Authors 153

Acknowledgments

In addition to Amos, this is a book about how our social group memberships shape our sense of self. My own identity formation owes to countless individuals both personal and professional. I would like to thank my doctoral supervisor Duane Garrett for his supernatural patience and wisdom in guiding an earlier version of this work. Many others read and offered valuable feedback along the way, among whom Daniel Carroll, Stephen Dempster, Daniel Timmer, Jarvis Williams, and Shane Parker deserve particular mention. This work also has been sharpened by conversations with Chris Porter, Peter Lau, Brian Tucker, and other members of the New Testament Social Scientific Commentary group at SBL. Several of my students were invaluable in the preparation of the manuscript. I would like to thank Drake Burrows, Janelle Bailey, Keith James, and Lance English for their careful attention.

I would also like to thank the leadership, faculty, staff, and students of Midwestern Baptist Theological Seminary and Spurgeon College, who have provided great encouragement and support. My parents, Michael and Darlene King, and my two brothers, C.J. and Adam, have walked with me through every step of this journey. I am deeply grateful for their steadfastness. Finally, I am thankful for my wife, Lauren, and our four children, Naomi, Benaiah, Ezra, and Judah. They are the greatest joy in my life. The completion of this project was made possible only through their ceaseless love and support. Dedicating this book to them is the smallest token of my gratitude.

Andrew M. King
Kansas City, MO
Spring 2020

ABBREVIATIONS

AB	Anchor Bible
ABD	D. N. Freedman, ed., *Anchor Bible Dictionary*. 6 vols. New York, 1992
ANE	Ancient Near East
ANEM	Ancient Near East Monographs
AUM	Andrews University Monographs
AUSS	*Andrews University Seminary Studies*
AYB	Anchor Yale Bible Commentaries
BASOR	*Bulletin of the American Schools of Oriental Research*
BASP	*Basic and Applied Social Psychology*
BBR	*Bulletin for Biblical Research*
BBRSup	Bulletin for Biblical Research, Supplements
BCAT	Biblischer Commentar über das Alte Testament
BDB	F. Brown, S. R. Driver and C. A. Briggs, *Hebrew and English Lexicon.* Oxford, 1907
BHHB	Baylor Handbook on the Hebrew Bible
Bib	*Biblica*
BibInt	*Biblical Interpretation*
BJPS	*British Journal for the Philosophy of Science*
BJSCP	*British Journal of Social and Clinical Psychology*
BJSP	*British Journal of Social Psychology*
BP	*Bulletin de Psychologie*
BSac	*Bibliotheca Sacra*
BT	*Bible Translator*
BTA	Bible and Theology in Africa
BTB	*Biblical Theology Bulletin*
BZAW	Beihefte zur Zeitschrift für die alttestamentliche Wissenschaft
CBQ	*Catholic Biblical Quarterly*
CBQMS	Catholic Biblical Quarterly Monograph Series
CBR	*Currents in Biblical Research*
CBSC	Cambridge Bible for Schools and Colleges
CC	Concordia Commentary
CRBS	*Currents in Research: Biblical Studies*
DOTP	M. J. Boda and J. G. McConville, eds. *Dictionary of the Old Testament Prophets*. Downers Grove, IL, 2012
EJSP	*European Journal of Social Psychology*
ESSP	European Studies in Social Psychology
EvT	*Evangelische Theologie*

ExpTim	*Expository Times*
FAT	Forschungen zum Alten Testament
HBT	*Horizons in Biblical Theology*
HUCA	*Hebrew Union College Annual*
ICC	International Critical Commentary
Int	*Interpretation*
JASP	*Journal of Abnormal and Social Psychology*
JBL	*Journal of Biblical Literature*
JBQ	*Jewish Bible Quarterly*
JESOT	*Journal for the Evangelical Study of the Old Testament*
JESP	*Journal of Experimental Social Psychology*
JETS	*Journal of the Evangelical Theological Society*
JNES	*Journal of the Ancient Near Eastern Society*
JPSP	*Journal of Personality & Social Psychology*
JSI	*Journal of Social Issues*
JSNTSup	Journal for the Study of the New Testament Supplement Series
JSOT	*Journal for the Study of the Old Testament*
JSOTSup	Journal for the Study of the Old Testament Supplement Series
LHBOTS	Library of Hebrew Bible/Old Testament Studies
LNTS	The Library of New Testament Studies
LXX	Septuagint
NAC	New American Commentary
NTOA	Novum Testamentum et Orbis Antiquus
OAN	Oracles against the Nations
OBT	Overtures to Biblical Theology
OTL	Old Testament Library
OtSt	*Oudtestamentische studiën*
OTWSA	*Die Outestamentiese Werkgemeenskap in Suid-Afrika*
RB	*Revue Biblique*
SBLDS	Society of Biblical Literature Dissertation Series
SBLMS	Society of Biblical Literature Monograph Series
SJT	*Scottish Journal of Theology*
SSI	*Social Science Information*
StBibLit	Studies in Biblical Literature (Lang)
STDJ	Studies in the Texts of the Desert of Judah
SUNT	Studien zur Umwelt des Neuen Testaments
TOTC	Tyndale Old Testament Commentary
TynBul	*Tyndale Bulletin*
TZ	Theologische Zeitschrift
WBC	Word Biblical Commentary
VT	*Vetus Testamentum*
VTSup	Supplements to Vetus Testamentum
WTJ	*Westminster Theological Journal*
WUNT	Wissenschaftliche Untersuchungen zum Neuen Testament
ZAW	Zeitschrift für die alttestamentliche Wissenschaft
ZTK	Zeitschrift für Theologie und Kirche

Chapter 1

Introduction

Human beings are social creatures. A cursory look at our world reveals countless subdivisions along ideological, cultural, and ethnic lines. The formation of social groups, necessitating group boundaries, allows group members to negotiate who they are. This sense of meaning is often framed in terms of opposition: "we" are distinct from "them." Though the expression of this opposition may be benign, there are countless historical examples of group differentiation that portend hostility and violence.[1] In either case, these groups provide an interpretation of the world for their members. Among the various means of identity formation for group members is the use of texts.[2] Authors can construct and embed a sense of identity for posterity. Though long dead, they can tell group members who they are and who they should be. This book explores the social identity construct embedded in one text from the Hebrew Bible, namely the book of Amos.

There is certainly no famine for words on the book of Amos. Already in 1959, James L. Mays could say,

> [Amos] has had more than his proportionate share of scholarly attention and Amos-studies are already on the way to becoming a small library on their own. The reason for this prodigious output is not far to seek. Amos is the first of the writing prophets, and so the point of departure for the study of the prophetic movement and its literature. His book is the testing ground for every thesis about the nature of prophecy and its developing history.[3]

---

1. See, for example, Neil Ferguson and Shelley McKeown, "Social Identity Theory and Intergroup Conflict in Northern Ireland," in *Understanding Peace and Conflict through Social Identity Theory: Contemporary Global Perspectives*, ed. S. McKeown, R. Haji, and N. Ferguson (New York: Springer, 2016), 215–27.
2. See Chapter 2.
3. James Luther Mays, "Words about the Words of Amos: Recent Study of the Book of Amos," *Int* 13, no. 3 (1959): 259. More recent bibliographies continue to

Amos has been mined with an eye towards questions of composition and redaction, both as an individual book and as part of the Book of the Twelve (Minor Prophets),[4] for its contribution to socio-historical reconstructions,[5] for its implications for ethics and issues of social justice,[6]

show the outward expansion of the trend. See Adrian van der Wal, *Amos: A Classified Bibliography*, 3rd ed. (Amsterdam: Free University Press, 1986); G. F. Hasel, *Understanding the Book of Amos: Basic Issues in Current Interpretations* (Grand Rapids: Baker, 1991); Henry O. Thompson, *The Book of Amos: An Annotated Bibliography*, ATLA Bibliographies 42 (Lanham, MD: Scarecrow, 1997); Roy F. Melugin, "Amos in Recent Research," *CRBS* 6 (1998): 65–101; M. Daniel Carroll R., *Amos, the Prophet and His Oracles: Research on the Book of Amos* (Louisville, KY: Westminster John Knox, 2002).

4. In addition to the commentaries, examples include Tchavdar S. Hadjiev, *The Composition and Redaction of the Book of Amos* (Berlin: de Gruyter, 2009); Marc Zvi Brettler, "Redaction, History, and Redaction-History of Amos in Recent Scholarship," in *Israel's Prophets and Israel's Past: Essays on the Relationship of Prophetic Texts and Israelite History in Honor of John H. Hayes*, ed. Brad E. Kelle and Megan Bishop Moore (New York: T&T Clark, 2006), 103–12; Aaron Schart, *Die Entstehung des Zwölfprophetenbuchs: Neubearbeitungen von Amos im Rahmen schriftenübergreifender Redaktionsprozesse*, BZAW 260 (Berlin: de Gruyter, 1998); Dirk U. Rottzoll, *Studien zur Redaktion und Komposition des Amosbuchs*, BZAW 243 (Berlin: de Gruyter, 1996).

5. Walter J. Houston, "Was There a Social Crisis in the Eighth Century?" in *In Search of Pre-Exilic Israel*, ed. John Day, JSOTSup 406 (London: T&T Clark, 2004), 130–49; J. Andrew Dearman, *Property Rights in the Eighth-Century Prophets: The Conflict and Its Background*, SBLDS 106 (Atlanta, GA: Scholars Press, 1988); Izabela Jaruzelska, "Social Structure in the Kingdom of Israel in the Eighth Century B.C. as Reflected in the Book of Amos," *Folia Orientalia* 29 (1992–1993): 91–117.

6. John Barton, *Understanding Old Testament Ethics: Approaches and Explorations* (Louisville, KY: Westminster John Knox, 2003); M. Daniel Carroll R., "Seek Yahweh, Establish Justice: Probing Prophetic Ethics: An Orientation from Amos 5:1–17," in *The Bible and Social Justice: Old Testament and New Testament Foundations for the Church's Urgent Call*, ed. Cynthia L. Westfall and Bryan R. Dyer, McMaster New Testament Studies (Eugene, OR: Wipf & Stock, 2015), 64–83; Daniel Timmer, "The Use and Abuse of Power in Amos: Identity and Ideology," *JSOT* 39, no. 1 (2014): 101–18; Walter J. Houston, *Contending for Justice: Ideologies and Theologies of Social Justice in the Old Testament* (London: T&T Clark, 2006); Phyllis A. Bird, "Poor Man or Poor Woman? Gendering the Poor in Prophetic Texts," in *Missing Persons and Mistaken Identities: Women and Gender in Ancient Israel*, OBT (Minneapolis: Fortress, 1997), 67–78; Donoso S. Escobar, "Social Justice in the Book of Amos," *Review and Expositor* 92, no. 2 (1995): 169–74; H. C. Roberts, "La Época de Amós Y La Justicia Social," *BTrans* 50 (1993): 95–106; H. Reimer, "Agentes y mecanismos de opresión y explotación en Amos," *Revista de Interpretación Bíblica Latinoamericana* 12 (1992): 69–81.

for its theological contributions,[7] and its place in the ongoing discussion of Israelite religion.[8] Though many of these works incorporate social-scientific methods of analysis, there has been little in the area of social psychology.[9] This may seem like an unremarkable claim in light of the relative obscurity of social psychology in biblical scholarship. But tools from this field, as will be shown, allow interpreters to ask new questions of the ancient text. Specifically, this book investigates the contribution of the book of Amos to the formation of social identity.

Amos offers its audience an interpretation of the world, inviting them—regardless of temporal or social location—to adopt its embedded norms and values.[10] More than simply describing events in the past, or reflecting

---

7. John Barton, *The Theology of the Book of Amos* (New York: Cambridge University Press, 2012); Gerhard Pfeifer, *Die Theologie des Propheten Amos* (Frankfurt: Peter Lang, 1995); Pfeifer, "Das Ja des Amos," *VT* 39, no. 4 (1989): 497–503; Robert D. Bell, "The Theology of Amos," *Biblical Viewpoint* 27, no. 2 (1993): 47–54; Donald L. Williams, "The Theology of Amos," *Review and Expositor* 63, no. 4 (1966): 393–403.

8. A. R. Davis, *Tel Dan in Its Northern Cultic Context*, Archaeology and Biblical Studies 20 (Atlanta, GA: SBL Press, 2013), 147–69; Jonathan S. Greer, "A Marzea and a Mizraq: A Prophet's Mêlée with Religious Diversity in Amos 6.4-7," *JSOT* 32 (2007): 243–61; M. Daniel Carroll R., "'For So You Love to Do': Probing Popular Religion in the Book of Amos," in *Rethinking Contexts, Rereading Texts: Contributions from the Social Sciences to Biblical Interpretation*, ed. M. Daniel Carroll R., JSOTSup 299 (Sheffield: Sheffield Academic, 2000), 168–89; Hans M. Barstad, *The Religious Polemics of Amos: Studies in the Preaching of Am 2,7b-8; 4,1-13; 5,1-27; 6,4-7; 8,14*, VTSup 34 (Leiden: Brill, 1984).

9. There have, however, been numerous investigations into the psychology of prophecy, but these ask different questions than will be pursued in the present work. See Paul M. Joyce, "The Book of Amos and Psychological Interpretation," in *Aspects of Amos: Exegesis and Interpretation*, ed. Anselm C. Hagedorn and Andrew Mein, LHBOTS 536 (New York: T&T Clark, 2011), 105–16; M. J. Buss, "The Social Psychology of Prophecy," in *Prophecy: Essays Presented to Georg Fohrer on His 65th Birthday, 6 Sept 1980*, BZAW 150 (Berlin: de Gruyter, 1980), 1–11.

10. The use of "audience" here is intentional to allow for both the acts of reading and hearing the book of Amos. On the matter of reading and listening to the text read aloud, see Ehud Ben Zvi, "Introduction: Writings, Speeches, and the Prophetic Books—Setting an Agenda," in *Writings and Speech in Israelite and Ancient Near Eastern Prophecy*, ed. Ehud Ben Zvi and Michael H. Floyd, Symposium 10 (Atlanta, GA: Society of Biblical Literature, 2000), 1–29. Ben Zvi rejects the notion that texts were *exclusively* read audibly. He finds the evidence for silent reading in the Hellenistic world suggestive for the literature of the Hebrew Bible. Where the texts were read aloud, Ben Zvi notes the identity-forming practice within the Yehud community.

upon the beliefs of a particular religious community, the book of Amos seeks to tell its audience who they are and who they can be in this world.[11] In short, the book of Amos, at some level, attempts to shape the identity of its audience.[12] The means by which this identity-formation occurs will be explored through the use of the Social Identity Approach in Chapter 2. I will argue that the book of Amos employs various identity-forming strategies to shape the boundaries, norms, and values of its audience.

Many works have focused on the construction, maintenance, and negotiation of identity in biblical literature (see Chapter 2), but to date there has not been a concentrated effort to do this with Amos. Thus, this project joins other works that trace the process of identity formation in scriptural texts.[13] My purpose is not to reconstruct supposed historical social dynamics behind Amos by means of its composition and redaction. Neither is this book a theology of Amos. I am not concerned simply with

---

11. Klyne Snodgrass discusses Scripture in the context of a hermeneutic of identity. He states, "Scripture tells us who we are, which is evident in the fact that Scripture is full of identity statements." Later he claims that Scripture is primarily about identity formation. Klyne Snodgrass, "Introduction to a Hermeneutics of Identity," *BSac* 168, no. 669 (2011): 4, 5. Also see Snodgrass, *Who God Says You Are: A Christian Understanding of Identity* (Grand Rapids: Eerdmans, 2018).

12. Despite limitation of literacy in the ancient world, Judith Lieu notes that "studies of identity in antiquity have focused on texts, not only because it is these that survive, but out of a recognition of the constructive role of texts in that world." Judith M. Lieu, *Christian Identity in the Jewish and Graeco-Roman World* (Oxford: Oxford University Press, 2004), 10. See also Benjamin D. Giffone, *"Sit at My Right Hand": The Chronicler's Portrait of the Tribe of Benjamin in the Social Context of Yehud* (New York: T&T Clark, 2016), 31–7.

13. Various approaches to the textual construction of identity have been posited. Louis Jonker, for instance, emphasizes the notion of "textual identities," whereby identity is negotiated, in part, through the available textual resources in a culture. Ole Jakob Filtvedt discusses textual constructions of identity in the sense that texts construct *notions* of identity. He distinguishes this general claim from the process of detailing how this construction occurs. His work focuses on the former, showing how texts create representations of reality that are analogous to that which is represented. Coleman Baker, following Paul Ricoeur, proposes a "narrative-identity approach" where the threefold process of prefiguration, configuration, and refiguration describe a reader's interaction with a text. See Louis C. Jonker, "Textual Identities in the Books of Chronicles: The Case of Jehoram's History," in *Community Identity in Judean Historiography*, ed. Gary N. Knoppers and Kenneth A. Ritsau (Winona Lake, IN: Eisenbrauns, 2009), 197–217; Ole Jakob Filtvedt, *The Identity of God's People and the Paradox of Hebrews*, WUNT 2/400 (Tübingen: Mohr Siebeck, 2015), 40–41; Coleman A. Baker, *Identity, Memory, and Narrative in Early Christianity: Peter, Paul, and Recategorization in the Book of Acts* (Eugene, OR: Pickwick, 2011).

the book's content, but with what it, as a text, *does*.[14] Thus, the focus is the embedded construction of identity in Amos as it interacts with its audience's sense of who they are.[15]

The significance of this study is not simply in the application of a new method to a biblical text. The question of what it means to belong to the people of God is one that must be posed anew to every generation. In this globalized world, where fear and xenophobia continue to rear their ugly head, one does well to consider the role of faith and religion in relation to social group norms and values. Miroslav Volf notes the damning effects of a blind merger of Christian and cultural commitments, stating, "Such sacralization of cultural identity is invaluable for the parties in conflict because it can transmute what is in fact a murder into an act of piety."[16] The tragic history of racial injustice in the United States, an issue far from resolved, often exposes the pious prejudice that emerges from the expectations of social groups.[17] Though these important questions are several steps removed from the present work, exploring aspects of social identity

---

14. See Lieu, *Christian Identity in Jewish and Graeco-Roman World*, 25. Speech-Act Theory has been used similarly to discover the affective power of language in the biblical texts. Though there may be overlap at points, the questions Speech-Act Theory asks are different from those in a Social Identity Approach. On Speech-Act Theory, see J. Eugene Botha, "Speech Act Theory and Biblical Interpretation," *Neotestamentica* 41 (2007): 274–94; Jim W. Adams, *The Performative Nature and Function of Isaiah 40–55*, LHBOTS 448 (New York: T&T Clark, 2006); Brevard S. Childs, "Speech-Act Theory and Biblical Interpretation," *SJT* 58 (2005): 375–92; Nicholas Wolterstorff, "The Promise of Speech-Act Theory for Biblical Interpretation," in *After Pentecost: Language and Biblical Interpretation*, Scripture and Hermeneutics 2 (Grand Rapids: Zondervan, 2001), 73–90; R. S. Briggs, "The Uses of Speech-Act Theory in Biblical Interpretation," *CRBS* 9 (2001): 229–76; Walter J. Houston, "What Did the Prophets Think They Were Doing? Speech Acts and Prophetic Discourse in the Old Testament," *Biblical Interpretation* 1 (1993): 167–88; Hugh White, "The Value of Speech Act Theory for Old Testament Hermeneutics," *Semeia* 41 (1988): 41–63.

15. All human identities, as Richard Jenkins states, "are, by definition, social identities. Identifying ourselves, or others, is a matter of meaning, and meaning always involves interaction: agreement and disagreement, convention and innovation, communication and negotiation." R. Jenkins, *Social Identity*, 4th ed. (London: Routledge, 2014), 18.

16. Miroslav Volf, *Exclusion and Embrace: A Theological Exploration of Identity, Otherness, and Reconciliation* (Nashville: Abingdon, 1996), 37.

17. See, for instance, Michael O. Emerson and Christian Smith, *Divided by Faith: Evangelical Religion and the Problem of Race in America* (Oxford: Oxford University Press, 2000).

formation in Amos will open the door to a more careful appropriation of the biblical texts in the discussion of religion, identity, and justice.[18]

Chapter 2 introduces the Social Identity Approach in detail, as well as its application in biblical studies. The tools provided by this method allow one to ask different questions of the text that yield insights for audiences entering the world of the text.[19]

Chapter 3 examines the dynamics of intergroup conflict in Amos as they relate to social identity. The Oracles against the Nations (1:3–2:16) and the confrontation with the priest Amaziah (7:10-17) serve as illustrations. In the latter case, it is shown that both Amos and Amaziah do not act as individuals, but as representatives of their social group. The conflict between social groups clearly frames a contrast between "us" and "them."

Chapters 4 and 5 explore an important dimension of identity-formation in Amos, namely the conception of time (past, present, future). Chapter 4 looks at Amos's use of the past, in continuity with the "present," as an othering strategy to expose the outgroup characterization of the addressees. Traditional identity markers presumed to define Israel as the people of God are dismantled. Chapter 5, on the other hand, looks towards Amos's conception of the future of Israel. Though the future is framed negatively for the majority of Israel, eschatological hope emerges for a remnant ingroup. The hopeful future of the "booth of David" provides the audience motivation to join this ingroup. Doing so would necessarily entail a change of behavior, for, to be part of the ingroup, audience members must adopt the norms and values of the group.

---

18. These dynamics of social identity were the impetus for Jan Bosman's doctoral dissertation: Jan Bosman, "Social Identity in Nahum: A Theological-Ethical Enquiry" (ThD diss., University of Stellenbosch, 2005). This was one of the first projects to employ a Social Identity Approach in the field of Old Testament studies.

19. The "world of the text" refers to the sense of a coherent reality constructed by the author(s)/editors of Amos. Peter Berger and Thomas Luckmann famously described the process of the social construction of reality; see their *The Social Construction of Reality: A Treatise in the Sociology of Knowledge* (New York: Doubleday, 1966). This concept has been related to social identity in various ways. Petri Luomanen provides a helpful summary of Berger and Luckmann as related to social identity in the New Testament. See Petri Luomanen, "The Sociology of Knowledge, the Social Identity Approach and the Cognitive Science of Religion," in *Explaining Christian Origins and Early Judaism: Contributions from Cognitive and Social Science*, ed. P. Luomanen, I. Pyysiäinen, and R. Uro, Biblical Interpretation 89 (Leiden: Brill, 2007), 201–8. Also see Titus Hjelm, *Social Constructionisms: Approaches to the Study of the Human World* (New York: Macmillan, 2014).

Though this book attempts to uncover the social identity dynamics embedded in the text, a cautionary word must be said about the appropriation of the proposed norms and values for contemporary audiences. I readily recognize the abundant diversity of social contexts within which audiences of the biblical text may exist. The goal of identity formation, as understood in this project, is not to suggest uniformity, as though social location is irrelevant. But for those who enter the world of the text, there is a certain construction of reality presented by the biblical author(s).[20] Thus this project does not entrust an interpretive community with the production of meaning, as in reader-response criticism.[21] Rather, the analysis will follow the rhetorical contour of the biblical text. I am by no means suggesting that my reading is the definitive interpretation of the book; nonetheless, the Social Identity Approach opens new lines of inquiry for audiences to be shaped by the text.

---

20. Ole Jakob Filtvedt states, "A text always carries with it some implied notion of the identity of those it addresses, it sometimes includes elaborate descriptions of persons or groups, it often somehow articulates what the author and the addressees have in common, and it is thus an apt tool for developing interpretive strategies for maintaining, negotiating and constructing identity." Filtvedt, *The Identity of God's People and the Paradox of Hebrews*, 40.

21. On reader-response criticism, see Eryl W. Davies, "Reader-Response Criticism and Old Testament Studies," in *Honouring the Past and Shaping the Future: Religious and Biblical Studies in Wales: Essays in Honour of Gareth Lloyd Jones*, ed. Robert Pope (Leominster, UK: Gracewing, 2003), 20–37. For a critique of reader-response, see John Barton, "Thinking about Reader-Response Criticism," *ExpTim* 113, no. 5 (2002): 147–51.

Chapter 2

The Social Identity Approach

"Identity" is a fundamental concept for human beings.[1] This much is clear from the wide range of fields that invoke identity. From religion and politics to gender and race, identity forms a central concept around which a sense of self may be situated.[2] Yet amidst the discussion of identity there can often be an assumed or underdeveloped theoretical framework employed. What exactly do we mean by "identity"? What does it mean to identify with a particular group? Moreover, how does this identification affect one's behavior? This chapter discusses important issues related to identity, leading to the specific framework of social identity employed throughout this work.

Social Identity

Historically, there have been numerous approaches to identity. For example, in sociological studies, the concept generally relates to the roles a person plays in the social world. Erving Goffman, a twentieth-century sociologist, likened people's social roles to actors on a stage, living out a public or group identity.[3] Other sociological perspectives, such as symbolic interactionism, examine how a person's identity is affected by

---

1. For a survey and history of identity studies, see Margaret S. Wetherell, "The Field of Identity Studies," in *The Sage Handbook of Identities*, ed. M. S. Wetherell and C. T. Mohanty (London: Sage, 2010), 3–26. Also see R. Jenkins, *Social Identity*.

2. A survey of the entries in the *Encyclopedia of Identity* shows the diversity of usage. See Ronald L. Jackson, ed., *Encyclopedia of Identity*, 2 vols. (Thousand Oaks, CA: Sage, 2010).

3. Erving Goffman, *The Presentation of Self in Everyday Life*, Anchor Books ed. (Garden City, NY: Doubleday, 1959). Also see David Shulman, *The Presentation of Self in Contemporary Social Life* (Thousand Oaks, CA: Sage, 2017).

social structures.⁴ In psychology, Erik Erikson's psychosocial developmental analysis is the best-known treatment of identity.⁵ The turn towards social psychology situated identity in terms of group membership. The theoretical framework employed here builds upon the foundation laid by social psychologists in understanding identity as a social phenomenon.⁶

The sense of identity outlined here operates within a particular model of "self." At the broader level of the structure is an individual's self-concept, which comprises "the totality of self-descriptions and self-evaluations subjectively available to the individual."⁷ Under the umbrella of one's self-concept is two specific components of identity: the personal and the social. In the former, one's identity is defined in terms of individual characteristics (e.g., lazy, respectable) as well as personal relationships (e.g., Jim's wife, Sandra's dad). The latter involves social categories such as nationality, occupation, religion, and so on.⁸ An individual will doubtlessly maintain a number of identities simultaneously.⁹ What is of particular

---

4. Thomas M. Brinthaupt, "Identity," in *International Encyclopedia of the Social Sciences*, ed. William A. Darity, Jr. (New York: Macmillan, 2008), 553; Jan E. Stets, "Identity Theory," in *Contemporary Social Psychological Theories*, ed. Peter J. Burke (Stanford, CA: Stanford University Press, 2006), 88–110.

5. Erik H. Erikson, *Identity: Youth and Crisis* (New York: W. W. Norton, 1968); Erikson, *Identity and the Life Cycle* (New York: W. W. Norton, 1994).

6. The biblical authors did not operate with social psychological categories; nevertheless, one can distinguish between social psychological theories and social psychological concepts. The latter serves as the premise, rather than the output, of the former. The phenomenon of groups seems to be intrinsic to humanity, and thus later articulations of analysis, if conducted properly, may prove useful for earlier instances of group behavior. See Ole Filtvedt, *The Identity of God's People and the Paradox of Hebrews*, 41–4.

7. Dominic Abrams and Michael A. Hogg, *Social Identifications: A Social Psychology of Intergroup Relations and Group Processes* (London: Routledge, 1998), 24.

8. Ibid., 25.

9. Regarding an individual's multiplicity of identities, Horrell states, "One cannot therefore speak simply of someone's 'identity' but must rather consider what aspects of identity are being considered and why these are relevant in a particular context." David G. Horrell, "'Becoming Christian': Solidifying Christian Identity and Content," in *Handbook of Early Christianity: Social Science Approaches*, ed. Anthony J. Blasi, Jean Duhaime, and Paul-André Turcotte (Walnut Creek, CA: AltaMira, 2002), 311. Abrams and Hogg point out that some of these identities may conflict. For example, someone's identity as a soldier may require a level of aggression that his or her identity as a Christian may deem inappropriate. See Abrams and Hogg, *Social Identifications*, 21; Jenkins, *Social Identity*, 7.

concern in this chapter is social identity, classically defined as "that part of the individual's self-concept which derives from their knowledge of their membership of a social group (or groups) together with the value and emotional significance attached to that membership."[10] According to this view, social groups are not "simply a passive context for individual behavior," but help shape and (re)define one's view of self.[11] Put simply, belonging to a group confers a sense of who one is and how one should behave.[12] Thus, those who position themselves as brokers of social identity are able to craft the norms, values, and boundaries of the group.

An Outline of the Social Identity Approach

Grappling with the complexities of social identity requires a degree of theoretical precision.[13] Just such a framework has been explored, tested, and applied in the Social Identity Approach (SIA) since the 1970s. The first step, which is now a standard tool used in a wide variety of fields, is Social Identity Theory (SIT). Later SIT was supplemented by Self-Categorization Theory (SCT), which explores the cognitive process of group formation. Together, these two theories make up what is known as the Social Identity Approach.

Beginnings of the Social Identity Approach

The Social Identity Approach began with the work of social psychologist Henri Tajfel.[14] Prior to the Second World War, Tajfel—a Polish Jew— moved to France to attend university. After only two years in France, Tajfel was drafted into the French army, only to be taken captive by

---

10. Henri Tajfel, *Human Groups and Social Categories: Studies in Social Psychology* (Cambridge: Cambridge University Press, 1981), 255.

11. S. Alexander Haslam, *Psychology in Organizations: The Social Identity Approach*, 2nd ed. (London: Sage, 2004), 17.

12. Abrams and Hogg, *Social Identifications*, 3. A social group is defined as three or more people who share the same social identity. They identify, evaluate, and define themselves in the same way, especially in contrast to people who are not in their group. See Michael A. Hogg, "Social Identity Theory," in Burke, ed., *Contemporary Social Psychological Theories*, 115–17.

13. Aaron Kuecker, *The Spirit and the "Other": Social Identity, Ethnicity and Intergroup Reconciliation in Luke–Acts*, LNTS 444 (New York: T&T Clark International, 2011), 25.

14. For a biographical sketch of Tajfel, see John C. Turner, "Henri Tajfel: An Introduction," in *Social Groups and Identities: Developing the Legacy of Henri Tajfel*, ed. W. Peter Robinson, International Series in Social Psychology (Oxford: Butterworth-Heinemann, 1996), 1–23.

German forces. The only factor that enabled his survival was the Germans' belief that Tajfel was French rather than a Polish Jew. Had his true identity been discovered he would most certainly have been killed, as tragically his family back home was. His perceived identity was the difference between life and death. In the post-war years, Tajfel studied the social psychology of intergroup behavior, earning his PhD from the University of London. Unpersuaded by the dominant framework of contemporary social psychologists who argued that intergroup phenomena were mere expressions of personality traits and individual differences, Tajfel sought to develop another explanation.[15]

Tajfel's personal experience illustrated a distinction in what he described later as an "interpersonal-intergroup continuum."[16] Regardless of his personal characteristics or the quality of his personal relationships with his German captors, it was his social category membership (French rather than Polish) that influenced their behavior and ultimately his fate.[17] This put the Germans' behavior more on the intergroup side of the continuum. On the other hand, Tajfel conceptualized that at the other extreme was social interaction governed purely by interpersonal behavior. This is where individual characteristics and personal relationships come into play. In his early work, he described this continuum as the difference between "acting in terms of self" versus "acting in terms of one's group."[18]

Much of Tajfel's work focused on categorization as it relates to stereotyping and prejudice.[19] This started with the study of "perceptual overestimation," which showed that perceptions of physical characteristics, such as the size of an object, were affected by the value and emotional significance attributed to them by the perceiver.[20] The underlying cognitive process of perceptual overestimation, he argued, corresponded to the cognitive aspects of stereotyping.[21] However, contrary to the reigning paradigm that studied individual cognitive functions only later to draw

15. Hogg, "Social Identity Theory," 112. Tajfel's first papers include Richard S. Peters and Henri Tajfel, "Hobbes and Hull—Metaphysicians of Behavior," *BJPS* 8 (1957): 30–44; Henri Tajfel, "Value and the Perceptual Judgement of Magnitude," *Psychological Review* 64 (1957): 192–203.

16. Henri Tajfel, "Social Identity and Intergroup Behavior," *SSI* 13 (1974): 65–93.

17. Turner, "Henri Tajfel," 3.

18. Tajfel, "Social Identity and Intergroup Behavior," 87–9.

19. See his early work, Henri Tajfel and S. D. Cawasjee, "Value and the Accentuation of Judged Differences," *Journal of Abnormal and Social Psychology* 59 (1959): 436–9; Henri Tajfel, "Quantitative Judgement in Social Perception," *BJSP* 50 (1959): 16–29; Tajfel, "Cognitive Aspects of Prejudice," *JSI* 25, no. 4 (1969): 79–97.

20. Turner, "Henri Tajfel," 12.

21. Ibid., 13.

conclusions about group behavior, Tajfel argued that the social group was the best starting point. This avoids the reductionistic explanations that arise from viewing a group as no more than the sum of its parts. Rather, a social group functioned differently.[22]

Though Tajfel was not the first to grasp the significance of social categorization for social psychology, his analysis became the most influential and lasting in the field.[23] This is due in part to his work at Bristol, which he led from 1967 until 1982. During this time, publications such as the *European Journal of Social Psychology* and the *European Monographs in Social Psychology* appeared under purview, allowing the discussion to reach a broader audience; but the beginnings of what came to be known as Social Identity Theory was Tajfel's article on social categorization published in 1972.[24] Here, he built upon previous empirical studies to explain the phenomenon of ingroup bias. The codification of SIT was the collaborative effort of Tajfel and his then doctoral student, and later colleague, John C. Turner.[25]

Social Identity Theory

At its core, Social Identity Theory suggests that categorization as a member of a particular group (1) leads to social comparison (seeking the meaning of one's group by comparison to another group); and (2) produces the desire for a positive distinctiveness of one's own group.[26]

---

22. Taylor and Brown distinguish between the individual as the focus of social psychological *research* and the individual as the focus of social psychological *theory*. They maintain that while social context must be considered in the process of research, an individualistic level of theorizing is entirely appropriate. See Donald M. Taylor and Rupert J. Brown, "Towards a More Social Social Psychology?" *BJSCP* 18 (1979): 173–80. Tajfel penned a rejoinder stating, "No one would deny that 'ultimately' we are concerned with 'individuals' who behave in one way or another. But a clear distinction must be made between theories which are 'individualistic' and one which is concerned with socially shared patterns of individual behaviour." Henri Tajfel, "Individuals and Groups in Social Psychology," *BJSCP* 18 (1979): 187.

23. Turner, "Henri Tajfel," 5.

24. Henri Tajfel, "La catégorisation sociale," in *Introduction á la psychologie sociale*, ed. S. Moscovici (Paris: Larousse, 1972), 272–302. For context, see Turner, "Henri Tajfel," 16.

25. See their seminal study: Henri Tajfel and John C. Turner, "An Integrative Theory of Intergroup Conflict," in *The Social Psychology of Intergroup Relations* (Monterey, CA: Brooks Cole, 1979), 33–47.

26. For the empirical underpinnings of these points, see the research cited in S. Alexander Haslam, Stephen D. Reicher, and Michael J. Platow, *The New Psychology of Leadership: Identity, Influence, and Power* (New York: Psychology Press,

If one's group does not contribute to a positive social identity, he or she can either move to another group or employ various strategies to reconceptualize their current group.

Regarding the first point, according to Tajfel, it is the fact of social comparison that links social categorization and social identity.[27] Just as it is true that "no man is an island," so too, says Tajfel, "no social group is an island."[28] Rather, "[the] characteristics of one's group as a whole… achieve most of their significance in relation to perceived differences from other groups and the value connotation of these differences."[29] It is in this environment where social identity is forged. One's sense of his or her group membership, along with the emotion and value attached to such identification, happens only when there are other groups present. In other words, there needs to be a "them" in order for there to be an "us." It is then only natural to weigh the defining features of one's own group over against other groups (i.e., social comparison). As noted above, SIT posits a tendency to accentuate perceived similarities of people belonging to the same group and differences of those belonging to different groups, also known as the meta-contrast principle.[30]

2011), 50. As Reicher notes, for Tajfel, strategies to better one's social location (i.e., social change) is the *raison d'être* of social identity theory. See Stephen D. Reicher, "Social Identity and Social Change: Rethinking the Context of Social Psychology," in Robinson, ed., *Social Groups and Identities*, 322. This, however, is not to indicate that ingroup bias is the *inevitable* result of categorization. The identification must be salient and relevant to one's self-concept to necessitate ingroup favoritism. For instance, an identification based on gender may not be a relevant feature in certain circumstances. Thus, favoring members of one's own gender may not result in increased positive distinctiveness. See Tajfel and Turner, "An Integrative Theory of Intergroup Conflict," 41.

27. Henri Tajfel, "Social Categorization, Social Identity and Social Comparison," in *Differentiation between Groups: Studies in the Social Psychology of Intergroup Relations*, ed. Henri Tajfel (London: Academic, 1978), 61–76.

28. Ibid., 66.

29. Ibid.

30. John C. Turner, "The Experimental Social Psychology of Intergroup Behaviour," in *Intergroup Behaviour*, ed. John C. Turner and H. Giles (Oxford: Blackwell, 1981); Hogg, "Social Identity Theory," 112; Penelope Oakes, S. Alexander Haslam, and John C. Turner, "The Role of Prototypicality in Group Influence and Cohesion: Contextual Variation in the Graded Structure of Social Categories," in *Social Identity: International Perspectives*, ed. Stephen Worchel et al. (London: Sage, 1998), 77–8. As Tajfel states, "When a classification is correlated with a continuous dimension, there will be a tendency to exaggerate the differences on *that* dimension between items which fall into distinct classes, and to minimize these differences within each of the classes." Tajfel, "Cognitive Aspects of Prejudice," 83.

The second point states that social categorization produces the desire for positive distinctiveness of one's group.[31] The behaviors motivated by this pursuit in Tajfel's analysis are based on a subjective belief structure that focuses on issues such as status (How does my group compare to other groups?), stability (How stable is the status relationship?), legitimacy (How legitimate is the status relationship?), permeability (How easy is it to change status by moving membership to an another group?), and cognitive alternatives (Is a different intergroup relationship conceivable?).[32] When the conditions for the preservation of positive social identity of one's group are absent, an individual will be motivated to leave the group.[33] In cases where one's social system is thought to be permeable, an individual will move from one social situation to another through the process of "social mobility."[34] This includes strategies both

---

31. John C. Turner and Katherine J. Reynolds, "The Story of Social Identity," in *Rediscovering Social Identity: Key Readings*, ed. Tom Postmes and Nyla R. Branscombe (New York: Psychology Press, 2010), 15. As Haslam et al. state, "This quest for *positive distinctiveness* means that when people's sense of who they are is defined in terms of 'we' rather than 'I', they want to see 'us' as different from and better than 'them' in order to feel good about who they are and what they do." S. Alexander Haslam et al., "The Social Identity Perspective Today: An Overview of Its Defining Ideas," in Postmes and Branscombe, eds., *Rediscovering Social Identity*, 343.

32. Michael A. Hogg, "Social Identity Theory," in *Encyclopedia of Social Psychology*, ed. R. F. Baumeister and K. D. Vohs (Thousand Oaks, CA: Sage, 2007), 2:902; Abrams and Hogg, *Social Identifications*, 24–6. Lacoviello et al., argue for a nuanced normative perspective of self-esteem enhancement vis-à-vis ingroup favoritism where ingroup favoritism, rather than simply being a result of categorization, conforms to ingroup norms. In groups that value and promote fairness, ingroup favoritism would not contribute to a member's positive self-conception. See Vincenzo Lacoviello et al., "The Impact of Ingroup Favoritism on Self-Esteem: A Normative Perspective," *JESP* 71 (2017): 31–41.

33. Tajfel, "Social Categorization, Social Identity and Social Comparison," 67. See also John C. Turner, "Social Comparison and Social Identity: Some Prospects for Intergroup Behaviour," *EJSP* 5, no. 1 (1975): 5–34. But as Haslam et al. note, individual mobility may be a valued feature of the group. Situations where individual mobility, as opposed to collective behavior, may be more conducive, *does not* always determine the strategy a group member will employ. Thus, one must assess the values of the group to better understand the dynamics of individual and collective mobility. See S. Alexander Haslam et al., "The Social Identity Perspective Tomorrow: Opportunities and Avenues for Advance," in Postmes and Branscombe, eds., *Rediscovering Social Identity*, 360.

34. Henri Tajfel, "Interindividual Behaviour and Intergroup Behaviour," in Tajfel, ed., *Differentiation between Groups*, 67.

actual and psychological, neither of which necessarily change the material status of the group.³⁵ In this, one may imagine a social group related to citizenship. If one's current identification does not yield a positive social identity, he or she can, in theory, take up citizenship in a different country where positive value is available, thus abandoning the old identity.³⁶ Yet, certain circumstances may prohibit individuals from leaving their country. In this case, it may be more conducive for individuals to remain in their country but simply identify less with their nationality in favor of another social identity. Thus, though their actual membership has not changed, psychologically they have moved to a new social location. This could conceivably involve seeking out those in their community who also share their new identity. In each of these cases the mobility occurs at the individual, not group, level. Nevertheless, it is the group that contributes to one's self-evaluation and so falls within the scope of social identity.

Perceived impermeable boundaries in a social system necessitate another way.³⁷ Here, two collective strategies, namely "social creativity" and "social competition," can enhance one's ingroup status, awarding a positive social identification. Social creativity involves changing one of three comparative features between a low-status ingroup and higher-status outgroups.³⁸ First, group members may shift the *point of comparison* with outgroups to another referent. Rather than dealing directly with the negative attributions of their own group, individuals emphasize other areas where their ingroup is superior. This may include present realities as well as the group's history and traditions.³⁹ For example, members of a losing sports team may not be able to gain positive distinctiveness based solely on their team's success. What they can do, however, is shift the point of comparison to another issue, such as how fair they play relative

---

35. Linda A. Jackson et al., "Achieving Positive Social Identity: Social Mobility, Social Creativity, and Permeability of Group Boundaries," *JPSP* 70, no. 2 (1996): 241; Tajfel and Turner, "An Integrative Theory of Intergroup Conflict," 43–4.

36. In this case, non-acceptance by the new group can lead to a feeling of marginality. For example, an individual dissatisfied with his or her identity as an African may move to America or Europe with the hopes of a more positive social identity. If this does not occur upon arrival, the individual will struggle again with a desire for a more positive social identity. See Abrams and Hogg, *Social Identifications*, 56.

37. Naomi Ellemers et al., "Social Identification and Permeability of Group Boundaries," *EJSP* 18, no. 6 (1988): 497–513.

38. Tajfel and Turner, "An Integrative Theory of Intergroup Conflict," 43–4.

39. Jutta Jokiranta, *Social Identity and Sectarianism in the Qumran Movement*, STDJ 105 (Leiden: Brill, 2013), 84; Tajfel, *Human Groups and Social Categories*, 340.

to the winning team. The point, then, becomes less about being the better team than being the fairer team.[40] If fairness becomes the most salient feature for the low-status group, they are able to maintain a positive social identity.

The second strategy of social creativity involves re-envisioning the perceived negative attributes of one's group as a positive feature. An example commonly noted is the "black is beautiful" campaign.[41] This movement sought to redefine the negative association of skin color as something favorable and even desirable. While no actual change to the group occurred, this strategy allowed members to gain a positive social identity from their membership in a low-status group.

The third social creativity strategy involves changing the comparative outgroup to another low-status group. Members of an ethnic minority group, for instance, rather than emphasizing the comparison with the majority group, may shift their focus to low-status members of their own ethnicity.[42] To illustrate this point, middle-class African Americans who compare themselves to middle-class whites with negative results may emphasize their positive group identification when set against urban, poor African Americans. From this standpoint, the middle-class African Americans are in a better social location than the comparison group. Again, no actual change to the group has occurred, only a re-conception enabling those with low group status to cope.[43]

Unlike the strategies of social creativity, social competition involves confronting an outgroup directly. This strategy is forged in situations where the relationship between groups is thought to be illegitimate and insecure/permeable (i.e., possible to change).[44] Revolutions are born from

---

40. On this process, see Gérard Lemaine, "Inégalité, comparaison et incomparabilité: Esquisse d'une théorie de l'originalité sociale," *Bulletin de Psychologie* 20 (1966): 24–32; Lemaine, "Social Differentiation in the Scientific Community," in *The Social Dimension: European Developments in Social Psychology*, ed. Henri Tajfel, ESSP (Cambridge: Cambridge University Press, 1984), 1:338–42.

41. Tajfel and Turner, "An Integrative Theory of Intergroup Conflict," 43–4. Also, see Tajfel, *Human Groups and Social Categories*, 284–5.

42. Tajfel and Turner, "An Integrative Theory of Intergroup Conflict," 43–4.

43. This example presumes that ethnicity is a salient group identification. There may be instances where another social identity is superordinate in the hierarchical identification structure. See, e.g., A. J. Fuligni, G. J. Rivera, and A. Leininger, "Family Identity and the Educational Persistence of Students with Latin American and Asian Backgrounds," in *Contesting Stereotypes and Creating Identities: Social Categories, Social Identities and Educational Participation*, ed. A. J. Fuligni (New York: Russell Sage Foundation, 2007), 211.

44. Haslam, Reicher, and Platow, *The New Psychology of Leadership*, 51.

a belief that those in power do not deserve to be there and should be replaced. Though sometimes violent, social competition can be expressed through other means such as passive resistance (e.g., Civil Rights movement, Gandhi, etc.).[45] The same process is active, but the form it takes can depend on the specific context. The goal is to ensure a positive social status for one's ingroup through the actual change of intergroup dynamics. As evident from this brief discussion on social mobility and social change, group members have a number of strategies to escape a perceived negative social identity, whether cognitively or in actuality.[46] And as Tajfel argued early on, the mere fact of social categorization is sufficient to produce social comparison.[47]

Self-Categorization Theory

The foundation for the study of social identity was laid by Tajfel and Turner in the 1970s. Yet the specific process of how groups are formed was yet to be explored in detail. Turner and his colleagues at Bristol took particular interest in the cognitive processes of social identity. The resulting model became known as Self-Categorization Theory (SCT), sometimes referred to as the Social Identity Theory of the Group.[48] Turner set out to define, psychologically, what a group is and what socio-cognitive processes lead to group identifications and behaviors.[49] In other words, what factors caused individuals to view themselves as a group and not merely as

45. Abrams and Hogg, *Social Identifications*, 26.
46. This is not to indicate that individuals identify with groups only to the extent that they serve one's personal self-interests. As with soldiers, one's group membership may actually jeopardize one's self-interest. Nevertheless, the potential cost may be a positive value of the group (i.e., patriotism). See Naomi Ellemers, "Social Identity Theory," in *Encyclopedia of Group Processes and Intergroup Relations*, ed. John M. Levine and Michael A. Hogg (Thousand Oaks, CA: Sage, 2010), 2:801.
47. As he states, "The characteristics of one's group as a whole (such as its status, its richness or poverty, its skin colour or its ability to reach its aims) achieve most of their significance in relation to perceived differences from other groups and the value connotation of these differences." Tajfel, *Human Groups and Social Categories*, 258.
48. John C. Turner, "Towards a Cognitive Redefinition of the Social Group," in *Social Identity and Intergroup Relations*, ed. Henri Tajfel (Cambridge: Cambridge University Press, 1982), 15–40; Turner, "Social Categorization and the Self-Concept: A Social Cognitive Theory of Group Behavior," in *Advances in Group Processes*, ed. E. J. Lawler (Greenwich, CT: JAI, 1985), 2:77–122; John C. Turner et al., eds., *Rediscovering the Social Group: A Self-Categorization Theory* (Oxford: Blackwell, 1987); Michael A. Hogg, "Self-Categorization Theory," in Levine and Hogg, eds., *Encyclopedia of Group Processes and Intergroup Relations*, 2:728–31.
49. Hogg, "Self-Categorization Theory," 729.

individuals? Moreover, what behaviors result from identification with a particular social group? In short, SCT is concerned with when, how, and why someone defines self in terms of "we" (social identity) rather than "I" (personal identity).[50] As Turner himself put it, "We are hypothesizing that social identity is the cognitive mechanism which makes group behaviour possible."[51]

Part of the process of activating one's social identity is the transition from thinking in terms of "I" to thinking in terms of "we." This move away from individualistic thinking is known as "depersonalization." Turner notes, "Depersonalization refers to the process of "self-stereotyping" whereby people come to perceive themselves more as the interchangeable exemplars of a social category than as unique personalities defined by their individual differences from others."[52] In other words, individuals perceive themselves not simply as singular members of a group, but rather, as psychological representatives of the group to which they belong.[53] It is in this process of self-stereotyping whereby the defining attributes and values of a group become the ideals a member seeks to embody. Their cognition, perception, and behavior are regulated by group standards rather than idiosyncratic personal norms.[54] In essence, "[through] depersonalization the group becomes the measure of *all* things to us."[55] This is a parallel process to the stereotyping of outgroups. Just as individuals in an outgroup are simply "one of them," so too depersonalization describes how someone in an ingroup is simply "one of us." This facilitates group cohesion and conformity.

To illustrate depersonalization, one may think of a military recruit on active duty. The recruit will begin to think of himself less in terms of "I" and more as a collective "we" as he perceives his membership in this group. This is why he may be willing to jeopardize, and even sacrifice,

---

50. Haslam, Reicher, and Platow, *The New Psychology of Leadership*, 52.
51. Turner, "Towards a Cognitive Redefinition of the Social Group," 21.
52. Turner et al., eds., *Rediscovering the Social Group*, 50.
53. This is not to suggest that the social identity of the group is static. In fact, it is this variability of group values that enables group members to shape and reshape the identity of the group (see below). It should also be noted that depersonalization does not necessitate an individual's perception of herself as a functional representative of the group, as in the case of a formal leader, but simply as a psychological representative. See Haslam, Reicher, and Platow, *The New Psychology of Leadership*, 52.
54. Michael A. Hogg, Elizabeth A. Hardie, and Katherine J. Reynolds, "Prototypical Similarity, Self-Categorization, and Depersonalized Attraction: A Perspective on Group Cohesiveness," *EJSP* 25, no. 2 (1995): 160.
55. Haslam, Reicher, and Platow, *The New Psychology of Leadership*, 53.

his own life for the values of the group, a fact that goes against maintenance of his personal interest. Depersonalization, however, does not mean group members lose their sense of self. Rather, this process describes how a change in one's view of self can be brought about in specific circumstances.[56]

The military recruit's identity as a soldier may require the use of violence or self-sacrifice, behaviors not mandated by his identity as a fan of his local sports team. Context determines the salience (i.e., relevance and significance) of a particular social identity.[57] When the recruit is behind enemy lines with his unit, his identity as a soldier is more salient than his other identities. But if this same recruit, who is Jewish, is on base with other soldiers, some of whom are also Jewish, his ethno-religious identity may become more prominent. He may tend to feel solidarity with his fellow Jews on the base. This sense could be strengthened if these individuals share common Jewish customs and rituals together. In each of these circumstances, the recruit operates within the parameters of a social group. When a social identity is activated, the process of depersonalization shows how the needs, norms, and values of the group supersede that of the individual.

While I have discussed the importance of context above generally, the question remains of when a particular identity becomes salient. Two contributing factors to categorization noted by social psychologists are "accessibility" and "fit."[58] The first of these, also called "perceptual

---

56. Craig McGarty, Ana-Maria Bliuc, and Renata Bongiorno, "Depersonalization," in Levine and Hogg, eds., *Encyclopedia of Group Processes and Intergroup Relations*, 1:197. This contrasts with deindividuation theory, which maintains that individuals lose their sense of individual identity in a crowd exhibiting violence and irrational behavior. These individuals, according to this theory, resort to a primitive state of being where hidden aggression is unhindered by cultural norms. For a summary of deindividuation theory, see Tom Postmes, "Deindividuation," in *Encyclopedia of Social Psychology*, ed. R. F. Baumeister and K. D. Vohs (Thousand Oaks, CA: Sage, 2007), 1:233–5. For a succinct critique of deindividuation, see Stephen D. Reicher, "The Determination of Collective Behaviour," in Tajfel, ed., *Social Identity and Intergroup Relations*, 58–63.

57. John C. Turner and Rina S. Onorato, "Social Identity, Personality, and the Self-Concept: A Self-Categorization Perspective," in *The Psychology of the Social Self*, ed. T. R. Tyler, R. M. Kramer, and Oliver P. John (New York: Psychology Press, 1999), 21; Abrams and Hogg, *Social Identifications*, 22.

58. Penelope Oakes, "The Salience of Social Categories," in Turner et al., eds., *Rediscovering the Social Group*, 117–41; J. C. Turner et al., "Self and Collective: Cognition and Social Context," *Personality and Social Psychology Bulletin* 20 (1994): 454–63.

readiness," describes how people are more likely to use categories in relation to particular groups based on their previous experiences and associated meanings of these groups.[59] People with a history of racism will tend to categorize members of other races (i.e., outgroups) based on prior expectations and ideology.[60] When people encounter someone from of another ethnicity, their social history facilitates their process of categorization. Moreover, a significant past experience with another race (violence, prejudice, etc.) strengthens their readiness to draw upon their social preconceptions. If a Caucasian female, for example, was once held at gunpoint by a Hispanic male, the categories of gender and race may become equally salient in a context where there are men, some of whom are Hispanic. Similarly, a woman who has fought tirelessly for gender equality in the workplace doubtlessly will have an increased readiness to employ the categorization of gender in a situation where women are the minority.

Alongside the accessibility of social identifications, the concept of "fit" equally contributes to social identity salience.[61] Fit refers to "the degree to which a social categorization matches subjectively relevant features of reality—so that the category appears to be a sensible way of organizing and making sense of social stimuli."[62] In other words, the principle of fit states that people will employ categories based on what makes sense in light of their expectations of groups and group members. There are two aspects of fit discussed in SCT, namely "comparative fit" and "normative fit."[63] With comparative fit, individuals are more likely to identify with a particular group to the extent that the perceived differences of the group are smaller than the differences with other groups in a particular context. In a room full of Democrat and Republican politicians, a Democrat will view the difference between herself and other Democrats in the room as far less than the differences with the Republicans present. Yet in a different context, such as a sporting event, that same individual may minimize the differences with a Republican who has turned out in support of her team over against fans of the opposing team. In that situation, the differences

---

59. Haslam, Reicher, and Platow, *The New Psychology of Leadership*, 65, 69; Turner, "Social Categorization and the Self-Concept," 102; Penelope Oakes, S. A. Haslam, and J. C. Turner, *Stereotyping and Social Reality* (Oxford: Blackwell, 1994).

60. See Haslam, Reicher, and Platow, *The New Psychology of Leadership*, 69.

61. Blanz argues that accessibility and fit are not independent but can mutually affect each other. See Mathias Blanz, "Accessibility and Fit as Determinants of the Salience of Social Categorizations," *EJSP* 29, no. 1 (1999): 43–74.

62. Haslam et al., "The Social Identity Perspective Today," 348.

63. Turner et al., "Self and Collective," 455; Haslam et al., "The Social Identity Perspective Today," 348–9.

between herself and others appear smaller because the identity as a sports fan is more salient. Thus, categorization provides the fundamental basis of one's social orientation to others.[64]

While comparative fit addresses the degree of perceived similarities and differences between groups and their members, normative fit describes the degree to which the content of a group member matches the perceiver's expectation of the nature of the group.[65] If content-related expectations are violated, social categorization will not follow. If, for instance, a Republican senator argues for significant tax increases on the wealthy, the perceiver may be less inclined to invoke the categorization of political party.[66] Thus, both the degree of differences between groups (comparative fit) and the nature of these differences (normative fit) contribute to category salience. It is important to note that neither fit nor accessibility are understood to be *sufficient* explanations for category salience.[67] They are simply pieces of the larger puzzle. Yet together, they provide important factors that aid category salience. As Turner concludes, "Thus given two equally 'fitting' categories the more 'accessible' category will become salient and given two equally 'accessible' categories the one that better 'fits' the perceptual data will become salient and, in general, salience depends on both accessibility and fit."[68]

Underlying the salience of a particular category is an understanding of what it means to embody the essence of the category itself. From a social identity perspective, group membership requires a certain level of conformity to a category prototype.[69] The concept of prototypicality

---

64. Oakes, Haslam, and Turner, "Role of Prototypicality in Group Influence and Cohesion," 80.

65. Penelope Oakes, John C. Turner, and S. Alexander Haslam, "Perceiving People as Group Members: The Role of Fit in the Salience of Social Categorizations," *BJSP* 30, no. 2 (1991): 127.

66. Haslam, Reicher, and Platow, *The New Psychology of Leadership*, 66.

67. Turner et al., "Self and Collective," 456.

68. Turner, "Social Categorization and the Self-Concept," 102. From the above, one can see a temporal element to the analysis. Since much of perceiver readiness and fit are based on previous experiences and expectations, both the past and the present are equally relevant to the salience of social categories. What happened in the past affects categorization in the present, but categorization in the present can reinterpret and redefine one's perception of the past. This works for the future as well. As Haslam, Reicher, and Platow state, "Categorization is not only about the past (prior experience) or the present (existing social organization), it is also about the *future*." Haslam, Reicher, and Platow, *The New Psychology of Leadership*, 69.

69. Oakes, Haslam, and Turner, "Role of Prototypicality in Group Influence and Cohesion," 75.

is the result of Eleanor Rosch's work on the psychological process of categorization.[70] In addition to exploring comparisons between categories, Rosch and her colleagues discovered that categories themselves have an internally graded structure. Contrary to the classical view, which understood all category members as possessing an even level of shared defining attributes, category members in actuality varied in typicality.[71] An eagle, for example, may be seen by Americans as more typical of the category "bird" than an ostrich. Nevertheless, both exist in the category of bird. Thus, one could say that an eagle is more prototypical (i.e., a better representation) of the category than an ostrich. It is not that members share a defining set of features, such as beaks and feathers, but that they are related through their similarity to a prototype.[72] Yet the comparative element is equally significant when discussing prototypicality. While an eagle may appear more prototypical than an ostrich, an ostrich will appear prototypical of birds when compared with a crocodile. At the human level, a group member may appear prototypically risky or prototypically cautious when compared with a more risky or cautious outgroup member.[73] The comparative context influences the perception of prototypicality.[74]

None of this is to imply, however, that prototypes are fixed in the context of a static group. They are, as Rosch noted in her work, "fictions" that are context dependent.[75] Thus, from the viewpoint of Self-Categorization Theory, prototypicality is emphasized more than prototypes. Nevertheless, to the perceiver the prototypes *appear* fixed in various situations. The context-dependent nature of categorization is enabled by the principles

70. Ibid. See Eleanor Rosch, "Principles of Categorization," in *Concepts: Core Readings*, ed. E. Margolis and S. Laurence (Cambridge, MA: MIT, 1978), 189–206.
71. Oakes, Haslam, and Turner, "Role of Prototypicality in Group Influence and Cohesion," 75.
72. Ibid.
73. M. A. Hogg, J. C. Turner, and B. Davidson, "Polarized Norms and Social Frames of Reference: A Test of the Self-Categorization Theory of Group Polarization," *BASP* 11, no. 1 (1990): 77–100; Oakes, Haslam, and Turner, "Role of Prototypicality in Group Influence and Cohesion," 85–6.
74. The context of the perceiver is equally significant in categorization. Barsalou and Sewell, for instance, studied categorization from the point of view of American and Chinese undergraduate students. While the American students perceived robins and eagles as more prototypical of birds, Chinese students viewed swans and peacocks as more typical. See L. W. Barsalou and D. R. Sewell, *Constructing Representations of Categories from Different Points of View*, Emory Cognition Projects Report 2 (Atlanta, GA: Emory University, 1984).
75. Oakes, Haslam, and Turner, "Role of Prototypicality in Group Influence and Cohesion," 80.

discussed above of accessibility and fit. A perceiver will more easily categorize a prototypical group member if they have had previous experience with the group than if it is the first encounter.

Thus, from the preceding discussion, a prototype may be defined as "a fuzzy set of attributes (perceptions, attitudes, feelings, and behaviors) that are related to one another in a meaningful way and that simultaneously capture similarities within the group and differences between the group and other groups or people who are not in the group."[76]

Texts and Identity

Language is a central component of identity formation.[77] We frame who we are, and who we are not, in part, with discourse. One of my basic premises is that texts aid the construction and negotiation of identity. Judith Lieu notes how the study of identity in antiquity has often focused on texts.[78] This is, in part, due to the accidental survival of texts from the ancient world. But more fundamentally, there is a general recognition of the constructive role that texts played in these societies. The Apostle Paul, for example, circulated letters prescribing various practices and matters of doctrine. The patterns established by his written instruction had the potential to influence the self-conceptions and behaviors of local groups of Christ-followers.[79] These written texts could shape communities. This phenomenon, however, is by no means limited to the study of identity in antiquity. In reality, any discursive practice has the potential to form social groups as well as facilitate identity negotiation and maintenance.[80] There is always an implied sense of identity in texts, both of the author and audience.[81] While the proximity of a text to its audience with relation to its original context is not unimportant, texts resist confinement to a local

---

76. Hogg, "Social Identity Theory," 118.

77. For a brief introduction, see A. De Fina, D. Schiffrin, and M. Bamberg, eds., *Discourse and Identity* (Cambridge: Cambridge University Press, 2006), 1–16. Also see Gary Taylor and Steve Spencer's "Introduction" to *Social Identities: Multidisciplinary Approaches*, ed. Gary Taylor and Steve Spencer (London: Routledge, 2004), 1–13.

78. Lieu, *Christian Identity in the Jewish and Graeco-Roman World*, 10.

79. See, e.g., Jack Barentsen, *Emerging Leadership in the Pauline Mission: A Social Identity Perspective of Local Leadership Development in Corinth and Ephesus*, Princeton Theological Monograph 168 (Eugene, OR: Pickwick, 2011).

80. Ruth Wodak et al., *The Discursive Construction of National Identity*, trans. Angelika Hirsch, Richard Mitten, and J. W. Unger, 2nd ed. (Edinburgh: Edinburgh University Press, 2009), 8.

81. Filtvedt, *Identity of God's People and Paradox of Hebrews*, 40.

environment.[82] Thus, embedded notions of identity in texts may be just as relevant to a foreign situation, whether by distance or time, as it was to its addressees.

The primary interest of the present work is not to trace the outworking of identity formation in specific historical settings, but rather, to explore the embedded notions of identity in the text of Amos. Though new and diverse social groups emerge in various contexts, Amos as a text seeks to reconfigure the audience's sense of self wherever they may be situated. Yet a purely cognitive understanding of one's group membership is not the goal. A proper understanding of social identification produces corresponding behavior.

Ruth Wodak and her coauthors catalogue several macrofunctions of discursive acts from the perspective of Critical Discourse Analysis. While some acts generate and perpetuate social situations, such as the formation of groups and establishment or concealment of power, other discursive practice may be effective in dismantling or even destroying the status quo.[83] Some texts may more readily lend themselves to one or the other by use of language of inclusion and exclusion. This coincides with the intergroup dynamics we will discover in the biblical text. Moreover, the cosmic scope of Amos—that is, the socially constructed reality—shows the all-encompassing nature of the world presented. It simply will not allow the status quo to remain. The text presents representations of reality audiences could recognize as potential ways of perceiving themselves.[84] Another way to say this is that the text puts forward "roles" and invites the audience to identify with those roles.[85] This is particularly subversive with respect to the elites encountering the book of Amos.[86] Those called by YHWH's name (Amos 9:12) are presented as a social group with a positive social identity. As one enters into the world of Amos, this social identity can motivate a desire for social mobility. The audience may then adopt the norms and values embedded in Amos as an attempt to conform to the patterns of prototypicality presented. The audience may choose to resist membership in this social group, but within the world of the text this breaks out against all reason. Thus, the constructive function of identity embedded in the text of Amos can be productive regardless of temporal or original social location.

82. Lieu, *Christian Identity in Jewish and Graeco-Roman World*, 4–5.
83. Wodak et al., *The Discursive Construction of National Identity*, 8.
84. Filtvedt, *Identity of God's People and Paradox of Hebrews*, 41.
85. Ibid.
86. On the reception and influence of the text of Amos in later periods, see Walter J. Houston, *Amos: Justice and Violence*, T&T Clark Study Guides to the Old Testament (London: T&T Clark, 2017), 83–96.

Application in Hebrew Bible Studies

The Social Identity Approach has yielded numerous insights in biblical studies, particularly in New Testament scholarship, as well as the study of Second Temple literature.[87] Although SIA has not received an equal reception in Hebrew Bible/Old Testament studies, some good work has been done. To orient my own project, I will briefly survey some of the major applications to date.

Jan P. Bosman

Writing from a post-apartheid South African context, Bosman applies a "multi-dimensional ideological-critical" approach to the book of Nahum. From this perspective, he argues that Nahum, often read as an ethnocentric text, actually yields an ethic of tolerance and responsible co-existence. Undergirding this thesis is the premise that social identity comprises the essence of what it means for a group to live ethically with other groups.[88] The specific approach taken combines a Social Identity Approach with both a synchronic and diachronic reading of the text, all the while keeping an eye towards its socio-political ideology and ancient Near Eastern context.

Bosman posits five working premises about social identity that he tests in the two strata of material he discerns in Nahum (pre-exilic material and exilic/post-exilic material).[89] The first premise is that all people have a social identity and belong to groups with basic group principles and beliefs. The second premise states that people in a group are motivated to act stereotypically according to their group principles. The third premise is that individuals in a group will always minimize differences between ingroup members and maximize differences in relation to the outgroup. The fourth premise is that the process of self-categorization is context dependent according to the meta-contrast principle. The fifth premise is that groups create their social identity by constructing textual identities. Together, says Bosman, these premises reveal a theological ethic in Nahum that rejects exclusivism. He does discover, however, some aspects of the text that he believes should be resisted, such as the use of Nahum to

---

87. See Coleman A. Baker, "Social Identity Theory and Biblical Interpretation," *BTB* 42, no. 3 (2012): 129–38; J. Brian Tucker and Coleman Baker, eds., *T&T Clark Handbook to Social Identity in the New Testament* (London: Bloomsbury, 2016); Samuel Byrskog, Raimo Hakola, and Jutta Jokiranta, eds., *Social Memory and Social Identity in the Study of Early Judaism and Early Christianity*, NTOA/SUNT 116 (Göttingen: Vandenhoeck & Ruprecht, 2016).

88. Jan Petrus Bosman, *Social Identity in Nahum: A Theological-Ethical Enquiry* (Piscataway, NJ: Gorgias, 2008), 3.

89. Ibid., 87–9.

legitimatize violence and dehumanization. Though his project can at times be overly complex, with a corresponding lacking coherence, Bosman attempts an innovative application of the Social Identity Approach to the Hebrew Bible.

Peter Lau

Lau's monograph *Identity and Ethics in the Book of Ruth: A Social Identity Approach* analyzes the characters in Ruth for the persuasive intent of the narrative for an "implied reader."[90] Thus, he combines a narrative-ethical and Social Identity Approach in his reading. He argues that both personal and social identity are operative in the narrative. Together, these both provide a foundation *for* ethical behavior and also being shaped *by* ethical behavior. The characters in the narrative themselves embody tensions between these expressions of identity. It is from this perspective that ethics may be derived. Through his study, the socio-historical context for the implied reader is central to understanding ethical influence of the text.

Louis C. Jonker

Over the years, Jonker has put forward numerous works interacting with identity construction in the Hebrew Bible, most notably Chronicles.[91] The burden of his work, as evidenced in his 2016 volume, *Defining All-Israel in Chronicles: Multi-Levelled Identity Negotiation in Late Persian-Period Yehud*, is to critically evaluate and implement "identity" as a heuristic tool in the interpretation of the Hebrew Bible. He rejects what he believes to be a reductionistic methodology that does not adequately consider the socio-historical context of the texts being studied, including provenance and composition. More than simply understanding

---

90. P. H. W. Lau, *Identity and Ethics in the Book of Ruth: A Social Identity Approach*, BZAW 416 (Berlin: de Gruyter, 2011), 43.

91. See the following works by Louis C. Jonker: "The Rhetorics of Finding a New Identity in a Multi-Cultural and Multi-Religious Society," *Verbum et Ecclesia* 24, no. 2 (2003): 396–416; "Refocusing the Battle Accounts of the Kings: Identity Formation in the Books of Chronicles," in *Behutsames Lesen: alttestamentliche Exegese im interdisziplinären Methodendiskurs; Christof Hardmeier zum 65. Geburtstag*, ed. Louis C. Jonker et al., Arbeiten zur Bibel und ihrer Geschichte 28 (Leipzig: Evangelische Verlagsanstalt, 2007), 245–75; "Textual Identities in the Books of Chronicles," 197–217; "Human Dignity and the Construction of Identity in the Old Testament," *Scriptura* 105 (2010): 594–607; *Defining All-Israel in Chronicles: Multi-Levelled Identity Negotiation in Late Persian-Period Yehud*, FAT 106 (Tübingen: Mohr Siebeck, 2016).

the surrounding environment of texts, however, Jonker seeks to show how the texts themselves contribute to the negotiation of identity in Persian Yehud. He implements a multi-levelled methodology built upon the belief that biblical texts are too complex for one or two methods of analysis to do them justice. His particular approach in his most recent monograph *All-Israel in Chronicles*, utilizes four specific methods as "road markers" on the way forward, including post-colonial analysis, insights from utopian studies, social memory, and social psychology.

With regards to the construction of identity, Jonker prefers the terminology of "identity negotiation." This, he says, portrays the dynamic nature of the process (i.e., a constructivist understanding of identity). Contrary to an essentialist understanding of identity (i.e., fixed and innate), Jonker argues that there is not a point where one's identity is fully realized. Rather, identity remains a fluid process. It is something that continues to be forged at the intersection of text and social context. Moreover, he embraces a multi-directional process of identity. It is not a linear project, but a dialogue between one's social context and one's subjective identification. In his view, "negotiation" better captures this process than "identity formation" or "identity construction."

To capture the dynamic nature of identity negotiation in literary sources, as well as the interrelationship between social groups and their texts, Jonker adopts the notion of "textual identities."[92] This concept follows the developments in research on discourse and identity, emphasizing the embeddedness of identity in social and discourse practices.[93] From this vantage point, the Chronicler is shown to present his material not as a retelling of the facts of the past, but rather "for the sake of self-categorization in a new present."[94]

Dominic S. Irudayaraj

Irudayaraj analyzes the violent description of the Arriving One in Isa. 63:1-6 in his book *Violence, Otherness and Identity in Isaiah 63:1-6: The Trampling One Coming from Edom*. Methodologically, he employs a Social Identity Approach, combined with Iconographic Exegesis.[95]

---

92. See Jonker, "Textual Identities in the Books of Chronicles."
93. See, e.g., De Fina, Schiffrin, and Bamberg, *Discourse and Identity*.
94. Jonker, "Textual Identities in the Books of Chronicles," 214.
95. The latter method was developed by Izaak J. de Hulster. He defines Iconographic Exegesis as "a historical method which…is intended to illuminate biblical texts (their contents, concepts, ideas, etc.) and their historical context (religious, social, cultural, political, economical [*sic*]) with the help of images in order to understand

While interpreters have grappled with how to understand Isa. 63:1-6 in the hopeful context of Isaiah 56–66, Irudayaraj proposes that the imagery functions "as a cipher for the prophetic revival of theological and social identities of the Yehud community."[96] The othering of one's "proximate neighbor" served to reify the ingroup's sense of self. According to Irudayaraj, the post-exilic Judean context of Third Isaiah made defining Israelite identity essential. The addition of Iconographic Exegesis, which essentially incorporates contemporaneous art forms into the interpretive process, supposedly provides a fuller picture of textual imagery. While Irudayaraj's analysis situates social identity in a socio-historical context, he does not develop the background information to the degree pursued in other works.

Jutta Jokiranta

Though not specifically within Hebrew Bible scholarship, Jokiranta's research on social identity makes a notable contribution to the study of Second Temple Judaism and the Dead Sea Scrolls.[97] In her book *Social Identity and Sectarianism in the Qumran Movement*, she states that the study of identity requires more than a simple study of beliefs and practices.[98]

---

the text as much as possible in the way the first receiving communities did." Izaak J. de Hulster, *Iconographic Exegesis and Third Isaiah*, FAT2 36 (Tübingen: Mohr Siebeck, 2009), 20, quoted in Dominic S. Irudayaraj, *Violence, Otherness and Identity in Isaiah 63:1-6: The Trampling One Coming from Edom*, LHBOTS 633 (New York: T&T Clark, 2017), 108.

96. Irudayaraj, *Violence, Otherness and Identity in Isaiah 63:1-6*, 5.

97. See, e.g., the following works by Jutta Jokiranta: "Black Sheep, Outsiders, and the Qumran Movement: Social-Psychological Perspectives on Norm-Deviant Behaviour," in Byrskog, Hakola, and Jokiranta, eds., *Social Memory and Social Identity in the Study of Early Judaism and Early Christianity*, 151–73; "Social-Scientific Approaches to the Dead Sea Scrolls," in *Rediscovering the Dead Sea Scrolls: An Assessment of Old and New Approaches and Methods*, ed. Maxine L. Grossman (Grand Rapids: Eerdmans, 2010), 246–63; "Social Identity Approach: Identity-Constructing Elements in the Psalms Pesher," in *Defining Identities: Who Is the Other? We, You, and the Others in the Dead Sea Scrolls. Proceedings of the Fifth Meeting of the IOQS in Groningen*, ed. Florentino García Martínez and Mladen Popović, STDJ 70 (Leiden: Brill, 2008), 85–109; "Prototypical Teacher in the Qumran Pesharim: A Social Identity Approach," in *Ancient Israel: The Old Testament in Its Social Context*, ed. Philip F. Esler (Minneapolis: Fortress, 2006), 254–63; Cecilia Wassen and Jutta Jokiranta, "Groups in Tension: Sectarianism in the Damascus Document and the Community Rule," in *Sectarianism in Early Judaism: Sociological Advances*, ed. David J. Chalcraft (London: Equinox, 2007), 205–45.

98. Jokiranta, *Social Identity and Sectarianism in the Qumran Movement*, 1.

To investigate the concept of identity in the Qumran community, Jokiranta employs a Social Identity Approach, studying the construction of both social and person identity in the *serakhim* (the rule documents) and the *pesharim*. Here, various strategies are employed to strengthen ingroup boundaries, form cohesive ingroup norms, and disparage outgroups. In her view, the *serakhim* not only reflect the sectarianism of the Qumran movement as a religious group, but also reflects the construction of the sectarian group itself. Thus, group members seek to adopt the sectarian social identity as evidenced in the rules. Identity-construction strategies in the *pesharim* include establishing continuity with the faithful in Scriptural traditions, aligning their own enemies with pagan enemies of God, and presenting the prototypicality of the Teacher of Righteousness. Together, these strategies evidence the value of questions raised by a Social Identity Approach.

Linda M. Stargel

In a recent monograph, Stargel employs a Social Identity Approach to ascertain the contribution of the "exodus story" to the construction of identity in the Hebrew Bible.[99] With over 120 direct references to the exodus, this narrative has a greater level of "mnemonic density" than any other single narrative theme.[100] To assess its significance for identity-construction, Stargel examines both the "primary exodus story" (Exod. 1:1–15:21) and eighteen "retold exodus stories" in the Pentateuch, Prophets, and Writings, employing a new heuristic tool. Specifically, this tool includes five dimensions of social identity applied to each passage: cognitive, evaluative, emotional, behavioral, and temporal. These categories, as she states, "not only represent collective identification processes present in narratives but they have the potential to mediate social identity to hearers."[101] Thus, the exodus story is able to influence social actors in subsequent time periods. Indeed, as Stargel asserts, it functions "not simply to safeguard the past but to persuade Israel of a still relevant, present and future collective identity."[102] Of all the works mentioned above, Stargel's is the broadest use of the Social Identity Approach in Hebrew Bible scholarship to date. The focus on narrative identity, however, limits the possible application of the specific method to certain base texts. Nevertheless, she

---

99. Linda M. Stargel, *The Construction of Exodus Identity in Ancient Israel: A Social Identity Approach* (Eugene, OR: Wipf & Stock, 2018).
100. Ibid., xvii.
101. Ibid., 29.
102. Ibid., 144.

ably demonstrates the suitability of SIA for the rich study of how biblical texts function, not just for the original audience(s), but for later readers and hearers.

Conclusion

This chapter presented the theoretical framework employed throughout this work. The chapter outlined the origins of the Social Identity Approach, comprised of Social Identity Theory and Self-Categorization Theory, along with the respective elements of each. At its core, SIT maintains that categorization as a group member leads to social comparison and a desire for positive distinctiveness of one's group. If a positive social identity is not derived from one's current group membership, an individual will pursue identification with another group, whether actually or psychologically. The permeability of group boundaries determines which approach an individual will take towards this end. For groups that do award a positive social identity, members will seek to conform to an ingroup prototype to become more representative of the group itself. Conversely, they will exaggerate the differences with outgroups (i.e., the principle of meta-contrast). This othering of outgroups facilitates the solidarity of a social group.

As this chapter has shown, the Social Identity Approach has great explanatory power within various group dynamics, especially intergroup conflict. As will be shown in Chapter 4, the book of Amos is laden with intergroup conflict, providing a ripe field for the application of this heuristic tool. The brief survey of applications of SIA in Hebrew Bible scholarship shows the potential for this approach for biblical literature. As a text, the textual construction of identity embedded in Amos is significant for its audience in shaping their sense of self. As they enter into the world of the text, they will discover who they are, and who they can be, as well as how they should live.

Chapter 3

THE PEOPLE OF GOD IN AMOS:
THE PROPHET AND PROTOTYPICALITY

The book of Amos is laden with conflict. Foreign nations do violence to one another. The elites in Israel extort, oppress, and abuse the lowly in their own society. Religious leaders silence the dissenting voice of the prophet. Despite their religious fervor, they stand as enemies of YHWH. The people of Israel love injustice and hate righteousness, perpetuating systems of self-aggrandizement. Indeed, they do not know how to do what is right (3:10a). From a social identity perspective, the differing descriptions of the groups in Amos serve to portray various outgroups as existing on the same plane. In short, they are *them*; they are not *us*. The othering of outgroups contrasts with the positive characteristics of the ingroup. This chapter will explore these group dynamics in the book of Amos. First, a summary of the intergroup conflict from a social identity perspective will be presented. A brief study of the Oracles against the Nations (1:3–2:16) will serve as an apt illustration. Second, the nature of both the ingroup and outgroup will be explored through an analysis of the confrontation with Amaziah, the priest at Bethel. This section shows that Amos and Amaziah are not primarily acting as individuals in the narrative, but rather are prototypes of their respective groups.

Intergroup Conflict from a Social Identity Perspective

There are a number of plausible factors that may contribute to intergroup conflict. One seemingly obvious example involves competition for scarce resources. If there is only so much of a resource available, one would expect groups in close proximity to engage in competition to secure it. Yet the findings of social psychological experimentation indicate that a scarcity of resources is not necessarily a precondition for intergroup conflict.¹ Rather, studies have shown that categorization as a group member, when paired with a desire for a positive ingroup distinctiveness, proved sufficient to generate ingroup bias and outgroup discrimination. Furthermore, hostility between groups can escalate when a group's desire for positive distinctiveness is frustrated or impeded by an outgroup.² And while the nature of the relationship between categorization and intergroup conflict remains a live question, Social Identity Theory remains a dominant tool for analysis.³

In the book of Amos, most of the conflict exists between social groups (nations, social classes, etc.), with a brief narrative involving two individuals (7:10-17). Throughout the book YHWH speaks with the first-person singular "I" to and about groups of peoples. Yet in all of this, an underlying group concept is apparent. YHWH does not act simply as an individual. He labors to establish the credibility of the prophet, who always hears and speaks his word (cf. 3:7). The eschatological restoration at the conclusion of the book does not end with YHWH standing alone, but with YHWH in relationship with a renewed people. In other words, there is always a group dynamic at work. As will be seen in the Bethel narrative, the two individuals involved are best understood in light of their social group membership. To illustrate this, I will first look at the collection of Oracles against the Nations (OAN).

Before turning to the OAN collection, the role of the superscription (1:1) and the motto (1:2) for understanding identity should be mentioned. The superscription identifies Israel as the focus of Amos's message.⁴ Set within the reigns of Uzziah, king of Judah, and Jeroboam the son of Joash, king of Israel, the book opens with an eye towards both the northern and southern kingdoms.⁵ This was a time of prosperity and relative security

---

1. See Robin R. Vallacher et al., *Attracted to Conflict: Dynamic Foundations of Destructive Social Relations* (London: Springer, 2014), 38.

2. Tajfel and Turner, "An Integrative Theory of Intergroup Conflict," 46.

3. For other explanations of intergroup conflict, see Susan Condor and Rupert Brown, "Psychological Processes in Intergroup Conflict," in *The Social Psychology of Intergroup Conflict: Theory, Research and Applications*, ed. Wolfgang Stroebe et al. (New York: Springer, 1988), 3–26.

4. For a discussion of Amos 1:1-2, see Karl Möller, *A Prophet in Debate: The Rhetoric of Persuasion in the Book of Amos* (New York: Sheffield Academic, 2003), 154–71; Jason Radine, *The Book of Amos in Emergent Judah*, FAT 45 (Tübingen: Mohr Siebeck, 2010), 7–11.

5. Hosea's superscription similarly includes both Judean kings (Uzziah, Jotham, Ahaz, and Hezekiah) and one northern king (Jeroboam the son of Joash). Though Micah's superscription only contains three southern kings, the message he received

for both kingdoms.⁶ The first mark of turbulence in the text comes with the mention of the earthquake two years following Amos's prophecy. From the beginning of the book the audience knows that devastation is on the horizon, an event so severe that it could provide a temporal marker for later generations.⁷ Following the superscription is a motto that announces the roaring of YHWH from Zion (1:2).⁸ Even before the earthquake is actualized in the world of the text, YHWH's voice brings destruction. The location of YHWH's roaring is identified as Zion and Jerusalem.⁹ This too makes a bold statement in the world of the text. James Linville notes the

---

is said to concern Samaria and Jerusalem. Tucker detects a compositional history to Amos's superscription, reflecting scribal concerns. He suggests that a shorter version of the superscription likely circulated at the head of the visions in Amos 7–9. See G. M. Tucker, "Amos the Prophet and Amos the Book: Historical Framework," in Kelle and Moore, eds., *Israel's Prophets and Israel's Past*, 90–1.

6. Levin attributes the description of the ill treatment of the poor in Amos to a date much later than eighth century BCE. Thus, the prophetic social criticism, in his view, are part of the Jewish and early Christian idealization of the godliness of the poor. See Christoph Levin, *Re-Reading the Scriptures: Essays on the Literary History of the Old Testament*, FAT 87 (Tübingen: Mohr Siebeck, 2013), 285–7; Levin, "Das Amosbuch der Anawim," *ZTK* 94 (1997): 407–36. Houston assesses the four major models used to explain the social conflict in ancient Israel and Judah in the ninth through eighth centuries BCE (rent capitalism, "ancient" class society, the tributary state, and the patronage system). He concludes that though each contains elements of truth, no single model can adequately account for all the facts. The establishment of the state, along with the increase in Assyrian dominance, led to an increase in taxation, especially in cities. In his view, these economic pressures gave rise to social conflict that forms the background of the eighth-century social critique. Houston, *Contending for Justice*, 18–51; Houston, "Was There a Social Crisis in the Eighth Century?" 130–49. For a survey of scholarly approaches to economics in ancient Israel, see Roger S. Nam, *Portrayals of Economic Exchange in the Book of Kings* (Leiden: Brill, 2012), 17–28.

7. This earthquake is also mentioned in Zech 14:5. See Carolyn J. Sharp, *Irony and Meaning in the Hebrew Bible* (Bloomington: Indiana University Press, 2009), 154.

8. The first two clauses in Amos 1:2 occur, with slight variation in word order, in Joel 3:16a-b. In Joel, the roaring of YHWH, which causes the heavens and earth to quake, stands alongside the hopeful claim that YHWH is a secure place for his people (3:16c-d). This conjoins with the exaltation of Jerusalem in Joel 3:17, 20-21. As will be seen, Amos's usage of YHWH's roar implies not security but devastation.

9. Many scholars identify the verse as a later addition based on the mention of Zion and Jerusalem. Paul, however, defends its authenticity. See Shalom M. Paul, *Amos*, Hermeneia (Minneapolis: Fortress, 1991), 36–7.

purposeful function of this setting, stating, "Geography is not neutral in this word-world."[10] But what significance does Jerusalem have in Amos 1:2 in the interpretation of what follows?

Scholars have traditionally sought to locate the *Sitz in Leben* of the motto.[11] For our purposes, however, it will suffice to note the destabilizing effect the mention of Judah's capital city at the outset of Amos's prophecy would have upon the sense of implied group identity in the book. The opening verses make clear that YHWH does not reside in the northern kingdom, as may have been expected, but in the South.[12] The coming rebuke is not an in-house affair. Rather, an outsider, Amos from Judah, delivers a message to the North from YHWH, who also emanates from Judah. Yet lest the audience assume that Judah is then an implied ingroup, the cosmic scope of YHWH's voice is noted in 1:2b-c—"the pastures of the shepherds mourn, and the top of Carmel withers."[13] This merism, as Shalom Paul notes, indicates the completeness of the destruction.[14] Judah, as made explicit in 2:4-5, is no more exempt from YHWH's roar of judgment than the northern kingdom. Thus, the audience starts with ambiguity regarding the implied ingroup in the book of Amos, a feature that is compounded by the following collection of Oracles against the Nations (1:3–2:16).

---

10. James R. Linville, *Amos and the Cosmic Imagination*, Society for Old Testament Study Monographs (Burlington, VT: Ashgate, 2008), 45.

11. See, for instance, James D. Nogalski, *Literary Precursors to the Book of the Twelve*, BZAW 217 (Berlin: Gruyter, 1993), 82–85; Hans Walter Wolff, *Joel and Amos*, Hermeneia (Philadelphia: Fortress, 1977), 119–22.

12. Scholars also note the significance of the order of kings in 1:1, with Uzziah king of Judah preceding Jeroboam king of Israel, as introducing a Judean audience. Möller, *A Prophet in Debate*, 169; Jörg Jeremias, *The Book of Amos: A Commentary*, trans. Douglas W. Stott (Louisville, KY: Westminster John Knox, 1998), 11; Francis I. Andersen and David Noel Freedman, *Amos: A New Translation with Introduction and Commentary*, AYB 24A (New York: Doubleday, 1989), 192.

13. The verb אבל could be understood either as "mourn" or "dry up." The LXX has ἐπένθησαν ("mourn"), a view followed by Anderson and Freedman, *Amos*, 226–7; M. Daniel Carroll R., "God and His People in the Nations' History: A Contextualised Reading of Amos 1–2," *TynBul* 47 (1996): 65–6; R. Reed Lessing, *Amos* (St. Louis: Concordia, 2009), 50. Scholars who understand it as "dry up" or "wither" include Eidevall, *Amos*, 92; Paul, *Amos*, 39–41; Duane A. Garrett, *Amos: A Handbook on the Hebrew Text*, BHHB (Waco, TX: Baylor University Press, 2008), 17; Wolff, *Joel and Amos*, 125.

14. Paul, *Amos*, 40.

Oracles Against the Nations (Amos 1:3–2:16)

The most extensive occurrence of intergroup conflict at a national level in Amos is the Oracles against the Nations in the first two chapters. This genre, also present in Isaiah 13–23, Jeremiah 46–51 (LXX 26–32), and Ezekiel 25–32, describes YHWH's judgment on seven of Israel's neighbors for various offenses.[15] Unlike other OAN collections in the Hebrew Bible, however, Amos opens the book with the indictment against foreign peoples, which includes Aram (1:3-5), Philistia (1:6-8), Tyre (1:9-10), Edom (1:11-12), Ammon (1:13-15), Moab (2:1-3), and Judah (2:4-5).[16] The extent and formulaic structure of the oracles in Amos make

---

15. For a brief introduction to the OAN genre, see Marvin A. Sweeney, "The Oracles Concerning the Nations in the Prophetic Literature," in *Concerning the Nations: Essays on the Oracles Against the Nations in Isaiah, Jeremiah and Ezekiel*, ed. Andrew Mein, Else K. Holt, and Hyun Chul Paul Kim (New York: Bloomsbury, 2015), xvii–xx. Gottwald argues that OAN is among the first forms of Israelite prophecy. Norman K. Gottwald, *All the Kingdoms of the Earth* (New York: Harper & Row, 1964), 49. Also see Gene M. Tucker, "The Social Location(s) of Amos: Amos 1:3–2:16," in *Thus Says the Lord: Essays on the Former and Latter Prophets in Honor of Robert R. Wilson*, ed. John J. Ahn and Stephen L. Cook, LHBOTS 502 (New York: T&T Clark, 2009), 273–84. On the structure, see also Andrew E. Steinmann, "The Order of Amos's Oracles Against the Nations: 1:3-2:16," *JBL* 111 (1992): 683–9; Robert B. Chisholm, Jr., "'For Three Sins…Even for Four': The Numerical Sayings in Amos," *BSac* 147, no. 586 (1990): 188–97; Karl Möller, "'Hear This Word Against You': A Fresh Look at the Arrangement and the Rhetorical Strategy of the Book of Amos," *VT* 50 (2000): 499–518.

16. The oracles against Tyre (1:9-10), Edom (1:11-12), and Judah (2:4-5) are generally considered secondary due to form and/or content. The Tyre oracle, for instance, indicts the nation for delivering another people group to Edom, which parallels the preceding charge against Philistia with similar language (1:6). The structure of the Tyre, Edom, and Judah oracles also deviates from the pattern of the others. Whereas the other oracles (Aram, Philistia, Ammon, Moab) have a brief charge for crimes and a longer punishment, these three reverse the pattern with a longer charge and abbreviated punishment formula. The substance of Judah's crimes (2:4) is a primary reason for its designation as an editorial insertion. It contains material generally considered deuteronomistic with its mention of the rejection of the law of YHWH (תורת יהוה). For a more extensive treatment of redaction in the OAN, see Hadjiev, *Composition and Redaction of Amos*, 42–59; Jakob Wöhrle, *Die frühen Sammlungen des Zwölfprophetenbuches: Entstehung und Komposition*, BZAW 360 (Berlin: de Gruyter, 2006), 93–7. Christensen reads the OAN against the background of an idealized Davidic empire. While he retains the authenticity of the Tyre and Edom oracle, he labels the Judah oracle a later insertion. Duane L. Christensen, *Transformations of the*

it unique in the broader OAN tradition. While each oracle varies in the details, they all follow a parallel pattern of divine speech formula ("Thus says YHWH"), graded numerical sequence ("For three sins of X, and for four"), a charge for crimes committed, and a punishment formula ("I will send/kindle fire"). Each nation is systematically tried and sentenced to death. The last nation targeted is Israel itself. The oracle against Israel deviates from the previous pattern in the charge and punishment formula.

Two notable issues pertaining to the oracles in Amos for our purposes include the basis for Amos's condemnation of the nations and the overall purpose of the oracles in the book as a whole. Together, these discussions will show the explanatory power of the Social Identity Approach.

The crimes charged against the nations range from human trafficking (Tyre, 1:6; Edom, 1:9) and brutality (Ammon, 1:13) to the rejection of YHWH's instruction and statutes (Judah, 2:4). The opening oracle indicts the Arameans for threshing Gilead with iron sledges.[17] While the crimes included are self-evidently heinous, scholars suggest a number of proposals for the rationale on which the nations are condemned. John Barton summarizes the options under four headings: (1) Nationalism and Covenant, (2) Logical Extension, (3) Universal Law, and (4) International Customary Law.[18] The first of these, Nationalism and Covenant, states that the nations are denounced for their opposition to Israel, YHWH's chosen people. This view presupposes a cultic provenance for the oracles.[19] Here, cultic functionaries would perform rituals designed to denounce Israel's

---

War Oracle in Old Testament Prophecy: Studies in the Oracles Against the Nations (Missoula, MT: Scholars Press, 1975), 57–72. Radine dates all of 1:3–2:5 between 553–538 BCE, thus connecting 1:2, with the destructive power of YHWH's roar, to the oracle against Israel in 2:6. The later oracles, he states, imitated the pattern of the original indictment of Israel. See Radine, *Book of Amos in Emergent Judah*, 11–22. For a defense of the authenticity of the entire collection, see Paul, *Amos*, 16–27.

17. The threshing of nations and peoples has parallels in the Assyrian royal inscriptions. It generally depicts the cruel treatment of the land and its inhabitants (cf. 2 Kgs 13:7). See Paul, *Amos*, 47. Wolff views the Gilead here as the area north of the Jabbok River. See Wolff, *Joel and Amos*, 154. On this oracle, also see Radine, *Book of Amos in Emergent Judah*, 172–5; C. L. Crouch, *War and Ethics in the Ancient Near East: Military Violence in Light of Cosmology and History*, BZAW 407 (Berlin: de Gruyter, 2009), 105.

18. See Barton, *Understanding Old Testament Ethics*, 109–14.

19. See, for instance, Ernst Würthwein, "Amos-Studien," *ZAW* 62 (1950): 10–52. For a critique of this view, see Göran Eidevall, "A Farewell to the Anticultic Prophet: Attitudes towards the Cult in the Book of Amos," in *Priests and Cults in the Book of the Twelve*, ed. Lena-Sofia Tiemeyer, ANEM 14 (Atlanta, GA: SBL, 2016), 102–4.

enemies and ensure victory in battle.[20] The offenses mentioned by Amos are thus committed ultimately against Israel. Another dimension of this view is that the nations are liable to YHWH because they were once vassals of Israel under the Davidic empire.[21] The difficulty with this view, however, is apparent. One may legitimately ask how Moab's desecration of the bones of Edom's king (2:1) is a personal affront to Israel. The suggestion that Edom was somehow allied with Israel lacks support.[22]

The second basis, Logical Extension, maintains that Israel's neighbors are under the same moral obligation Israel is known to owe YHWH. This view retains an Israel-focus, but not in terms of cult or covenant.[23] Israel would thus retain its privileged position as the covenant people of YHWH, but the nations nevertheless are responsible from an ethical perspective in light of the obligations of the covenant. The ethical requirements known to Israel are equally binding upon its neighbors. This, says Barton, would be a startling innovation in Israel, at least as far as popular opinion is concerned. Barton, however, rejects this view in an effort to preserve the rhetorical potency of the collection for an Israelite audience.[24] If the condemnation of Israel is to come as a surprise (see below), the verdict announced against the nations must accord with popular belief. What comes as a surprise is not that Israel's neighbors are guilty of the crimes common among all peoples, but rather that Israel should be equally

---

20. Bentzen argues that the OAN are similar in form and arrangement to the pattern of curses found in Egyptian execration texts, thus providing a link to a cultic context. Aage Bentzen, "The Ritual Background of Amos i 2-Ii 16," *OtSt*, no. 8 (1950): 85–99; Arvid S. Kapelrud, *Central Ideas in Amos* (Oslo: Aschehoug, 1956), 17–33. Also, Henning Graf Reventlow, *Das Amt des Propheten bei Amos*, FRLANT 80 (Göttingen: Vandenhoeck & Ruprecht, 1962), 56–75. For a response, see Meir Weiss, "The Pattern of the 'Execration Texts' in the Prophetic Literature," *Israel Exploration Journal* 19, no. 3 (1969): 150–7.

21. See Max. E. Polley, *Amos and the Davidic Empire: A Socio-Historical Approach* (New York: Oxford University Press, 1989). For a summary of this view, see Paul Noble, "Israel among the Nations," *HBT* 15 (1993): 56–61.

22. As noted in Wolff, *Joel and Amos*, 163.

23. F. C. Fensham, "Common Trends in Curses of the Near Eastern Treaties and Kudurru-Inscriptions Compared with Maledictions of Amos and Isaiah," *ZAW* 75 (1963): 155–75. This view is more prominent in Clements's earlier work, but later he seems to move towards what Barton labels Universal Law. See R. E. Clements, *Prophecy and Covenant*, Studies in Biblical Theology 43 (Eugene, OR: Wipf & Stock, 1965), 40–4; Clements, *Prophecy and Tradition* (Atlanta, GA: Westminster John Knox, 1975), 65.

24. Barton, *Understanding Old Testament Ethics*, 111–12.

as liable for their own actions. The third basis, Universal Law, states that nations are subject to divine law which derives from YHWH's sovereignty over humankind.[25] Shalom Paul states this clearly:

> All of mankind is considered the vassal of the Lord whose power, authority, and law embrace the entire world community of nations. His sovereignty is not confined merely to the territorial borders of Israel and Judah. Offenses against him are punished directly, wherever they are committed and whoever the guilty party may be. The Lord enforces the law he authors and imposes punishments against his rebel vassals. His law binds all peoples, for the God of Israel is the God of all the nations.[26]

The fourth basis noted by Barton, International Customary Law, maintains that nations infringe customs of war accepted—or believed to be accepted—by all civilized nations.[27] These international norms, though not explicitly legislated, relied upon conventional morality. This is the view espoused by Barton. The advantage of this position, he says, is that it allows for the rationality of Amos's condemnation in the sense that the nations are not judged by a standard of which they would not recognize.[28] In other words, each nation was thought to know these actions in war were immoral, but nevertheless disregarded the norms. The Ammonites, for example, knew that ripping open pregnant women in an attempt to expand their territory (1:13) was against conventional standards of warfare. No special form of legislation was needed. All civilized nations would agree, but the Ammonites violated this norm anyway. Other instances, especially in light of the final form of the text, pose more trouble for Barton's view. The Judah oracle in 2:4, for example, does not fit the international customary law framework with its religious orientation. Barton recognizes the anomalous nature of the Judah oracle, but is content to dismiss it as a secondary addition and move on.[29] Though Barton provides a substantive

---

25. So Eidevall, *Amos*, 100; Paul R. Raabe, "Why Prophetic Oracles Against the Nations?" in *Fortunate the Eyes That See: Essays in Honor of David Noel Freedman in Celebration of His Seventieth Birthday*, ed. Astrid B. Beck (Grand Rapids: Eerdmans, 1995), 234; Andersen and Freedman, *Amos*, 231–2.

26. Paul, *Amos*, 46.

27. See Jeremy M. Hutton, "Amos 1:3–2:8 and the International Economy of Iron Age II Israel," *Harvard Theological Review* 107 (2014): 81–113.

28. Barton, *Understanding Old Testament Ethics*, 113.

29. Barton states, "It is hard to believe that Amos could not have found some more definite sin with which to charge Judah, and, in any case, the tone of general disapprobation for disobedience to law is quite out of keeping with the indictment of the other nations for war crimes (foreign nations) and social injustice (Israel)." Barton, *Understanding Old Testament Ethics*, 96.

survey of international law in the ancient Near East, his proposal for the oracles in Amos remains hypothetical.[30]

Paul Noble affirms Barton's claim that the nations were not judged by a standard unknown to them, but nevertheless finds fault with the international customary law explanation as overly anthropocentric.[31] By this description he means that this view places the onus of developing the moral norms on humans. In Amos, then, YHWH is simply responding to this breach of humanly constructed norms. Against this, Noble locates the standard of national judgment in YHWH himself, a point which he says is an integral component to the book's conception of God.[32] Thus Noble links the basis of judgment to YHWH's law, albeit in a general sense. The nations may not have known the specific laws enacted by YHWH, but they were aware that extreme instances of wrongdoing, such as those charged against them in Amos, were rightly condemnable.[33] As Noble states, "Yahweh's judgment is therefore just, because it is based upon a standard which they could have known and ought to have lived by."[34]

Before providing an evaluation of the basis of the OAN from a social identity perspective, I will survey several proposals for overall purpose of the OAN in their present context. Most of these proposals build their argument on a particular understanding of the literary structure and organization of the unit.[35] As noted above, the seven oracles that precede the indictment of Israel share common stylistic features. This has led to much debate regarding the logic of the oracles' arrangement. Though questions of authenticity are not unimportant, the analysis here is concerned with the final form of the text. I will discuss the relevant details before providing an evaluation from a Social Identity Approach.

Regarding the purpose of the OAN, a very common view is that the oracles in Amos draw the audience in with what Robert Alter calls a "rhetoric of entrapment."[36] According to this tactic, the implied Israelite audience would be in agreement with the pronouncement of judgment upon neighboring nations. The Judah oracle, the seventh nation addressed, would be an especially welcomed climax to the series. Yet the surprise comes when the supposed climax turns out to be a pseudo-climax, Israel

---

30. Eidevall, *Amos*, 100.

31. Noble, "Israel Among the Nations," 63–4. So too Möller, *A Prophet in Debate*, 190.

32. Noble, "Israel Among the Nations," 64.

33. Ibid.

34. Ibid., 65.

35. For a detailed introduction to the structural features of OAN, see Andersen and Freedman, *Amos*, 206–18.

36. Robert Alter, *The Art of Biblical Poetry* (New York: Basic Books, 1985), 144.

being the real target of the indictment.[37] This view is expressed at length in Karl Möller's rhetorical study of Amos.[38] He argues that the book as a whole is designed to persuade its audience through a debate constructed in the text between the prophet and his eighth-century audience. The OAN introduce this debate with the rhetorical trap, moving from foreign nations (Arameans, Philistines, Phoenicians) to Israel's blood relatives (Edomites, Ammonites, Moabites), to Israel's sibling nation (Judah) before arriving at the target (Israel).[39] The goal of the book of Amos, in Möller's view, is to exhort pre-exilic Judah to not follow the mistake of the northern kingdom in shunning the call to return to YHWH. The place of the OAN in this schema is to trap the audience into condemning the other nations before themselves facing scrutiny for their own crimes.[40]

Maintaining the climax view, Shalom Paul argues that the oracles link together to form a "concatenous literary pattern."[41] This pattern ties each oracle to both the preceding oracle and subsequent oracle by means

---

37. The deviation from the expected 6 + 1 pattern has led many to doubt the unity of the section. This factors, for instance, into Harper's rejection of the authenticity of the oracle against Judah. See William R. Harper, *A Critical and Exegetical Commentary on Amos and Hosea*, ICC 23 (Edinburgh: T. & T. Clark, 1905), 44. On the other hand, Linville emphasizes the thematic unity of the section, labeling it the "Poem against the Nations." James R. Linville, "What Does 'It' Mean? Interpretation at the Point of No Return in Amos 1–2," *BibInt* 8 (2000): 400. Freedman suggests that intentional deviations from established patterns of repetition may serve specific rhetorical functions. See David Noel Freedman, "Deliberate Deviation from an Established Pattern of Repetition in Hebrew Poetry as a Rhetorical Device," in *Divine Commitment and Human Obligation: Selected Writings of David Noel Freedman*, ed. John R. Huddlestun (Grand Rapids: Eerdmans, 1997), 2:205–12.

38. Möller, *A Prophet in Debate*, 175–216.

39. Ibid., 194–5.

40. Hadjiev rejects the climax view, claiming that the present literary context is directed towards a later Judean audience. As such, the mention of northern Israel after the Judah oracle "would serve more as an anticlimax than anything else." Hadjiev, *Composition and Redaction of Amos*, 57. Yet within the world of the text, compositional issues aside, Israel appears to be the target, as indicated in the superscription ("The words of Amos...which he saw *concerning Israel*," 1:1 [emphasis added]). It would thus be fitting to interpret the OAN collection within a literary context of an indictment against northern Israel. For methodological considerations regarding synchronic reading, see Daniel H. Ryou, *Zephaniah's Oracles Against the Nations: A Synchronic and Diachronic Study of Zephaniah 2:1–3:8*, Biblical Interpretation 13 (Leiden, Netherlands: Brill, 1995), 1–7.

41. Shalom M. Paul, "Amos 1:3–2:3: A Concatenous Literary Pattern," *JBL* 90, no. 4 (1971): 397–403; Paul, *Amos*, 13–15. Christensen suggests that Paul's

of catchwords, phrases, and ideas. The mention of Tyre forsaking the covenant of brotherhood (לא זכרו ברית אחים) in 1:9, for instance, precedes Edom's hostility against its brother (רדפו בחרב אחיו) in 1:11. "Brother" is thus a keyword that links these two oracles. Another example is the nearly verbatim phrase in both the Aram oracle (1:5) and the Philistia oracle (1:8) regarding the cutting off of inhabitants (הכרתי יושב מבקעת־און ותומך שבט מבית עדן מאשקלון). In fact, the only link that does not contain an identical word or phrase is between Edom (1:11-12) and Ammon (1:13-15). Paul resolves this tension by positing a conceptual parallel between Edom's pursuing its "brother" with a "sword" and Ammon's ripping open pregnant women, presumably also with a sword.[42] Together, says Paul, the oracles against foreign nations form "one grand prolegomenon" to the surprise oracle against Israel. The force of the literary pattern is that the audience is propelled forward with each subsequent nation until the Judah oracle, after which they must reckon with the crimes of Israel, the *raison d'être* of Amos's commission.[43]

M. Daniel Carroll R. acknowledges Paul's concatenous pattern is plausible but asks if the poetics of the texts might not invite the audience to appreciate a degree of discontinuity in the series.[44] Noting Tyre's place as the third oracle and Edom's place as the fourth, Carroll R. suggests that the graded numerical sequence that governs the introduction of each oracle may function at the larger level. The entire unit then would consist of two interlocking sections of the three/four pattern. This could cause the audience to slow down at the Edom oracle, with its extended charge, and then again at the final Israel oracle. The purpose of this arrangement is to include Israel in the somber fate of guilty nations. When considered alongside the complex features of the section, the OAN, says Carroll R., show "Israel as enmeshed within several entwining webs of structural devices that make it part of this world of nations and their history."[45] Several of the themes introduced in the opening chapters of Amos recur throughout the book, such as military disaster, reversal of historical tradition (e.g., the exodus tradition), and the refusal to listen to YHWH.

---

concatenous literary pattern may be the result of two separate structural patterns composed by the poet. See Duane L. Christensen, "Prosodic Structure of Amos 1–2," *Harvard Theological Review* 67, no. 4 (1974): 436.

42. Paul, "Amos 1:3–2:3," 402.

43. Paul, *Amos*, 76. Also see Robert H. O'Connell, "Telescoping N + 1 Patterns in the Book of Amos," *VT* 46 (1996).

44. Carroll R., "God and His People," 63.

45. Ibid.

Another point discussed by Carroll R. that is relevant here is a self-identification process he posits for the audience of Amos.[46] The readers/hearers of the text, in light of the lack of details present, may come to identify with the victims of the atrocities in the acts condemned. Some of the oracles may have originally included Israel as the target of the war crimes mentioned. So, when Aram is charged with threshing Gilead, Amos's audience could resonate as those too who have been victimized in their past. But the twist comes when those who come to identify with the victims are shown themselves to be victimizers of those within their borders. In sum, Carroll R. views both continuity and discontinuity between Israel and the nations. They are, on the one hand, the covenant people of God, but on the other hand, they behave in like manner with other peoples of the world.

Similarly, Noble argues for both continuity and discontinuity with the portrayal of Israel among the nations. He makes a case for the unity of the section, arguing that the OAN frame Israel and Judah, called "classic Israel," as both formally assimilated *among* many nations as well as distinguished *from* the nations. Their common place among the nations is evidenced by the common literary elements in the unit, such as the graded numerical sequence. Just as the other nations are accountable to YHWH for extreme wrongdoing, so too Judah and Israel will be held accountable for their crimes. In this sense there is no difference between the people of God and the rest of humanity. In another sense, however, classic Israel is distinct from the other nations. In the Judah oracle (2:4-5), says Noble, the people are "marked out from [their] pagan neighbours through being aware of and responsible to the law of Yahweh in a way in which the surrounding nations evidently are not."[47] The Israel oracle (2:6-16), which also resembles the OAN pattern, is differentiated from the others with an extended theological reflection on their offenses. This differentiation is especially evident, Noble states, in the historical retrospect in 2:9-12, where YHWH recounts his victory over and dispossessing of the mighty Ammonites on Israel's behalf. In sum, Noble argues that the purpose of the 1:3–2:16 is to answer the fundamental question "What does it mean to be the people of God?" The answer is that classic Israel, as the people of God, are recipients of YHWH's grace, and are therefore under his law.[48] For Amos, this warranted a prophetic word of judgment against the two Yahwistic nations.

46. Ibid., 64.
47. Noble, "Israel Among the Nations," 69.
48. Ibid., 74.

Noble provides a good starting point for an evaluation of the OAN. From a social identity perspective, the question of "What does it mean to be the people of God?" lies at the center of the identity-forming capacity of the book. While this issue will be addressed more fully below, the relationship of the OAN to this question is instructive. As stated previously, one's social identity is, in part, shaped by the existence of, and relation to, outgroups. The collection of oracles in Amos 1–2 situates the embedded social identity in an international context where an audience, especially in light of the heinous crimes, is invited to align itself with the favorably represented group.[49] The desire for positive distinctiveness of one's group, as noted by Tajfel, leads to social comparison.[50] This tenet of the Social Identity Approach provides a helpful lens through which to reevaluate the questions of the basis for the nations' guilt as well as the function of the OAN in the book as a whole.[51]

Whatever the original basis for condemning the foreign nations, the present form of the text does not explicitly identify the rationale. It is simply assumed that these crimes warrant YHWH's judgment. This may actually be significant for my analysis when combined with Noble's point about the extreme nature of the nations' crimes.[52] The offenses of the foreign nations are not minor offenses. Threshing an entire region (1:3), facilitating the exile of an entire population (1:6, 9), desecrating human

---

49. Communication theorists describe the process of audiences aligning with characters in a text as "identification" and "transportation." By identification, these studies refer to the empathic responses to characters and audience may feel as they share the character's identity and experiences. Transportation, on the other hand, is where audiences enter into a text and temporarily lose access to the real world, being engrossed by an alternate reality. These two concepts, though related, have been distinguished. See Nurit Tal-Or and Jonathan Cohen, "Understanding Audience Involvement: Conceptualizing and Manipulating Identification and Transportation," *Poetics* 38 (2010): 402–18.

50. Tajfel, "Social Categorization, Social Identity and Social Comparison," 61–76.

51. In his discussion of the purpose of oracles against foreign nations, Raabe presents three helpful methodological considerations. First, the complex nature of the material contained in these units should open the possibility that a given oracle might serve several concurrent purposes simultaneously. Second, one should take seriously the present shape of the oracles in their present literary context. Of course, the placement of the oracles in Jeremiah in the MT (46–51) and LXX (25–31) present an interesting case. Finally, one should allow the rest of the book to inform the interpretation of a specific oracle. See Raabe, "Why Prophetic Oracles against the Nations?" 236–57.

52. See Noble, "Israel Among the Nations," 64.

dignity both in its earliest stages (1:13) and latter state (2:1), all point to the severity of the charges. Even Judah's crimes are extreme in the sense that they had rejected a central component of their identity, namely YHWH's instruction (2:4). And while these offenses differ in specifics from one another, they collectively show the outgroup status of the nations as a whole in two ways. First, the oracles allow no ethical distinction between each nation. Judah's religious defection (2:4), according to Amos, is in the same category with Ammon's violence against pregnant women for the purpose of territory expansion (1:13). This may appear to be disproportionate from an "objective" standpoint, but when understood from a social identity perspective, this is an effective othering strategy. There is no gradation of wrong behavior among outgroups. The indictment against Israel (2:6-16) then takes on a powerful force as they too are shown, perhaps contrary to expectation, to be equally an outgroup. Thus, by extension, the manifestation of social injustice within Israel is analogous in YHWH's sight to violence against pregnant women by Ammon and the enslavement of people groups by Philistia and Tyre.

Second, there is no distinction within a particular foreign nation between the actual agents of the violence and the general population, a common othering strategy in the Hebrew Bible.[53] An audience unfamiliar with the nation of Ammon would assume based on Amos's description that all Ammonites are brutish and violent.[54] These othering strategies illustrate the social identity principle of meta-contrast, which states that group members tend to accentuate perceived similarities of people belonging to the same outgroup.[55] Through the first seven oracles, the

---

53. Bosman notes how ethnocentric behavior can increase when group identity is threatened, especially as it relates to international conflict. In his study of Nahum, Bosman detects, to use M. Sternberg's term, a "self-critical ethnocentrism." While this is more veiled in Nahum, Amos explicitly implicates Israel as one of the nations condemned. See Bosman, *Social Identity in Nahum*, 171–2, 248–9. Esler states that "[the] closer behaviour is to the intergroup extreme, the greater the tendency to treat outgroup members as 'undifferentiated items in a unified social category'" Philip F. Esler, "Group Norms and Prototypes in Matthew 5.3-12: A Social Identity Interpretation of the Matthaean Beatitudes," in Tucker and Baker, eds., *T&T Clark Handbook to Social Identity in the New Testament*, 161.

54. Part of ancient Near Eastern literature, such as in Assyrian royal propaganda, involved portraying the Enemy as a unified group. By opposition to the throne, the Enemy is intrinsically guilty, as manifested by their actions. For an illustration of this strategy, see Andrew M. King, "Did Jehu Destroy Baal from Israel? A Contextual Reading of Jehu's Revolt," *BBR* 27, no. 3 (2017): 309–32.

55. Tajfel, "Cognitive Aspects of Prejudice," 83. Hogg and Abrams explain ethnocentric stereotypic perceptions in terms of a desire for positive distinctiveness

text's audience would be drawn into this othering strategy, viewing the nations all on the same plane. Yet the climax in the Israel oracle (2:6-16) is especially potent as the historic ingroup turns out to be no more favored than every other outgroup.

The revelation that Israel is an outgroup is a jarring feature of the text. In order for an outgroup to be formed, there must first be a sense of ingroup membership.[56] The turn against Israel in 2:6, which was already hinted at in 1:1-2, leaves the audience wondering where the ingroup is to be found. If the ingroup does not exist on the national level, a recurring theme throughout the rest of Amos (cf. 3:1; 9:7), the audience is required to look elsewhere. Thus, the OAN introduce a central question to the identity of the people of God, albeit negatively. While the nature of the ingroup in Amos is explored later in the book, the audience at this point comes to see violence and injustice as an outgroup norm. By contrast, the implied ingroup presumably avoids and resists these behaviors.

The Confrontation at Bethel (Amos 7:10-17)

Amos 7–9 contains a series of five visions regarding YHWH's judgment of Israel. Visions 1–4, with a slight variation in the third, begin with the opening formula "this is what the Lord YHWH showed me."[57] These visions are commonly subdivided in three sets. The first pair of visions (7:1-3, 4-6) reveals the destruction brought by a locust plague (7:1) and a judgment by fire (7:4) respectively. The terrible scenes move the prophet to intercede for the people, pleading "Lord YHWH please forgive! How

---

of one's group. It is important, they state, that both ingroup and outgroup stereotypes reflect well on self. See Abrams and Hogg, *Social Identifications*, 74. Some studies have noted factors such as group size affecting perceptions of outgroup homogeneity. See, e.g., Suzanne C. Thompson et al., "Perceptions of Attitudinal Similarity in Ethnic Groups in the U.S.: Ingroup and Outgroup Homogeneity Effects," *EJSP* 27, no. 2 (1997): 209–20; Alberto Voci, "Perceived Group Variability and the Salience of Personal and Social Identity," *European Review of Social Psychology* 11, no. 1 (2000): 177–221. Haslam and Oakes, on the other hand, maintain the importance of social identity salience for perceived homogeneity. See S. Alexander Haslam and Penelope J. Oakes, "How Context-Independent Is the Outgroup Homogeneity Effect? A Response to Bartsch and Judd," *EJSP* 25, no. 4 (1995): 469–75.

56. As Tajfel states, "In order for the members of an ingroup to be able to hate or dislike an outgroup, or to discriminate against it, they must first have acquired a sense of belonging to a group which is clearly distinct from the one they hate, dislike or discriminate against." Tajfel, "Social Identity and Intergroup Behavior," 66–7.

57. This formula appears in 7:1, 4, 7, and 8:1.

can Jacob stand? He is small." Amos's intercession is effective in both instances, causing YHWH to relent of the readied destruction (7:3, 6).[58]

The second pair of visions (7:7-9; 8:1-3) contains the revelation of an object, followed by a dialogue between YHWH and Amos. YHWH asks, "Amos, what do you see?" The prophet rightly identifies the objects, אנך (7:8) and a basket of summer fruit (8:2), but does not grasp the meaning of either.[59] Before any intercession can occur, YHWH announces the total judgment of Israel in language reminiscent of exodus tradition.[60] Whereas he had relented and passed over the guilt of the people in the first pair of visions, he does so no longer.

The final vision (9:1-4) differs in form and style from the previous four.[61] Here Amos sees YHWH standing beside "the altar," declaring the destruction to come. There is no other visual representation and no dialogue between the deity and the prophet. YHWH simply announces that there will be no safe place for the people to hide when he fixes his "eyes upon them for evil and not for good" (9:4c).

Situated between the third and fourth visions is a narrative detailing an interaction between Amos and the priest of Bethel, Amaziah (7:10-17). Apart from the superscription in 1:1, this section provides the most information about the background and context of Amos's message.[62] The

---

58. As Jeremias notes, YHWH's "repentance" does not indicate that his punishment is unjustified. Jörg Jeremias, *Die Reue Gottes: Aspekte alttestamentlicher Gottesvorstellung*, Biblische Studien 65 (Neukirchen–Vluyn: Neukirchener Verlag, 1975), 40–8.

59. The interpretation of the *hapax legomenon* אנך is a classic crux in Hebrew Bible scholarship. On the interpretative options, see H. G. M. Williamson, "The Prophet and the Plumb-Line: A Redaction-Critical Study of Amos 7," in *In Quest of the Past: Studies on Israelite Religion, Literature, and Prophetism*, ed. A. S. van der Woude, OTS 26 (Leiden: Brill, 1990), 105–13.

60. Sharp, *Irony and Meaning in the Hebrew Bible*, 154.

61. Some scholars question the original inclusion of Amos 9:1-4 in the collection of visions based on the formal structural differences of this unit. Eidevall, for instance, notes the difference in form, as well as the expectation of finality proclaimed at the end of the fourth vision ("the end has come," 8:2). He states that after the fourth vision, no continuation in the series is expected. Eidevall, *Amos*, 224. In spite of this, he acknowledges the present form of the book portrays 9:1-4 as some kind of continuation of the previous visions. Thus, "[from] the reader's perspective, it is the fifth vision" (224). Paul maintains the place of the fifth vision in the collection. See Paul, *Amos*, 225.

62. Even still there is not an extensive amount of information regarding the prophet in the narrative. It does not seem to fit the genre of a "prophetic biography." See below.

unit is connected to the previous vision through the use of the *wayyiqtol* form in 7:10. While no historical claim about the sequence of visions and the event recorded is necessitated, the form sets the story in the context of the visions as a whole.[63] But whereas the previous visions were recounted from Amos's perspective, the episode here is taken up by a narrator. The section unfolds in three parts as Amaziah's complaint to Jeroboam II regarding Amos (7:10-11) is followed by the priest's direct address to the prophet (7:12-13) and Amos's response (7:14-17). Both Amaziah's report and Amos's response show that there is a deeper level than a mere historical recounting of events. The episode as a whole can be described, with Patrick Miller, as a "conflict of perspectives" between Amaziah and Amos.[64] Their view of the world, and more especially what is good and what is to be rejected, is evident in their speech and behavior.[65] In other words, the text reflects a conception of social identity. The features of the narrative define the boundaries of the ingroup and the outgroup. This embedded construction of social identity is realized as both Amaziah and Amos are shown to be prototypical members of their respective groups, Amaziah the outgroup and Amos the ingroup. As such, the text employs several othering strategies, while also enhancing the positive value of Amos's ingroup status. The audience is thus invited to conform to the values of the ingroup, which, among other behaviors, entails obedience to YHWH.

Amaziah's Complaint (7:10-11)

Amaziah's report to the king contains a charge of sedition. He gives a summary quote of Amos supposedly announcing the death of Jeroboam by the sword and exile of the nation (v. 11). This conspiracy is so repulsive to Amaziah that he states the land itself is unable to bear Amos's words (v. 10). The content of Amaziah's report contains aspects of Amos's message presented thus far in the book. The death of the king, though not a direct quote of an extant oracle, is made explicit in the judgment announced at the conclusion of the third vision ("I will rise against the house of Jeroboam with the sword," v. 9). Moreover, the king would

---

63. Garrett, *Amos*, 218. Most commentators note the catchword "Jeroboam" in 7:9 and 7:10 as a reason for the present placement of the narrative.

64. Patrick D. Miller, "The Prophetic Critique of Kings," *Ex Auditu* 2 (1986): 84–5.

65. I am aware that the representation of both parties is filtered through the editor(s) of Amos. Nevertheless, the interest of the present work is the embedded sense of identity within the text of Amos. Thus, I will explore the different portrayals within the world of the text.

certainly be included in the judgment announced more generically on the elites in earlier sections in the book. The language from the exodus tradition draws together this connection. Part of the phrase used in 7:8 to announce judgment on Israel (לא־אוסיף עוד עבור לו), mentioning the house of Jeroboam, parallels the judgment proclaimed in the dirge in 5:17 (אעבר בקרבך). In both instances, the time of YHWH's patience has ended, and he would no longer pass over their iniquity. The second half of Amos's message in Amaziah's report declares the exile of Israel from her land.

Amaziah's summary of Amos is brief, but it is interesting to note both what he includes and what he omits. Thus far in the book, the condemnation announced against the elites are presented in a general fashion. Amaziah takes these general statements about the future judgment of the nation and its leadership and turns it into a direct threat against Jeroboam.[66] Moreover, he omits any charge of guilt, including the social injustice shot through the book, as well as the religious dimension of Amos's prophecy. These alterations can be explained in several ways. First, it can be argued that Amaziah here quotes an unrecorded proclamation of Amos in its brief but exact form. This seems unnecessary, however, in light of the close approximation to judgment announced elsewhere. In 7:9, for example, Amos pronounced the end of Jeroboam's house. It would be no less a threat for Amos to declare the end of Jeroboam's dynasty than it would be to proclaim the death of the king himself.[67] Regarding the second half of Amaziah's report, it is clear that exile is a common theme in Amos's message, so this portion would not be novel (cf. 1:5; 4:2-3; 5:5, 27; 6:7; 7:17; 9:4). Second, Amaziah could simply be using exaggerated rhetoric as a political maneuver to elicit the king's immediate action.[68] Jeroboam may be less concerned with the ravings of a southern prophet criticizing the treatment of the poor, than a message of assassination and insurrection. Even though Amaziah is aware that a Judean prophet was virtually powerless to incite an international conflict resulting in the deportation of Israel, all that mattered would be the rhetorical effect to evoke the king's action.

While both the above explanations of Amaziah's report are plausible, Amaziah's message may reflect his underlying conception of his social

---

66. Eidevall, *Amos*, 207.

67. James Luther Mays, *Amos: A Commentary*, OTL (Philadelphia: Westminster John Knox, 1969), 135.

68. See F. O. García-Treto, "A Reader-Response Approach to Prophetic Conflict: The Case of Amos 7:10–17," in *The New Literary Criticism and the Hebrew Bible*, ed. J. C. Exum and D. J. A. Clines, JSOTSup 143 (Sheffield: JSOT, 1993), 120.

group membership. Though he is a religious functionary, his orientation is not ultimately towards the deity, but towards the king. For him, the king is central to his group's sense of meaning. A threat against the nation, Amaziah's ingroup, can rightly be summarized as a direct threat leveled against the king. Unlike Amos, who derives his ingroup identity in relation to YHWH (see below), Amaziah embodies the outgroup status of the northern kingdom. This becomes more evident in his direct address to the prophet.

Amaziah's Address (7:12-13)

Amos 7:12-13 initiates the direct confrontation between Amaziah and the prophet. Following the prose clause (ויאמר אמציה אל־עמוס), the remainder of the section is Amaziah's reported speech. He addresses Amos as a "seer" (חזה),[69] furthering the connection of the narrative to the broader context of the visions.[70] Amaziah commands Amos to flee to Judah, where he is to prophesy (נבא) and earn his bread (אכל־שם לחם). The reason Amaziah forbids the southern prophet from conveying his message in Bethel is because "it is the king's sanctuary and it is a temple of the kingdom." This latter point gives a sense for how Amaziah categorizes Amos, as well as how he views his own social location.[71] Social categorization occurs within, and is predicated upon, specific social contexts.[72] This suggests that stereotyping is not limited to a fixed and universal set of attributes, but rather involves group conceptions that are continually adapted according to the social context, as well as the perspective of

---

69. Some take this in a derogatory sense, as though Amaziah is refusing to acknowledge Amos's prophetic status. Cohen, for instance, says that Amos would have resented this lesser title. See Simon Cohen, "Amos Was a Navi," *HUCA* 32 (1961): 177. Yet the occurrence of the word elsewhere in the Hebrew Bible shows that it need not be understood negatively (e.g., 2 Sam. 24:11; 2 Chron. 9:29). So Paul, *Amos*, 240–1; J. Alberto Soggin, *The Prophet Amos: A Translation and Commentary*, trans. John Bowden (London: SCM, 1987), 127. Wolff goes further, stating that the word itself was a term of respect. See Wolff, *Joel and Amos*, 311.

70. Paul, *Amos*, 240–1. Garrett notes the irony of Amaziah calling Amos a "seer of visions," since the context makes clear that this is exactly what he is. See Garrett, *Amos*, 220. Also, see H. C. O. Lanchester and S. R. Driver, *The Books of Joel and Amos*, 2nd ed., CBSC (Cambridge: Cambridge University Press, 1915), 210.

71. Andrew Davis notes that nowhere does Amaziah invoke any of the Bethel traditions historically associated with the sanctuary. Rather, "for [Amaziah] the king's patronage of the site is decisive for its identity." Davis, *Tel Dan in Its Northern Cultic Context*, 149.

72. See Oakes, "The Salience of Social Categories," 117–41.

the perceiver.[73] We can assume that there were prophets in the northern kingdom whose oracles would have been welcomed at the Bethel sanctuary.[74] The issue is not with prophecy as such. The issue is the disparity between the kind of ministry Amos carries out and the kind of person recognized as a prophet in Israel. In other words, from Amaziah's perspective, Amos violates the principle of normative fit.[75] Amos claims to speak for the deity but, in Amaziah's eyes, is opposed to the very thing that makes the northern kingdom what it is.[76]

Perhaps Amos's words could have been tolerated somewhere else. The emphasis on place in Amaziah's speech lends a particular significance to this aspect of social identity.[77] Amos is to flee to "the land of Judah"; it is there (שם) he is to eat his bread, and there (שם) he is to prophesy. But he should no longer prophesy at Bethel because it is a royal sanctuary (מקדש־מלך) and a national temple (בית ממלכה). The repetition of the root מלך describes the overarching issue. The affairs of the northern kingdom,

---

73. Naomi Ellemers and Ad Van Knippenberg, "Stereotyping in Social Context," in *The Social Psychology of Stereotyping and Group Life*, ed. R. Spears et al. (Cambridge, MA: Blackwell, 1997), 234.

74. 1 Kgs 22:1-28 is illustrative. On the brink of war with Syria, Jehoshaphat the king of Judah allies with the king of Israel to retake Ramoth-gilead. Before they set out, Jehoshaphat asks Israel's king to inquire of a prophet. Ahab gathers four hundred prophets who announce victory for the coalition, which was a welcomed message. But when YHWH's prophet, Micaiah, is summoned, his announcement is not favorable and thus rejected, eventually costing Ahab his life. The content-related expectation maintained by the kings was violated according to the principle of normative fit. The behavior of Micaiah in prophesying against the coalition shows that he belongs to a different social group.

75. Blanz, "Accessibility and Fit," 43–74; Oakes, Turner, and Haslam, "Perceiving People as Group Members," 125–44.

76. Though Amaziah's official political capacity is not clear, it is reasonable to assume that he was motivated to protect state interests. Izabela Jaruzelska makes the case that cult personnel functioned by royal appointment in Israel. This is supported elsewhere in the biblical text (1 Kgs 12:31-32; 13:33). As such, it would be in Amaziah's best interest, if not part of his official duties, to warn of any political trouble at his site. See Izabela Jaruzelska, "Amasyah—prêtre de Béthel—fonctionnaire royal (essai socio-économique préliminaire)," *Folia Orientalia* 31 (1995): 53–69. Also see Joseph Blenkinsopp, *Sage, Priest, Prophet: Religious and Intellectual Leadership in Ancient Israel*, Library of Ancient Israel (Louisville, KY: Westminster John Knox, 1995), 79. Mays refers to Amaziah as Jeroboam's royal chaplain. Mays, *Amos*, 136.

77. Noble draws attention to the significance of location in Amaziah's address in "Amos and Amaziah in Context: Synchronic and Diachronic Approaches to Amos 7–8," *CBQ* 60, no. 3 (1998): 429.

including its religious life, are politically oriented.[78] The difference between Amaziah and Amos, however, should not be defined in terms of a secular–sacred distinction.[79] For although Amaziah's message is devoid of *explicit* theological content, he was operating according to the current religious structure at play in Bethel. The system of religion he mediated as a priest embodied the essence of the nation. He also presumably benefits socially and economically from the operation of the sanctuary (cf. 2:8). It may be impossible to disentangle the threads of the socio-religious dynamics involved.[80] Together, these components defined the values of Amaziah's social group.

Despite the report of sedition from Amaziah, there is no response recorded from the king. Jeroboam's absence is a conspicuous feature of the narrative. Amos is not reticent to condemn the actions of the elites. It would seem like a missed opportunity to indict Jeroboam by omitting a response if one were available. However the king responded, the editors could frame it as further evidence of the corruption in Israel at the highest level, especially if the king too called for the silence of the prophet. Göran Eidevall explains the absence of Jeroboam's response in terms of genre.[81] In his view, contrary to the episode as a prophetic biography, the unit is best described as a "dispute narrative," focusing on words not events.[82] But one could imagine an additional report describing the words

---

78. Ibid., 429.

79. See ibid., 429–31; Jeremias, *The Book of Amos*, 138; Mays, *Amos*, 136; Miller, "The Prophetic Critique of Kings," 85. Miller's work on Israelite religion notes the complexity of categorizing the nature of Israel's cult. Nevertheless, he often appeals to "state religion" corresponding to the supposed development of the Israelite cultus. See Patrick D. Miller, *The Religion of Ancient Israel*, Library of Ancient Israel (Louisville, KY: Westminster John Knox, 2000). The bifurcation of "official/state religion" and "popular religion" is problematic on a sociological level. See F. Stavrakopoulou, "'Popular' Religion and 'Official' Religion: Practice, Perception, Portrayal," in *Religious Diversity in Ancient Israel and Judah*, ed. J. Barton and F. Stavrakopoulou (London: T&T Clark, 2010), 37–58.

80. See Clifford Geertz, *The Interpretation of Cultures: Selected Essays* (New York: Basic, 1973), 90; M. Daniel Carroll R., *Contexts for Amos: Prophetic Poetics in Latin American Perspective*, JSOTSup 132 (Sheffield: JSOT, 1992), 56–63.

81. Eidevall, *Amos*, 204–5, 207–8.

82. Ibid., 208. For the biographical approach, see Soggin, *The Prophet Amos*, 6–12; John D. W. Watts, *Vision and Prophecy in Amos* (Grand Rapids: Eerdmans, 1958), 1–2, 32; Andersen and Freedman, *Amos*, 763. Tucker labels the narrative "a story of prophetic conflict." Gene M. Tucker, "Prophetic Authenticity: A Form-Critical Study of Amos 7:10-17," *Int* 27, no. 4 (1973): 430. See also Roy F. Melugin, "Prophetic Books and Historical Reconstruction," in *Prophets and Paradigms: Essays in Honor*

of Jeroboam that would not intrude upon this focus. While it may be that no report was available, a better explanation may reflect the embedded social identity in the narrative.

The king simply may not have been needed for the group dynamics to be realized in the Bethel narrative. Rather, the unit may function to contrast the two social groups in terms of their prototypical members: Amaziah and Amos. Amaziah here is viewed not simply as an individual, but as an exemplar of his socio-religious group.[83] While he may have had an official duty to report seditious activity to the royal authorities, his address to Amos seems to go beyond this. In his justification of the sanctity of the Bethel sanctuary, Amaziah is responding to a threat against his social identity. He takes a threat against the throne personally because it is a threat against the group to which he is a member and derives his sense of self. As a priest, Amaziah can be considered a high-identifier with the group. As such, the threat to his social group would invoke a more derogating reaction than someone less-identified with the group.[84] Amaziah's appeal to the royal patronage of the Bethel cult leaves little need for Jeroboam to be present. Amaziah is representative of the group as a whole. The king and the priest become, in essence, interchangeable. When Amaziah instructs Amos to flee, the audience can imagine the priest's words with the voice of Jeroboam echoing in the background.

Many commentators understand Amaziah's command to flee to Judah as a friendly attempt to save Amos's life.[85] The prophet's harsh words

---

of Gene M. Tucker, ed. Stephen Breck Reid (Sheffield: Sheffield Academic, 1996), 75–6. Wolff calls the section an *apophthegma*, which is "an historical episode... presented solely for the purpose of making intelligible a pointed prophetic oracle by explaining the circumstances of its origin." Wolff, *Joel and Amos*, 308.

83. That Amaziah and Amos are representative in some form in the narrative is a point noted by many commentators. See, for instance, Robert R. Wilson, *Prophecy and Society in Ancient Israel* (Philadelphia: Fortress, 1980), 140–1; Blenkinsopp, *Sage, Priest, Prophet*, 134–8; Eidevall, *Amos*, 212; John H. Hayes, *Amos: The Eighth-Century Prophet; His Times and His Preaching* (Nashville: Abingdon, 1988), 233; Wolff, *Joel and Amos*, 309; James K. Hoffmeier, "Once Again the 'Plumb Line' Vision of Amos 7:7-9: An Interpretive Clue from Egypt," in *Boundaries of the Ancient Near Eastern World: A Tribute to Cyrus H. Gordon*, ed. Meir Lubetski, Claire Gottlieb, and Sharon Keller, JSOTSup 273 (Sheffield: Sheffield Academic, 1998), 317.

84. Nyla R. Branscombe et al., "The Context and Content of Social Identity Threat," in *Social Identity: Context, Commitment, Content*, ed. N. Ellemers, R. Spears, and B. Doosje (Oxford: Blackwell, 1999), 46–50.

85. Würthwein, "Amos-Studien," 20–1; Mays, *Amos*, 136–7; Wolff, *Joel and Amos*, 311; Hayes, *Amos*, 233–4; Paul, *Amos*, 241–2. Against this, see Soggin, *The*

against the northern kingdom would jeopardize his safety; so Amaziah, then, is looking out for his wellbeing by encouraging him to leave. In addition to the group dynamics discussed above, this interpretation fails on several accounts. First, this view draws too sharp a distinction between Amaziah's correspondence to Jeroboam and his address to Amos. Though the message is directed towards Jeroboam, it nevertheless frames Amos as a menace in the land. What would warrant a change in tone when he interacts with Amos directly? It may be noted that Amaziah does not order the arrest or execution of Amos, but simply instructs him to continue his prophetic ministry in his home country. While this is true, imprisonment and execution are not the only options for intergroup hostility. Various othering strategies can be equally effective towards identity maintenance. What mattered for Amaziah was eliminating the perceived threat to his social group. Sending Amos away would accomplish this just as well.

The second argument against Amaziah's expulsion as a friendly gesture is Amos's association with those oppressed in Israel. Like the Nazarites who were forced to drink wine against their vow of abstinence, prophets are commanded to be silent in 2:12. These crimes perpetrated by Israel's elites are described in succession to the OAN collection, thus putting Israel's offenses on par with the war crimes of the nations. The means of coercion upon the Nazarites and prophets is not explicit, but social pressure, or even the threat of violence, is likely. Those in power are described as hating the one who advocates for righteousness in the gate (5:10).[86] In their many transgressions they also silence those who are wise (5:13).[87] Amos in the Bethel narrative follows the pattern of the one

Prophet Amos, 132; Harper, *Critical and Exegetical Commentary on Amos and Hosea*, 170; Douglas K. Stuart, *Hosea–Jonah*, WBC 31 (Waco, TX: Word, 1987), 376.

86. The Hebrew (שנאו בשער מוכיח ודבר תמים יתעבו) could indicate the object of hatred at the gate is the poor and oppressed themselves. But as Anderson and Freedman note, there is no need for the exploiters to hate their miserable victims. Andersen and Freedman, *Amos*, 498–9. Rather, it appears that there is a third party (the prophet?) arguing for justice, legal or otherwise. In return for their righteous deeds they are despised.

87. I follow Anderson and Freedman, that the silence of the prudent is not voluntary but forced. Otherwise, it would make little sense for the prophet, who proclaimed his message when Israel was at the height of corruption, to deliver his oracles at all. He should rather be silent. On the other hand, like the reprover in the gate, the prudent are despised and silenced by those in power. See Andersen and Freedman, *Amos*, 505. Gary Smith translates the verse, "Therefore, at that time the prosperous person will be silent, for it will be an evil time." Gary V. Smith, "Amos 5:13: The Deadly Silence of the Prosperous," *JBL* 107, no. 2 (1988): 289–91. He thus renders שכל as "prosperous"

who speaks truth but is silenced. In other words, he is put alongside the oppressed elsewhere. Thus, to portray Amaziah as in some sense an ally of Amos would undermine the tension between the oppressors and the oppressed in the book.

A final argument against Amaziah's friendly exile is Amos's response. The prophet replies to Amaziah with a harsh and graphic prediction. The nation is not simply verbally reprimanded, but Amaziah and his family are singled out for violence and death. If Amaziah was looking out for the wellbeing of Amos, this would be, to say the least, an ungrateful response. It is more likely that the expulsion of Amos was a hostile action on the part of Amaziah, as expected from a perspective of intergroup conflict. The clash of prototypical members leads to this form of othering. But Amaziah does not get the last word.

Amos's Response (7:14-17)

In response to Amaziah's command to leave Bethel, Amos rejects Amaziah's assumption regarding his prophetic status with a series of four verbless clauses in 7:14.[88] The first two, stated negatively, deny that Amos was/is a prophet (לא־נביא אנכי ולא בן־נביא), while the second two describe his vocation (כי־בוקר אנכי ובולס שקמים). The major interpretive issue with the verbless clauses here is the implied sense of time.[89] Should the clauses

---

(cf. Deut. 29:8; Josh. 1:7; 2 Kgs 18:15) and relates the "evil time" to the coming day of judgment based on a chiastic arrangement of 5:1-17. Also, Jared J. Jackson, "Amos 5:13 Contextually Understood," *ZAW* 98, no. 3 (1986): 434–5; Carroll R., *Contexts for Amos*, 233–4. Paul renders the verb יִדֹּם not as "keep silent," but from the homonymous root דמם, "to moan," which fits a chiastic structure that begins and ends with lament. Paul, *Amos*, 175–6. The problem is that Paul must excise the hymn fragment in 5:8-9 to make the chiasm work. This is not satisfactory in my view.

88. The interpretation of Amos 7:14 is another notorious crux in Hebrew Bible scholarship and has been the subject of numerous publications. Ridge provides a comprehensive summary in David B. Ridge, "On the Possible Interpretation of Amos 7:14," *VT* 68 (2018): 1–23. Also see Michael Seleznev, "Amos 7:14 and the Prophetic Rhetoric," in *Babel und Bibel*, ed. L. Kogan et al., vol. 1, Ancient Near Eastern, Old Testament and Semitic Studies, Orentalia et Classica 5 (Moscow: Russian State University of the Humanities, 2004), 251–8.

89. For a succinct overview of the syntactic issues related to verbless clauses, see Cynthia L. Miller, "Pivotal Issues in Analyzing the Verbless Clause," in *The Verbless Clause in Biblical Hebrew: Linguistic Approaches*, ed. M. O'Connor and Cynthia L. Miller, Linguistic Studies in Ancient West Semitic 1 (Winona Lake, IN: Eisenbrauns, 1999), 10–15. Wilson summarizes the major scholarly views in Daniel J. Wilson, "Copular Predication in Biblical Hebrew" (MA thesis, University of the Free State, 2015), 8–34.

be understood as past tense, present tense, or some variation? Without a verbal form marked for tense, contextual factors must be considered. Even still, there are no definitive contextual indicators, leaving the question open. I will briefly summarize the views before stating my own understanding, which supports the approach to social identity discussed here.

The past-tense interpretation claims that Amos was not a prophet previously but became one when YHWH called him.[90] The latter two verbless clauses then describe his occupation *before* he received the call to be a prophet. Some who hold this view claim that the verbless clauses are subordinate to ויקחני יהוה ("But YHWH took me") in v. 15. This view puts the emphasis on YHWH's initiative to change Amos's status from a non-prophet to a prophet. There are two specific problems raised for this position. First, it is generally maintained that היה is required if the clause is set in either a past or future time, the unmarked form being the present.[91] But as David Ridge states, citing Deut. 26:5 and 2 Chron. 33:1 as examples, "There is no justification for the claim that nominal clauses cannot independently refer to a past event without a form of the verb היה."[92] The second problem raised is the implication that a past-tense denial of the first two clauses would naturally lead towards a present affirmation involving *both* clauses (i.e., not formally a prophet or a member of the prophetic guild, but now a prophet and a member of the prophetic guild).[93] Since it is not widely held that Amos was a member of a prophetic guild (בן־נביא), the past-tense interpretation faces difficulty.[94] Yet this problem is not insurmountable, even without recourse to a specialized meaning of

---

90. The LXX attests to this translation. Scholars representative of a past-tense rendering include Paul, *Amos*, 243–47; H. H. Rowley, "Was Amos a Nabi?" in *Festschrift Otto Eissfeldt zum 60. Geburtstag, 1. September 1947*, ed. Johann Fück (Halle: Max Niemeyer, 1947), 191–8; Würthwein, "Amos-Studien"; Jeremias, *The Book of Amos*, 139–40; Mays, *Amos*, 137–9; Rudolf Smend, "Das Nein des Amos," *EvT* 23, no. 8 (1963): 416–18; Kapelrud, *Central Ideas in Amos*, 7.

91. B. K. Waltke and M. O'Connor, *An Introduction to Biblical Hebrew Syntax* (Winona Lake, IN: Eisenbrauns, 1990), 72; Rüdiger Bartelmus, *HYH: Bedeutung und Funktion eines hebräischen "Allerweltwortes"* (St. Ottilien, Germany: Eos, 1982), 80–235; E. Gass, "'Kein Prophet bin ich und kein Prophetenschüler bin ich': Zum Selbstverständnis des Propheten Amos in Am 7:14," *TZ* 68 (2012): 12.

92. Ridge, "On the Possible Interpretation of Amos 7:14," 16. He later concludes, "Simply, there is no significant evidence that the rules of Hebrew grammar make a simple past-tense interpretation of the nominal clauses in v. 14 impossible" (18).

93. On the phrase בן־נביא, see Wilson, *Prophecy and Society in Ancient Israel*, 140–1; Blenkinsopp, *Sage, Priest, Prophet*, 134–8.

94. See Linville, *Amos and the Cosmic Imagination*, 144. See also G. R. Driver, "Affirmation by Exclamatory Negation," *JNES* 5 (1973): 108.

נביא in the sense of a "professional prophet" as supposed by Ernest Vogt.[95] It would suffice to say that the first two verbless clauses deny any former association with the prophetic sphere, whether active or affiliated, and the second two clauses identify Amos's vocation. With that information in mind, Amos can point to a definitive event in v. 15 that resulted in a change in status. Once he had no responsibility to speak YHWH's word, but then YHWH commissioned him. While this is not definitive, it is indeed plausible.

The present-tense interpretation of the verbless clauses argues that Amos straightforwardly denies being a prophet. This could be in the sense that though he prophesies, he cannot be considered a "prophet" in a formal sense.[96] On the other hand, Amos could affirm that he is indeed a prophet, but just not in the sense assumed by Amaziah (i.e., professional prophet). Though Amos clearly bears the marks of a prophet (he is instructed by YHWH "to prophesy to my people Israel" in 7:15), he denies that he is a prophet for hire or beholden to a prophetic guild. On the contrary, his economic status is secure due to his vocation as a herdsman and tender of Sycamore trees. Eidevall maintains this interpretation, viewing the question not in terms of legitimate vocation, but in terms of authority.[97] The debate between Amos and Amaziah in the narrative, he says, centers on both where and how Amos should be allowed to prophesy. Essentially, Amos rejects the notion that Amaziah has jurisdiction over him because he is not a professional prophet under his supervision. Rather, he is economically independent, a point made by the vocational references in the second two verbless clauses. A problem with this view is that the

---

95. So Ernest Vogt, "Waw Explicative in Amos 7," *ExpTim* 68 (1957): 301–2.

96. Scholars maintaining a present-tense translation include Eidevall, *Amos*, 209; Wolff, *Joel and Amos*, 312–13; Linville, *Amos and the Cosmic Imagination*, 144; Dirk U. Rottzoll, "2 Sam 14,5—Eine Parallele Zu Am 7,14f.," *ZAW* 100 (1988): 413–15; Martha E. Campos, "Structure and Meaning in the Third Vision of Amos (7:7-17)," *Journal of Hebrew Scriptures* 11 (2011): 14–15; Sigo Lehming, "Erwägungen zu Amos," *ZTK* 55, no. 2 (1958): 162–9; Matitiahu Tsevat, "Amos 7:14—Present or Preterit?" in *The Tablet and the Scroll: Near Eastern Studies in Honor of William W. Hallo*, ed. Mark E. Cohen, Daniel C. Snell, and David B. Weisberg (Bethesda, MD: CDL, 1993), 256–8; Joseph Blenkinsopp, *A History of Prophecy in Israel*, rev. ed. (Louisville, KY: Westminster John Knox, 1996), 255–6 n. 20. Zevit argues that Amos denies being a court prophet under Judean patronage, but affirms his status as an independent prophet. See Ziony Zevit, "A Misunderstanding at Bethel: Amos 7:12-17," *VT* 25, no. 4 (1975): 783–90; Zevit, "Expressing Denial in Biblical Hebrew and Mishnaic Hebrew, and in Amos," *VT* 29, no. 4 (1979): 505–9.

97. Göran Eidevall, *Amos*, AYB 24G (New Haven, CT: Yale University Press, 2017), 208–10.

intervention of YHWH in v. 15 seems to imply a change in status ("But YHWH took me"). Hans Wolff claims, however, that this does not mean Amos forfeited his profession.[98] In his view, the economic independence is a central component of Amos's self-justification. Since the imperatives and prohibition in v. 13 occur within the present, those who hold this view maintain that a continuation of this tense fits best.[99]

Others have understood the verse differently apart from the past/present-tense discussion. Richardson asserts that לֹא in the first verbless clause should be understood as the emphatic particle לֻא, as attested in Ugaritic.[100] Rather than denying that he is a prophet, Amos would then strongly affirm he is indeed a prophet, but just not a member of the prophetic guild. Similarly, G. R. Driver claims that Amos's denial functions on a rhetorical level, actually affirming he is a trained prophet.[101] From a different perspective, John D. W. Watts argues that the tense of the verbless clauses is actually unimportant relative to the mood of the verse.[102] Noting the recurrence of אנכי, "I," with reference to Amos, and the repetition of YHWH in the passage, Watts says the point is not Amos's status, but YHWH's authority. It is YHWH who commissioned Amos and thus Amaziah has no right to countermand this order.

Admittedly, the interpretation of the verbless clauses is no easy matter. Shalom Paul rightly states, "If an unambiguous solution were available, the problem would have been resolved ages ago."[103] And while there is no one clear answer, several indications favor a past-tense understanding of the verbless clauses.[104] First, the verbless clauses in v. 14 do appear to be subordinated to the *wayyiqtol* verb in v. 15, implying a sequence of events.[105] In the narrative, Amos states that he was, and perhaps still is, a herdsman, but YHWH called him to prophesy to Israel. He was one

---

98. Wolff, *Joel and Amos*, 314.

99. Gass, "'Kein Prophet bin ich und kein Prophetenschüler bin ich,'" 10–12.

100. H. Neil Richardson, "Critical Note on Amos 7:14," *JBL* 85, no. 1 (1966): 89.

101. Driver, "Affirmation by Exclamatory Negation," 108. Also, P. R. Ackroyd, "Amos 7:14," *ExpTim* 68, no. 3 (1956): 94.

102. Watts, *Vision and Prophecy in Amos*, 9–12.

103. Paul, *Amos*, 247.

104. Ridge maintains the grammatical plausibility of both a past or present tense of the verbless clauses. See Ridge, "On the Possible Interpretation of Amos 7:14," 17–18.

105. So R. Bach, "Erwägungen zu Amos 7,14," in *Die Botschaft und die Boten: Festschrift für Hans Walter Wolff zum 70. Geburtstag*, ed. J. Jeremias and L. Perlitt (Neukirchen–Vluyn: Neukirchener Verlag, 1981), 203–16. Contra Gass, "'Kein Prophet bin ich und kein Prophetenschüler bin ich.'"

thing, but now he is doing something else. He may not be a professional prophet, as perhaps supposed by Amaziah, but he does indeed deliver oracles from YHWH. If Amos wished to deny simply being a member of a prophetic guild, it seems like there would be an easier way to do so rather than denying that he is a prophet altogether. In my view, Wolff too quickly dismisses the force of the *wayyiqtol* in v. 15.[106] YHWH's initiative does not simply describe a past event for the sake of the present context. Rather, it brings about a change in Amos's status. He also bears the marks of a prophet by interceding for the people and announcing YHWH's judgment. This is different from those who may simply peddle their oracles for money. Amos is identified with those who speak for YHWH.

Second, the latter two verbless clauses identifying Amos's vocation would be an odd response to Amaziah's charge unless one attributes a specialized meaning to נביא. In this scenario the priest's instruction to "eat bread" in Judah would be matched by Amos's refusal to identity as a paid prophet (נביא). But if נביא does not imply an economic component, why would he need to reject the association, especially since he was originally addressed as חזה?[107]

Third, as will be shown in the subsequent chapters, history plays an important role in the identity-forming strategy of Amos. In the confrontation here, as noted above, Amos and Amaziah appear to stand not simply as individuals but as representatives of their respective groups. Amaziah embodies a reality that stands opposite to what the people Israel were called to be (cf. 2:9-12; 3:1-2). To the contrary, Amos symbolizes a reverse narrative. Israel was graciously called by YHWH yet refused to live accordingly (4:6-11). Amos was called by YHWH and walked the pathway of obedience. Israel comes to Bethel to multiply transgression (4:4), but Amos comes to Bethel to expose their transgression. In both cases, what seems to be at issue is not merely behavior, but a change of status. The response of each to YHWH's call reflects their respective social identity membership. Israel has become an outgroup and Amos has joined, or become more representative of, the ingroup. Thus, Amos's very status as a prophet against Israel, in addition to his words, stands as an indictment.

106. Cf. Wolff, *Joel and Amos*, 314.

107. The view that the second clause (ולא בן־נביא) contains an explicative *waw*, which would clarify the meaning of the first clause, should be rejected. There is no firm evidence that נָבִיא implies both a professional and non-professional status. The explicative ו is argued in Vogt, "Waw Explicative in Amos 7." Against this view, see Ridge, "On the Possible Interpretation of Amos 7:14," 10–12.

This notion of obedience is a significant feature, albeit an implicit one, in the identity-forming strategy of the Bethel narrative. If Amos is envisioned as a prototypical group member, he may provide a model of conforming to a central ingroup norm for later audiences. Scholars have recognized the central role that prototypes of the past have in shaping the beliefs and values of the group at later points in time, that is, collective memory.[108] Phillip Esler and Ronald Piper state, "Group prototypes and exemplars from the past tell the members who they are, what they should believe and who they should become."[109] Amos's obedience, which is described in terms of divine initiative ("YHWH took me," 7:15), contrasts with the outgroup depicted elsewhere in the book. For audiences desiring a positive social identity, the prophet's obedience establishes an ingroup norm they can conform to.

The commission Amos received from YHWH was to prophesy to "my people Israel" (עמי ישראל). What does this phrase reveal about the nature of Israel in Amos? Francis I. Andersen and David Noel Freedman provide an exhaustive study of the word "Israel" with all its variations in the book of Amos.[110] Their express purpose is to determine the intended referent of each occurrence, whether the northern kingdom alone, or the northern and southern kingdoms together. They conclude that when Israel appears by itself, the northern kingdom only is envisioned, but when the word appears with modifiers (בית, בתולת, עמי) it refers to a broader understanding that may include the southern kingdom.[111] The phrase "my people Israel" in Amos 7:15 by their own admission is "an apparent anomaly" for this thesis.[112] Nevertheless, they maintain that YHWH commissioned Amos to both the northern kingdom and his own country. Amaziah's command for Amos to flee to Judah, however, seems to stand against this. YHWH called Amos to go from Judah to "my people Israel," but Amaziah commands Amos to go from "my people Israel" to Judah. This opposing instruction appears to make the northern kingdom the focus. This does not mean that a wider audience is excluded from the words of YHWH, but simply that they are not enshrined in the phrase here.

---

108. See Philip F. Esler and Ronald A. Piper, *Lazarus, Mary and Martha: Social-Scientific Approaches to the Gospel of John* (Minneapolis: Fortress, 2006), 23–44; Baker, *Identity, Memory, and Narrative in Early Christianity*, 16–17.
109. Esler and Piper, *Lazarus, Mary and Martha*, 37.
110. Andersen and Freedman, *Amos*, 98–139.
111. See especially Andersen and Freedman, *Amos*, 126.
112. Andersen and Freedman, *Amos*, 118.

Another study that explores the concept of Israel in Amos is by J. Gordon McConville.[113] His particular focus is on the nature of Israel in the visions and the narrative in Amos 7–9. The prophet's intercession in the first two visions with appeal to the smallness of "Jacob" opens the question of what it means to be Israel. He concludes that "Amos uses the concept of a historic 'Israel' to call into question false notions of Israel that prevail in his day."[114] Amaziah's words reveal the equation of "Israel" with the northern state. When he refers to "the land," for instance, Amaziah echoes Deuteronomic language, but with a different meaning.[115] Rather than referring to the land as YHWH's gift to his covenant people, Amaziah defines the land strictly as the northern state, in contrast to "the land of Judah" where Amos should depart to. Contrary to Amaziah's conception, says McConville, "Israel" cannot be reduced simply to the northern kingdom. Judah too may be included, along with others to follow.[116] The exchange, especially with the phrase "my people Israel," evidences the reality that YHWH's Israel is not the same as Amaziah's Israel.[117]

The appellation "my people Israel" embodies a tension regarding the relationship of YHWH and the nation. The construction is used four times in the book (7:8, 15; 8:2; 9:14). The eschatological restoration of Israel detailed in 9:11-15 contains the phrase (9:14). At that time YHWH will cause his people to flourish without fear of future dispossession. This is the context one may expect for the phrase. Two instances, however, occur in unambiguous contexts of judgment. The first of these is in the third vision where YHWH sets אנך in the midst of "my people Israel" (7:8). The following verse describes the desolation of Israel's sanctuaries and the sword raised against Jeroboam (v. 9). The second instance of the phrase in a judgment context is in the fourth vision where YHWH announces, "the end has come upon my people Israel" (8:2).[118] The final instance of the phrase in the confrontation between Amaziah and Amos proves more difficult.

---

113. J. Gordon McConville, "How Can Jacob Stand? He Is So Small!" in Kelle and Moore, eds., *Israel's Prophets and Israel's Past*, 132–51. Also, Robert Khua Hnin Thang, *The Theology of the Land in Amos 7–9* (Cumbria, CA: Langham Monographs, 2014), 53.
114. McConville, "How Can Jacob Stand?" 113.
115. Ibid., 145–6.
116. Ibid., 150.
117. Ibid., 147.
118. Regarding the announcement of 8:2, Wolff says, "Everything that is said elsewhere concerning Israel's future is an interpretation of this harshest of statements." Wolff, *Joel and Amos*, 103.

Does YHWH's commission to Amos to prophesy to "my people Israel" (7:15) contain an expectation of judgment or hope? As argued throughout the present work, judgment is the predominant tone in Amos with future hope glimpsed in 5:4, 6, 14, 15 and only realized in 9:11-15. One could argue that in the context of the Bethel narrative (and the visions as a whole!), a latent note of judgment is presupposed. Amos's commission to prophesy is only necessary because there is a problem in the nation—a problem that is evidenced in Amaziah's response. McConville's claim that the text contains two perspectives of what constitutes Israel is plausible.[119] But the narrative shows that the two groups envisioned by Amaziah and YHWH are both outgroups. Amaziah's Israel and the people Amos addresses are under the same death sentence; however, the question remains as to why YHWH speaks of "*my people* Israel." In Hosea, the symbolic naming of Gomer's third child, לא עמי, "Not My People," is an effective rhetorical strategy in the othering of Israel (Hos. 1:8-9).[120] Appeal can be made to the historic and covenantal component of the relationship.[121] In Amos 3:1, YHWH addresses Israel as those he brought up from the land of Egypt. It is this unique relationship that increases the people's culpability of judgment (3:2). Nevertheless, YHWH's history with the nation, in some sense, weds them together.[122] Yet the present state of the nation makes it barely recognizable in relation to the idealized ingroup norms of justice and righteousness. Perhaps it is the dissonance of the phrase "my people Israel" in contexts of judgment that serves to open the possibility of a reconfiguration of Israelite identity.[123]

---

119. Also Patrick D. Miller, "What Do You Do with the God You Have? The First Commandment as Political Axiom," in *Shaking Heaven and Earth: Essays in Honor of Walter Brueggemann and Charles B. Cousar*, ed. C. R. Yoder et al. (Louisville, KY: Westminster John Knox, 2005), 36–7.

120. See Diana V. Edelman, "YHWH's Othering of Israel," in *Imagining the Other and Constructing Israelite Identity in the Early Second Temple Period*, ed. Ehud Ben Zvi and Diana V. Edelman, LHBOTS 591 (New York: T&T Clark, 2014), 54–5; J. P. Kakkanattu, *God's Enduring Love in the Book of Hosea: A Synchronic and Diachronic Analysis of Hosea 11:1-11*, FAT 2/14 (Tübingen: Mohr Siebeck, 2006), 106.

121. Mays, *Amos*, 7.

122. An analogous statement is made in John 2:16. Jesus finds the Jerusalem temple filled with merchants and money-changers doing business. Though the place is filled with corruption, Jesus refers to the temple as "my father's house." From his perspective, the historic function of the temple, though its present operation was corrupt, retained its status as God's place.

123. The last instance of the phrase in the eschatological restoration (9:14) shows how the redefinition of Israel is made possible by the malleable usage of the phrase. For example, the restored people, framed in Davidic terms, includes other nations

The designation of the outgroup as "My People Israel" may be viewed as an argument against the thesis presented here. According to this view, it would be inappropriate for YHWH to refer to an outgroup as "my people," a phrase we would expect to identify the ingroup. But in light of YHWH's authority and ownership, expressed in the covenant relationship, this phrase is less surprising. Israel and Judah are in once sense YHWH's people. He delivered them from Egypt and established them in the land. Yet as seen in 3:2, this is not good news for the people. The occurrence of this phrase in contexts of judgment evidences this alternate understanding.[124] Clearly, in this sense the northern kingdom is not YHWH's people, a point made clear by Amaziah's representation of the group. Nevertheless, YHWH makes plain that Jeroboam has no more authority than the voiceless nations in the OAN collection. The people are not accountable ultimately to the king, but to YHWH. Thus, the phrase can be explained in terms of history and authority. This phrase may also open the invitation for outgroup members to once again join the ingroup and live rightly as the people of YHWH. Similar to restoration envisioned in Hosea, those who were called "not my people" can be called, "children of the living God" (cf. Hos. 2:1 [Eng. 1:10]).

In the final stage of the Bethel narrative, Amos prophesies disaster for Amaziah, his family, and the nation (7:16-17). He begins with a familiar call to "hear the word of YHWH" (cf. 3:1; 4:1; 5:1). Amaziah had previously summarized Amos's message in his report to the king, but here

among the people of God (vv. 11-12). Daniel Timmer supports this view, arguing that the possession of "the remnant of Edom" in Amos 9:12 refers positively to a non-violent establishment of a divinely initiated relationship. Here, Edom is adopted into God's people under the reign of the future Davidic ruler. See Daniel Timmer, *The Non-Israelite Nations in the Book of the Twelve: Thematic Coherence and the Diachronic–Synchronic Relationship in the Minor Prophets* (Leiden: Brill, 2015), 55–61. Similarly, Ulrich Kellermann, "Der Amosschluss als Stimme deuteronomistischer Heilschoffnung," *EvT* 29 (1969): 169–83; Wolff, *Joel and Amos*, 353. Dicou rejects the notion that Amos envisions a positive future for Edom as part of the restored people of God. See Bert Dicou, *Edom, Israel's Brother and Antagonist: The Role of Edom in Biblical Prophecy and Story*, JSOTSup 169 (Sheffield: Sheffield Academic, 1994), 29–31.

124. The same understanding explains the call to prepare to meet your God in 4:12. The judgment for their obstinance will be executed by YHWH himself, who has authority to do so. The covenant relationship makes Israel accountable to no other. The same one who called for Israel to return is the same one who will judge them. Rather than a hopeful restoration envisioned in 4:12, the context supports a view of judgment. Contra Walter Brueggemann, "Amos IV 4-13 and Israel's Covenant Worship," *VT* 15, no. 1 (1965): 1–15.

Amos summarizes Amaziah's prohibitive command to no longer prophesy against Israel. Such suppression will result in the devastation of war. Amaziah's family will dwindle (cf. 5:3; 6:9) and he himself will be exiled to an unclean land. Scholars have often noted the great irony that a priest, presumably concerned with issues of purity, will end up in an unclean place.[125] Though Amaziah tried to compel Amos to leave Israel because the land could not bear his words (7:10, 12), it is in fact Israel who would leave the land because of their rejection of Amos's words.

Amos gets the last word in the confrontation. The audience is never told what happens to the prophet, or even if the prophecies regarding Amaziah, Jeroboam, and the nation are ever realized. Yet the book has labored to show the inevitability of YHWH's word. It is as natural as the fear that comes with the war horn (3:6). The fact that two vision sequences remain after the narrative indicates that YHWH has not said all there is yet to say. The confrontation as a whole reveals a truth about social identity from a divine perspective, namely that not just any socio-religious membership will do. The only group within the world of the text that provides a positive social identity is the group of which Amos is prototypical. The ingroup, which alone is able to provide ultimate safety, is marked by obedience to YHWH. Even in a hostile environment, the ingroup enacts YHWH's will. The outcome of association with the outgroup, on the other hand, is nothing less than destruction. Audiences entering into this textual world confront these dynamics. Regardless of time or location, membership in the ingroup involves speaking truth to power. The prophetic task, as Walter Brueggemann states, serves as a destabilizing presence that opens a new way of imagining reality.[126] As a prototypical member of his group, Amos models the norms for the implied ingroup.

Though my focus here is not on Old Testament ethics, a word must be said about the identity-forming strategy of Amos and the graphic violence depicted in the text. The audience may shudder to hear Amos's announcement that Amaziah's wife would be ravaged by soldiers while his sons and daughters are cut down by the sword (7:17). Such a disturbing pronouncement alone may invoke an instinctive repulsion to thought of sharing membership in this group. Indeed, the violence in the Hebrew Bible has generated much literature calling for reinterpretations

---

125. On the land in this passage, see Thang, *The Theology of the Land in Amos 7–9*, 100–101.

126. Walter Brueggemann, *A Social Reading of the Old Testament: Prophetic Approaches to Israel's Communal Life*, ed. Patrick D. Miller (Minneapolis: Fortress, 1994), 221–44.

and resistance to various degrees.[127] Though much more could be said, several points will suffice.

First, the violence announced by Amos is descriptive, not prescriptive for his group. The prophet is not calling for the ingroup to enact the violence that results from Amaziah and Israel's wrongdoing. Rather, the mention of exile to an unclean land implies the agency of a foreign nation. This meshes with the notion of the Adversary (צָר) mentioned in 3:11 and the nation raised up to oppress Israel in 6:14. As is the case elsewhere in the Hebrew Bible, YHWH uses a foreign nation to judge his own people. It is probable that the implied ingroup would endure the same fate as their countrymen. This leads to a second point, namely the indiscriminate nature of war. The guilt may rest largely with the elites, but invading armies do not make such distinction. The northern kingdom would be oppressed from Lebo-hamath to the Brook of the Arabah (6:14), which envisions the entirety of the kingdom of Israel.[128] That Amaziah's family would be victims of the onslaught is a tragic reality of invasion. The fact that Amos singles out the priest's family could be explained within the context of the dispute. Since Amaziah called for the silence of the prophet, Amos tells him how close to home the coming judgment will hit. Third, Amos's announcement shows the fact that judgment is inevitable, but not necessarily a celebrated reality. In the world of the text, judgment is a logical, though sometimes delayed, consequence of wrongdoing. Amaziah, prototypical of his group, acted in such a way where there could be no other outcome. In the same way, Amos is compelled to speak the word of YHWH. The lion had roared, so he could do nothing but prophesy. Lastly, someone may ponder the question in light of the depths of injustice described in the book of Amos. Those who enter into the world of the text are exposed to systems of oppression where people are traded as

---

127. See, for instance, Julia M. O'Brien and Chris Franke, eds., *The Aesthetics of Violence in the Prophets*, LHBOTS 517 (London: T&T Clark, 2010); T. M. Lemos, *Violence and Personhood in Ancient Israel and Comparative Contexts* (Oxford: Oxford University Press, 2017); L. Julia Claassens, "God and Violence in the Prophets," in *The Oxford Handbook of the Prophets*, ed. Carolyn J. Sharp (Oxford: Oxford University Press, 2016), 334–49; Susanne Scholz and Pablo R. Andiñach, eds., *La Violencia and the Hebrew Bible: The Politics and Histories of Biblical Hermeneutics on the American Continent* (Atlanta, GA: SBL, 2016); M. Daniel Carroll R. and J. Blair Wilgus, eds., *Wrestling with the Violence of God: Soundings in the Old Testament*, BBRSup 10 (Winona Lake, IN: Eisenbrauns, 2015); Eric A. Seibert, *The Violence of Scripture: Overcoming the Old Testament's Troubling Legacy* (Minneapolis: Fortress, 2012).

128. Paul, *Amos*, 221.

commodities (2:6; 8:6) and the poor are grossly abused (2:7; 5:11, 12). While not downplaying or normalizing violence, one can suspect that those who have endured the yoke of such systems may more readily understand YHWH's judgment.[129]

Conclusion

This chapter explored various dynamics of intergroup conflict. A clear instance of this is the opening collection of Oracles against the Nations, which culminates in an indictment of the northern kingdom. Here it was demonstrated that the principle of meta-contrast is at work to frame all the nations, including Israel, as outgroups. The destabilizing effect of this strategy is to draw boundaries of who "we" are not. As the first major section in the book, the audience is left searching for an ingroup with which they can positively identify. Though ingroup norms are evident throughout, the confrontation with Amaziah the priest at Bethel illustrates the lines between "us" and "them." It was shown that both Amos and Amaziah stand not just as individuals, but as prototypical representatives of their respective groups. For audiences entering the world of the text, the desire for positive distinctiveness would lead them to identify with the favorable group. Though the people remain historically linked to YHWH ("My People," 7:8, 15; 8:2), their behavior marks them as an outgroup that will be destroyed. Conformity to ingroup norms and values may thus influence the audience's own behavior to stand alongside the lone prophet against a system that calls for their silence.

---

129. See M. Daniel Carroll R., "'I Will Send Fire': Reflections on the Violence of God in Amos," in Carroll and Wilgus, eds., *Wrestling with the Violence of God*, 131–2.

Chapter 4

HISTORY AND SOCIAL IDENTITY IN AMOS

All Prophetic texts contain images of the past. They describe people, places, and events within a divinely ordered course of history. Some texts include more extensive narrative units, while others are more fragmentary. In either case, the Prophetic books in their current form provide perspectives of a contextualized past, both in the pre-exilic and post-exilic periods.[1] The use of the past, however, is not presented merely as an objective series of linear events. Rather, the past is instrumentalized for the sake of the "present." Judgment oracles are announced and/or experienced because of the people's previous behavior towards YHWH and each other. Future deliverance in the Prophets, similarly, is often predicated upon YHWH's relationship with the people in the past and present. Whether an audience is looking backward or forward, the Prophetic books orient them to what it means to belong to the people of God. In other words, social identity in the Hebrew Bible always has a temporal dimension.

The temporal nature of social identity has received attention only relatively recently.[2] One of the fruits of this study has been an appreciation for the social shape of the past. One example is the presentation of a shared

---

1. Christopher Seitz states, "No one will contest that, in terms of simple intelligibility, the prophets' message and the form of that message will be misunderstood without a sense of historical referentiality." Christopher R. Seitz, *Prophecy and Hermeneutics: Toward a New Introduction to the Prophets*, Studies in Theological Interpretation (Grand Rapids: Baker, 2007), 195.

2. See Marco Cinnirella, "Exploring Temporal Aspects of Social Identity: The Concept of Possible Social Identities," *EJSP* 28, no. 2 (1998): 227–48; Susan Condor, "Social Identity and Time," in Robinson, ed., *Social Groups and Identities*, 285–315. In biblical studies, works that consider temporal factors include Stargel, *The Construction of Exodus Identity in Ancient Israel*; Kar Yong Lim, *Metaphors and Social Identity Formation in Paul's Letters to the Corinthians* (Eugene, OR: Wipf & Stock, 2017); Matthew J. Marohl, *Faithfulness and the Purpose of Hebrews: A Social*

history for group members. With a narrative that invokes a common past, the engineers of history can construct group boundaries and norms in historical terms.³ They are able to define for the group who they are and, just as importantly, who they are not. This can take the form of various discursive strategies. Eviatar Zerubavel, for example, explores the shape of the past in the historical ordering of events. There is a general tendency to organize the past in ways that produce continuity with the present. For example, the so-called Nazi Third Reich is so named to present a supposed continuity with the second German empire, glossing over the intervening non-imperial 15 years between them. This continuity served to legitimate and situate the Nazi project within the broader scope of the nation's history. The latter is framed as the chronological successor of the former.⁴ Though this example shows the ills that may accompany the social use of the past, many positive examples could be cited as well.

In the hands of the Prophets, the past is used to construct Israel's social identity. These books tell group members where they have come from, and where they are going. Since the respective presentation of Israel's history is not one among competing versions, an unresisting audience entering the world of the text must negotiate identity within the specific framework provided. As the only valid version of their history, the prophetic retelling excludes alternate forms of remembering. They are not interested, for instance, in Aram, Assyria, or Egypt's recollection of events. The past serves only to explain and legitimate their interpretations. In this sense, the biblical authors are entrepreneurs of identity.⁵

As with other Prophetic books, the book of Amos employs the past to shape the audience's sense of self. Their shared history explains their present status vis-à-vis YHWH. Yet as will be seen below, this historical

---

Identity Approach, Princeton Theological Monograph 82 (Eugene, OR: Pickwick, 2008); Filtvedt, *The Identity of God's People*; Philip F. Esler, *Conflict and Identity in Romans: The Social Setting of Paul's Letter* (Minneapolis: Fortress, 2003).

3. James H. Liu and Denis J. Hilton, "How the Past Weighs on the Present: Social Representations of History and Their Role in Identity Politics," *BJSP* 44, no. 4 (2005): 537–56.

4. Eviatar Zerubavel, *Time Maps: Collective Memory and the Social Shape of the Past* (Chicago: University of Chicago Press, 2003), 37–54. Also see William L. Shirer, *The Rise and Fall of the Third Reich: A History of Nazi Germany* (New York: Simon & Schuster, 1988), 90–7.

5. As Haslam, Reicher, and Platow state, "The past does not determine who we are. Rather, it provides a number of resources that we can draw on in order to create a contemporary understanding of ourselves." Haslam, Reicher, and Platow, *The New Psychology of Leadership*, 178.

continuity between those in the "present" and those in the past puts them at odds with the ingroup. Works on Amos typically relate discussions of time to either the background, composition, and use of traditions (past) or the Day of YHWH concept (past/future).[6] Yet this neglects the identity-forming potential of the book's temporal orientation. This chapter explores the usage of the past in Amos. First, I will briefly introduce the concept of social memory as an additional heuristic tool for exploring identity-construction in the book. Though social memory, or collective memory as it has also been called, has been used in various—and sometimes contradictory—ways, it will be shown to provide a beneficial framework for thinking about the past in this analysis. Second, I will look at five specific usages of the past in Amos (2:9-12; 3:1-2; 4:6-11; 5:26-27; 9:7), seeking to detail their identifying-forming strategy. As will be seen, Amos weaponizes the past as an othering strategy. Each instance exposes, albeit in different ways, the outgroup status of the addressees. Audiences desiring positive distinctiveness within the world of the text can discern the norms and values that define outgroup members. This in turn sheds light on the boundaries and behaviors that mark the ingroup.

Social Memory

There are several ways of studying the past. Some modern historians continue the path laid by eighteenth-century German historians emblemized by Leopold von Ranke's history *"wie es eigentlich gewesen"* ("the way it essentially was").[7] Beyond simply seeking a reconstruction of historical periods and events, others look to phenomena of individual and

---

6. See the history of research in Carroll R., *Amos, the Prophet and His Oracles*, 3–30; Houston, *Amos*, 53–80. Also see Gary V. Smith, "Continuity and Discontinuity in Amos' Use of Tradition," *JETS* 34, no. 1 (1991): 33–42; John J. Collins, "History and Tradition in the Prophet Amos," *Irish Theological Quarterly* 41, no. 2 (1974): 120–33; Barton, *The Theology of the Book of Amos*, 52–106.

7. Leopold von Ranke, *The Theory and Practice of History*, ed. Georg G. Iggers (New York: Routledge, 2011), 86. Iggers notes how the word *eigentlich* has commonly been misunderstood in the English-speaking world. Some take it to mean that von Ranke called for historians to accept nothing less than a purely factual reconstruction of the past. Yet von Ranke elsewhere clarifies an *essential* meaning is what makes an account historical. See Georg G. Iggers, introduction to *The Theory and Practice of History*, xiv. For a thorough overview and evaluation of approaches to the history of Israel, see Megan Bishop Moore, *Philosophy and Practice in Writing a History of Ancient Israel*, LHBOTS 435 (London: T&T Clark, 2006). Also, Megan Bishop Moore and Brad E. Kelle, *Biblical History and Israel's Past: The Changing Study of the Bible and History* (Grand Rapids: Eerdmans, 2011).

social remembering of the past. The study of memory has a long history. Classical philosophers such as Aristotle discussed memory in terms of its material structure. Augustine's use of autobiography introduced a new genre for the remembered past.[8] The study of the social nature of memory, however, is generally attributed to the work of Maurice Halbwachs in the 1920s, although this did not arise in a vacuum.[9] As a student of the French philosopher Henri Bergson and sociologist Emile Durkheim, Halbwachs was exposed to their critique of what they considered deficiencies in transcendentalist accounts of time and space regarding memory. But whereas Bergson locates memory in the subjective experience of the individual, and Durkheim in social organization, Halbwachs argues that memory itself is structured *by* social arrangements.[10] Memory is conditioned through interactions with others within a social framework. As he states, "No memory is possible outside frameworks used by people living in society to determine and retrieve their recollections."[11] Childhood memories are an apt illustration of this point. When reflecting upon these memories, even if by oneself, it is impossible to parse objective facts from the amalgam of stories and tales shared within one's community, as well as subsequent social experiences.[12] Was I always a happy child? Have I always been a fan of that sports team? Did I live in the same house all throughout my upbringing? Questions like these are inaccessible through "objective recollection." Rather, what is heard from one's social groups, what Zerubavel calls "mnemonic others," influences a person's remembering of their own stories.[13]

---

8. See Samuel Byrskog, "Philosophical Aspects on Memory: Aristotle, Augustine and Bultmann," in Byrskog, Hakola, and Jokiranta, eds., *Social Memory and Social Identity*, 23–47; Janet Coleman, *Ancient and Medieval Memories: Studies in the Reconstruction of the Past* (Cambridge: Cambridge University Press, 1992).

9. Maurice Halbwachs, *Les Cadres Sociaux de La Memoire* (Paris: Librarie Felix Alcan, 1925). In their history of memory studies, Olick, Vinitzky-Seroussi, and Levy seek to correct what they view as a "misleading narrative about the origins of contemporary memory studies." Jeffrey K. Olick, Vered Vinitzky-Seroussi, and Daniel Levy's "Introduction" to *The Collective Memory Reader*, ed. Jeffrey K. Olick, Vered Vinitzky-Seroussi, and Daniel Levy (Oxford: Oxford University Press, 2011), 9–10. For a biographical sketch of Halbwachs, as well as a summary of his contribution, see Lewis A. Coser's "Introduction" to *On Collective Memory*, by Maurice Halbwachs, trans. Lewis A. Coser (Chicago: University of Chicago Press, 1992), 1–34.

10. Olick, Vinitzky-Seroussi, and Levy, "Introduction," 9–10.

11. Halbwachs, *On Collective Memory*, 43.

12. Olick, Vinitzky-Seroussi, and Levy, "Introduction," 18.

13. Eviatar Zerubavel, *Social Mindscapes: An Invitation to Cognitive Sociology* (Cambridge, MA: Harvard University Press, 2009), 83.

Over time, constructions of the past can shape a person's view of oneself in the present.[14] This can work both in positive and negative ways. An individual who grows up in a loving home will have memories that reflect the safety and stability of that environment. Studies on trauma and memory, on the other hand, have uncovered the tragic effects abuse can have upon one's view of self later in life.[15] Another example may be found at the level of national consciousness. The Hebrew Bible provides an example in Deut. 6:20-21: "When your son asks you in the future, 'What is the meaning of the testimonies and the statutes and the rules that YHWH our God has commanded you?' then you shall say to your son, 'We were Pharaoh's slaves in Egypt. And YHWH brought us out of Egypt with a mighty hand.'" Future generations, far removed from the events of the exodus, would remember through this retelling that Egypt is an enemy and an oppressor but that YHWH is the liberator of their people. Rituals, and other concrete manifestation of memory, provide a tangible sense of the past with enduring relevance for the present and the future. The fact that this exchange from Deuteronomy 6 continues as part of the Haggadah liturgy in contemporary Jewish communities is a testament to the potency of its social function.[16] The memory of the exodus, especially in its conception of identity, is socially shaped and socially lived. It is not "they" who were slaves in Egypt, but "we." In each of these cases, socially shaped memory of the past affects how people understand themselves in the present.[17]

Social memory has served as a theoretical framework in a number of studies of ancient history and texts.[18] It has been popularized through

14. Cognitive psychologists refer to the process of how our minds store and recall specific information as "episodic memory." This is distinct from semantic memory, which is concerned with facts about how the world is apart from emotion or reference to time and place. See the classical article, Endel Tulving, "Episodic and Semantic Memory," in *Organization of Memory*, ed. E. Tulving and W. Donaldson (San Diego: Academic, 1972), 381–403.

15. See Richard J. McNally, *Remembering Trauma* (Cambridge, MA: Harvard University Press, 2005).

16. Jan Assmann, *Cultural Memory and Early Civilization: Writing, Remembrance, and Political Imagination* (New York: Cambridge University Press, 2011), 1–4.

17. Olick, Vinitzky-Seroussi, and Levy, "Introduction," 19; Zerubavel, *Social Mindscapes*, 91–2.

18. See Sandra Hübenthal, "Social and Cultural Memory in Biblical Exegesis: The Quest for an Adequate Application," in *Cultural Memory in Biblical Exegesis*, ed. Pernille Carstens, Trine B. Hasselbalch, and Niels P. Lemche, Perspectives on Hebrew Scriptures and Its Contexts 17 (Piscataway, NJ: Gorgias, 2012), 175–99. Also, Hans M. Barstad, "History and Memory: Some Reflections on the 'Memory

the work of Egyptologist Jan Assmann,[19] and in biblical studies, Ehud Ben Zvi.[20] While studies in this field maintain significant differences and various nuances, the reason for inclusion of the social memory here is to emphasize the constructive nature of the past in Amos. The assumption here is that the use of these memories was purposeful, even if one cannot uncover the meaning with absolute certainty. As will be seen below, the memories invoked in Amos, alongside other purposes, serve to construct a sense of self for the audience. This is not done ultimately at an individual level, but at the social level. As readers and hearers enter the world of the text, they must negotiate where they belong. Whose history is my history? Whose people are my people? Whose fate is my fate? All of these questions find answers for those who are patient. With these preliminary matters aside, Amos's use of the past will be explored.

The Past in Amos

In Amos, the past is utilized largely as an othering strategy to delimit the boundaries and norms of the perceived outgroup. The temporal orientation takes its cue from the superscription, which sets the world of the text within an eighth-century BCE context.[21] From this perspective, the

Debate' in Relation to the Hebrew Bible," in *The Historian and the Bible: Essays in Honour of Lester L. Grabbe*, ed. Philip R. Davies and Diana V. Edelman, LHBOTS 530 (London: T&T Clark, 2010), 1–10.

19. Jan Assmann, *Das kulturelle Gedächtnis: Schrift, Erinnerung und politische Identität in frühen Hochkulturen* (Munich: Beck, 1992); Assmann, *Cultural Memory and Early Civilization*; Assmann, *Religion und kulturelles Gedächtnis. zehn Studien* (Munich: Beck, 2000), published in English as *Religion and Cultural Memory: Ten Studies*, trans. R. Livingstone (Stanford, CA: Stanford University Press, 2006).

20. See, for instance, Ehud Ben Zvi, *Social Memory Among the Literati of Yehud*, BZAW 509 (Berlin: de Gruyter, 2019); Ben Zvi, "On Social Memory and Identity Formation in Late Persian Yehud: A Historian's Viewpoint with a Focus on Prophetic Literature, Chronicles and the Deuteronomistic Historical Collection," in *Texts, Contexts and Readings in Postexilic Literature: Explorations into Historiography and Identity Negotiation in Hebrew Bible and Related Texts*, ed. Louis C. Jonker, FAT 2/53 (Tübingen: Mohr Siebeck, 2011), 95–148; Ehud Ben Zvi and Christoph Levin, "Remembering the Prophets through the Reading and Rereading of a Collection of Prophetic Books in Yehud: Methodological Considerations and Explorations," in *Remembering and Forgetting in Early Second Temple Judah*, FAT 85 (Tübingen: Mohr Siebeck, 2012), 17–44.

21. In Prophetic books that contain them, the superscriptions appear to be an initial reference that orients the message historically. While he rejects the use of the superscriptions to determine authorship and provide historical reconstruction,

formative experience of the exodus (2:10; 3:1), wilderness wandering (2:10; 5:25), and possession of the land of the Amorites (2:9-10), as well as events such as the destruction of Sodom and Gomorrah (4:11) stand in the distant past. Other instances are depicted as occurring in the recent past. The reclamation of Lo-debar and Karnaim (6:13), for instance, fits within the eighth-century narrative of Israel's military expansion (cf. 2 Kgs 14:25). Likewise, the series of afflictions in 4:6-11 that served to turn the addressees back to YHWH is presented as occurring within living memory.

While the eighth-century context comprises the background, the specific strategy Amos employs consistently merges the distant and recent pasts with the present. In Amos 3:1, for example, the oracle takes the form of a second-person indictment ("you"). Though the message is directed to the addressees, they are subsequently described as "the whole family that I brought up from the land of Egypt." The implied audience is thus projected back into the charter narrative of the exodus. The past and the present, for Amos, is part of an integrated whole.[22] This continuity, however, does not necessitate a favorable categorization. In fact, in line with the larger message of the book as understood here, the past serves primarily to define the outgroup. Thus, ingroup behavioral norms are mediated more by "who we are not" than "who we are." Those desiring a positive sense of self within this world are inclined to adopt the implied, that is, contrary, ingroup norms. At points these ingroup behaviors are exhibited by YHWH, who is positioned as a prototypical group member. Thus, both continuity and discontinuity in Amos's use of the past are weaponized as an othering strategy against addressees.

Ehud Ben Zvi acknowledges the role they have in invoking interpretive frames of reference within which the reading community would situate the message. Ehud Ben Zvi, "Studying Prophetic Texts against Their Original Backgrounds: Pre-Ordained Scripts and Alternative Horizons of Research," in Reid, ed., *Prophets and Paradigms*, 125–35. He says elsewhere, "In fact, [superscriptions] provided the rereaders with authoritative, interpretative keys that, to a large extent, governed the set of potential interpretations that the texts were allowed to carry." E. Ben Zvi, *Hosea*, FOTL 21A/1 (Grand Rapids: Eerdmans, 2005), 32.

22. Zerubavel argues that the cognitive blending of the past and the present is inevitable in our mental processes. He states, "Despite the conventional grammatical distinction between the past and present tenses, the past and the present are not entire separate entities. The notion that we could actually identify a point prior to which everything is 'then' and subsequent to which everything is 'now' is an illusion." Zerubavel, *Time Maps*, 37.

2:9-12

After the turn in the Oracles against the Nations to Israel itself (2:6-8), YHWH justifies the judgment historically. His gracious actions in the past on behalf of Israel required a correlative response that was now lacking. YHWH speaks in the first person in 2:9, describing his destruction of the mighty Amorite "from before them." The identity of this group is specified in 2:6 as Israel. The text puts the defeat of the Amorite, here used as a collective, in the hands of YHWH. Thus, it was not Israel who could claim victory, for YHWH defeated the peoples before them. While 2:9 envisions the time of the conquest under Joshua, the shift comes in 2:10 from the third-person reference ("them") to the second-person ("you," plural). YHWH states, "And I brought *you* up from the land of Egypt…" The seemingly jarring shift in person has led many scholars to regard 2:10-12 as a later addition.[23] The collapse of the past and the present, however, may function to draw in the audience in like fashion to the 7 + 1 pattern of the OAN. YHWH talks first about "them" before turning directly to "you."[24] Thus, his actions in the past were not simply for the benefit of another, but directly involve the addressees.

This direct address continues through v. 11, describing YHWH's provision in the exodus, wilderness wandering, conquest, and institution of the prophetic office. Yet despite these measures, the people directly counteract the kindness of YHWH. He raised up Nazarites and prophets (2:11), but the people forced the Nazarites to break their vows and sought to silence the prophets (2:12). More than simply raising the emotional appeal of the indictment in 2:9-11, the text says something about the identity of the addressees. Though they once received the benefits of ingroup membership as the people of God (deliverance, land, provision), their collective behavior marks them as an outgroup. The temporal association indicates that it is not simply individual actions that are in view, but identity. The current generation is implicated in a long history of working against YHWH. This was not simply the rebellion of previous generations. The cumulative effect of guilt falls squarely on the addressees. Since their exodus, the people have moved from Egypt to an outgroup status.

---

23. For a summary of arguments, see Hadjiev, *Composition and Redaction of Amos*, 48–50. Andersen and Freedman state that the change in number is inconsequential due to the frequency of such phenomenon in Hebrew composition. See Andersen and Freedman, *Amos*, 328. So too, Hayes, *Amos*, 115.

24. Möller argues that the shift contributes to the *pathos* of the text, especially heightened by the rhetorical question at the end of v. 11. See Möller, *A Prophet in Debate*, 206–7.

A number of commentators have drawn attention to the unusual order of events in these verses.[25] The conquest appears first in YHWH's actions (2:9) only then to be followed by the exodus event itself (2:10). While this order could be the result of redactional activity, the sequence is intelligible in context. James Mays draws attention to the logic of this order, which he says emphasizes Israel's existence in the land as solely the result of YHWH's action.[26] The inclusio of "Amorite" in vv. 9 and 10 supports this. YHWH destroyed the Amorites so he could give the "land of the Amorite" to the Israelites. Since life in the land is central to Amos's indictment, YHWH's power in gifting it has priority.[27] But more than simply creating a debt of gratitude, YHWH's actions model ingroup behavior.[28] When Israel was weak, in contrast to the strong Amorites, YHWH acted on their behalf. The assumption is that the people should follow this example.[29] But rather than helping the weak in their midst, the people trample and abuse the poor and needy (2:6-8).[30] Thus, YHWH is shown to serve a prototypical function for the implied audience. Their actions, however, are consistent with their outgroup status. And as an outgroup, Israel will meet a similar fate as the Amorites (2:14-16). The collapse of the past ("them") and the present ("you") in these verses creates a sense of continuity with the trans-temporal social group. The audience will either adopt the ingroup norms represented by YHWH or find themselves outside the ingroup.

3:1-2

The opening verse of Amos 3 sounds the first call to "hear" (שמעו) YHWH's word of judgment (cf. 3:13; 4:1; 5:1; 8:4). The people are addressed in several ways. In addition to the imperative to hear "the word which YHWH spoke," the addressees are specified in two prepositional

---

25. See Hadjiev, *Composition and Redaction of Amos*, 48–9; Wolff, *Joel and Amos*, 141; William Rainey Harper, "The Utterances of Amos Arranged Strophically," *Biblical World* 12, no. 3 (1898): 179–80. Eidevall suggests that the order may be for rhetorical effect. Göran Eidevall, *Amos*, AYB 24G (New Haven, CT: Yale University Press, 2017), 117.

26. Mays, *Amos*, 50.

27. For a defense of the land as a gift, see Thang, *The Theology of the Land in Amos 7–9*, 32–5.

28. Noble views the purpose of the historical retrospect as primarily stressing the indebtedness of Israel-Judah. He acknowledges, however, a substantial degree of truth to the other functions presented by scholars. See Noble, "Israel Among the Nations," 71, 80–1 n. 57.

29. Similarly, Möller, *A Prophet in Debate*, 207–8.

30. See Smith, "Continuity and Discontinuity," 38.

constructions, as well as an intervening vocative. The first prepositional phrase refers to the word "which YHWH spoke *against you*" (אשר דבר יהוה עליכם). The 2mp suffix continues the direct address in 2:10-13. Thus, the implied audience is yet again confronted with the fact that they are the target of the indictment. YHWH further specifies this group with the vocative "people of Israel" (בני ישראל). This designation for the present generation is then supplemented with the second prepositional phrase "against the whole family that I brought up out of the land of Egypt" (על כל־המשפחה אשר העליתי מארץ מצרים).[31]

Like 2:10, Amos 3:1 establishes continuity between the addressees and the exodus generation. While this could be explained simply in terms of the collectivist orientation of ancient Israel,[32] the rhetorical impact of these verses shows the particular relevance for the implied audience. The exodus in Amos constitutes the formative component of the people's sense of self. This event, as Ronald Clements says, "was dominant in Amos's understanding of who Yahweh was, and what he required of his people."[33] The addressees are not invited by Amos to reflect upon YHWH's actions on behalf of another people. Rather, they themselves are identified directly with this foundational reality.

The continuity between the past and the present in v. 1 is supplemented with the statement of 3:2a regarding YHWH's exclusive relationship with the addressees. This intimate relationship is expressed with the phrase "you only have I known" (רק אתכם ידעתי). Scholars debate the precise connotation of the verb ידע in this verse. The context implies more than simply a cognitive function on the part of YHWH. Herbert Huffmon argues that Hittite and Akkadian parallels lend weight to a covenantal meaning.[34] In addition to cognate verbs in treaty texts, he cites several

---

31. Schmidt attributes this verse to deuteronomistic redaction. See Werner H. Schmidt, "Die deuteronomistische Redaktion des Amosbuches," *ZAW* 77, no. 2 (1965): 178–82. Against this, see Norbert Lohfink, "Was There a Deuteronomistic Movement?" in *Those Elusive Deuteronomists: The Phenomenon of Pan-Deuteronomism*, ed. Linda S. Schearing and Steven L. McKenzie, JSOTSup 268 (Sheffield: Sheffield Academic, 1999), 42–5.

32. On Israel as a collectivist society, see Lau, *Identity and Ethics in the Book of Ruth*, 20–5. More generally, Harry C. Triandis, *Individualism and Collectivism*, New Directions in Social Psychology (New York: Routledge, 2018), 43–80; Triandis, "Collectivism and Individualism as Cultural Syndromes," *Cross-Cultural Research* 27, no. 3–4 (1993): 155–80.

33. Clements, *Prophecy and Covenant*, 46.

34. Herbert B. Huffmon, "The Treaty Background of Hebrew Yāda'," *Bulletin of the American Schools of Oriental Research* 181 (1966): 31–7; Herbert B. Huffmon and Simon B. Parker, "A Further Note on the Treaty Background of Hebrew Yāda',"

biblical examples thought to demonstrate this meaning. In Gen. 18:19, for instance, YHWH says to Abraham, "For I have known him (ידעתיו) so that he may instruct his sons and his house after him and they will keep the way of YHWH..." Huffmon also includes Jer. 1:5, where YHWH declares, "Before I formed you in the womb I knew you (ידעתיך)." Since the knowing of YHWH involves setting Jeremiah apart as holy, Huffmon states, "The sense seems to be that Jeremiah had been officially recognized as Yahweh's agent, as his functionary."[35] These texts lead Huffmon to suggest a covenant meaning for Amos 3:2. The verb in this passage, says Huffmon, defines the exclusive YHWH–Israel relationship in terms of a suzerain–vassal treaty, the violation of which results in the covenant curses.[36]

Against the view advocated by Huffmon, Seock-Tae Sohn argues that ידע in Amos 3:2 implies the common notion of the intimacy of a marital relationship rather than a legal one.[37] He faults Huffmon for drawing a false parallel between ידע and Akkadian *idû*, since the latter does not carry the level of intimacy expressed in sexual relations.[38] Moreover, Sohn states that Huffmon's supposed biblical parallels are in fact unrelated. Genesis 18:19, says Sohn, is related more to YHWH's election of Abraham than it is to the concept of covenant. According to Sohn, when used of Israel, ידע most often denotes the intimate relationship between YHWH and the nation in the sense of a husband and wife. He argues that this marital connotation makes sense in Amos 3:2. The sin of the people is thus not a violation of the covenant, but the betrayal of this familial relationship. Some instances in Hosea, a contemporary of Amos, employ a similar usage of the term (e.g., Hos. 2:22 [Eng. 2:20]).

In light of the discussion, how should the use of ידע in Amos 3:2 be evaluated? It seems that Sohn rightly questions some of the biblical examples Huffmon cites in support of the covenantal interpretation. It is difficult to see, for instance, how YHWH would recognize Jeremiah as a

---

Bulletin of the American Schools of Oriental Research, no. 184 (1966): 36–8. Also, see Paul, *Amos*, 101–2. Following Huffmon, Boyle understands the verses as part of a larger covenant lawsuit in the book of Amos. She may, however, overstate the legal case. See Marjorie O'Rourke Boyle, "Covenant Lawsuit of the Prophet Amos: 3:1–4:13," *VT* 21, no. 3 (1971): 342–5.

35. Huffmon, "The Treaty Background of Hebrew Yāda'," 34.
36. Ibid., 34–5.
37. See Seock-Tae Sohn, *The Divine Election of Israel* (Grand Rapids: Eerdmans, 1991), 24–6.
38. Ibid., 26 n. 36.

legitimate covenant partner while he was still in the womb.³⁹ The sense, rather, seems to be that YHWH had elected the prophet for a purpose even before he was born. Likewise, the reference to YHWH's knowledge of Abraham in Gen. 18:19 does not appear to support Huffmon's thesis. The verb in this verse, as Sohn notes, emphasizes Abraham's election, not the covenantal relationship.⁴⁰

Nevertheless, parallels with Hosea, a contemporary of Amos, indicate that the covenantal sense is not altogether foreign to this corpus.⁴¹ Huffmon correctly understands Hos. 13:4 to bear a covenantal meaning. YHWH declares to Israel, "…you know no God but me and besides me there is no savior" (ואלהים זולתי לא תדע). The first half of the verse puts this relationship's origin in the land of Egypt. The occurrence of a covenantal sense of ידע in the context of a memory of Egypt could support Amos's use of covenantal language in 3:2. Moreover, in light of Amos's references to the exodus, wilderness wandering, and entry into the land, it would be difficult to imagine these traditions existing in complete isolation from the covenant at Sinai.⁴² Thus, a covenantal interpretation is certainly plausible here in Amos.

---

39. Contra Holladay who states, "'Know' here then implies both intimacy and a covenantal bond; Yahweh chooses [Jeremiah] to be his spokesman and obligates him thereby." William L. Holladay, *Jeremiah 1: A Commentary on the Book of the Prophet Jeremiah, Chapters 1–25*, Hermeneia (Minneapolis: Fortress, 1986), 33.

40. Sohn, *The Divine Election of Israel*, 26 n. 36.

41. Some scholars continue to debate whether the notion of covenant was active prior to the eighth and seventh centuries BCE. See, for instance, Ernest W. Nicholson, *God and His People: Covenant and Theology in the Old Testament* (Oxford: Clarendon, 1986), 3–117; John Barton, "Covenant in Old Testament Theology," in *Covenant as Context: Essays in Honour of E. W. Nicholson*, ed. A. D. H. Mayes and R. B. Salters (Oxford: Oxford University Press, 2003), 23–38. Hasel, on the other hand, argues for the plausibility of covenant in the eighth century. Hasel, *Understanding the Book of Amos*, 72–5. In light of the skepticism of covenant, Brueggemann states, "Israel's theological self-presentation is not constrained by such critical judgments, but presents itself from the outset as Yahweh's covenant people." W. Brueggemann, *Theology of the Old Testament: Testimony, Dispute, Advocacy* (Minneapolis: Fortress, 1997), 418. Nevertheless, the question is not if covenant *could* serve as the background for the broader message, but whether it is intended here.

42. Widengren claims that the absence of Moses and the covenant at Sinai in Amos results from the circulation of Mosaic traditions among the northern tribes, to whom Amos did not belong. Geo Widengren, "Israelite-Jewish Religion," in *Historia Religionum: Handbook for the History of Religions*, ed. C. J. Bleeker and G. Widengren, Religions of the Past (Leiden: Brill, 1969), 1:275. This seems problematic, however, in light of Amos's grasp of other northern traditions.

On the other hand, there are two problems for Sohn's view. First, he seems to neglect the intimate relationship that can be expressed through covenant agreement in the ancient world.[43] Treaty partners could use familial, and even affectionate terms, to describe the relationship. Second, and perhaps more significant, the absence of marital imagery in the immediate context of Amos 3, as well as elsewhere in the book, makes this primary sense unlikely in 3:2. Therefore, while certainty is evasive, one can conclude, at minimum, that ידע here implies an intimate relationship that has a long history. If a covenantal reading is granted, the kind of "knowledge" that YHWH possesses embeds both blessings and curses in the relationship itself. YHWH's commitment to this relationship is evidenced throughout Amos in his provision, protection, and patience towards the people. The statement in Amos 3:2a reminds the addressees that they stand in a unique place with relation to God. What that entails, however, is shown to be different from what may be expected.

The special relationship between YHWH and the addressees is specified further with the claim that YHWH knows only Israel "from all the nations of the earth." This phrase magnifies the exclusivity of the relationship. This, however, does not imply that YHWH did not have dealings with other peoples (cf. 1:3–2:3; 9:7). But the exodus event, in some sense, marked Israel as a distinct people with a distinct identity. The significance of the exodus in the history of Israel cannot be overstated. Ronald Hendel says that "it is the gracious act of the great lord for his people *on which rests the superstructure of Israelite belief and practice*."[44] Amos brings the realization of this identity not in terms of abstract history, but participation. In essence, the sense that Amos presents is that the addressees themselves were known by YHWH from the beginning.[45] This continuity of the past and the present puts into sharp relief the norms of the implied audience and their present behavior.

---

43. Kelle, for example, demonstrates that love language can function within the context of suzerain-vassal treaties. See Brad E. Kelle, *Hosea 2: Metaphor and Rhetoric in Historical Perspective*, Academia Biblica 20 (Atlanta, GA: SBL, 2005), 113–18.

44. Ronald S. Hendel, "The Exodus in Biblical Memory," *JBL* 120, no. 4 (2001): 601 (emphasis added).

45. Another dimension of this temporal orientation is a recollection of a unified past between the northern and southern kingdoms. Appeal to the exodus in relation to "the whole family" that was brought up from Egypt reconfigures the boundaries of the target group. See Radine, *Book of Amos in Emergent Judah*, 23. This strategy intimates that the boundaries of the ingroup are not drawn simply along sociopolitical lines. Also see Noble, "Israel Among the Nations," 72.

The unique and exclusive relationship between YHWH and the addressees affirmed in 3:2a is immediately brought into tension in 3:2b. YHWH states that this exclusive relationship would be the basis not of their protection, but of their punishment. The specific iniquities (עון) in view are not specified but may be linked with the transgressions (פשע) in 2:6-8, as well as the historic acts in 2:12.[46] This surprising turn of events radically reconceptualizes the intersection of group identity and temporal orientation. Unlike Hosea, who holds some fondness of Israel's early experience (cf. Hos. 2:17d [Eng. 2:15]), Amos frames this period negatively in terms of the people's responsiveness to YHWH.[47] Moreover, the continuity between the past and the present concerning their sin further contributes to the outgroup status of the addressees.[48] In essence, Amos says that the sin of the people is not new. Indeed, the norms of their social identification make it impossible for them to behave properly (Amos 3:10). Amos 3:2 embodies the tension between Israel's election and their current outgroup status.

4:6-11

Amos 4 begins with the third call to "hear" (cf. 3:1, 13; 5:1).[49] The addressees, implied in the 2mp imperative, are immediately designated

---

46. The noun עון is used only here in Amos. The verb פקד, used in 3:2b, is connected in v. 14b with the פשע, substantiating a connection between these terms for sin/transgression. Lam analyzes both of these terms in relation to the metaphors reckoning or accounting. See Joseph Lam, *Patterns of Sin in the Hebrew Bible: Metaphor, Culture, and the Making of a Religious Concept* (Oxford: Oxford University Press, 2016), 134–5.

47. The view of Israel's early history in Hosea, however, is not monolithic. The love relationship described in Hos 11:1, expressed in the exodus from Egypt, is contrasted with the nation's perpetual idolatry in 11:2. See Roy E. Garton, "Rattling the Bones of the Twelve: Wilderness Reflections in the Formation of the Book of the Twelve," in *Perspectives on the Formation of the Book of the Twelve: Methodological Foundations, Redactional Processes, Historical Insights*, ed. R. Albertz, J. D. Nogalski, and J. Wöhrle, BZAW 433 (Berlin: de Gruyter, 2012), 243–7.

48. Rowley claims that the reckoning of the people's sin in Amos 3:2 is YHWH's gracious chastening as evidence of his divine love. Yet this underplays the pervasive outgroup categorization of Israel throughout the book. Rather than gracious chastisement, YHWH's judgment would leave little more than evidence that they had been ravaged by the Deity (3:12). See H. H. Rowley, *The Biblical Doctrine of Election* (London: Lutterworth, 1948), 53.

49. Möller notes the structuring function of the call to hear in 3:1, 4:1, and 5:1 as each introducing new sections. He evaluates and critiques Jeremias who views 4:1-3 as the conclusion of the "Samaria cycle" in 3:9–4:3. See Möller, *A Prophet in Debate*, 92–7.

"cows of Bashan" (4:1b).⁵⁰ The addressees are further specified by a relative clause and three participial clauses. These cows of Bashan are those "on the mountain of Samaria," "who oppress the poor," "crush the needy," and command their husbands to bring refreshments. The theme of oppression and injustice continues the indictment from chs 2–3. After a critique of cult in vv. 4-5, the text presents a series of plagues in vv. 6-11.⁵¹

The plagues form a historical retrospect, as YHWH recounts a series of calamities designed to evoke repentance. Each strophe begins with 1cs perfect verbs with YHWH as the subject and concludes with the refrain "but you did not return to me declares YHWH." The frequent 2mp suffixes throughout the section keep the addressees in view. They are projected back onto the events as if they themselves are culpable for responding to the warnings. Though the plagues mentioned would occupy a significant amount of time, perhaps greater than a single generation, the addressees are responsible for the cumulative rejection of YHWH's warnings. In this way, the temporal orientation of the section is similar to what we discover in 3:1-2. Together the five strophes of 4:6-11 collapse the past and the present to show the obstinance of the people.⁵² They are like the fool in

---

50. The identification of the "cows of Bashan" has received much attention. The most common view is that the "cows of Bashan" refer to the elite women of Samaria who perpetrate and embody injustice in the land. See Eidevall, *Amos*, 136–8; Brian Irwin, "Amos 4:1 and the Cows of Bashan on Mount Samaria: A Reappraisal," *CBQ* 74, no. 2 (April 2012): 231–46; Barton, *Theology of the Book of Amos*, 79; Terence Kleven, "The Cows of Bashan: A Single Metaphor at Amos 4:1-3," *CBQ* 58 (1996): 215–27; Wolff, *Joel and Amos*, 205–6; Andersen and Freedman, *Amos*, 416–17. Garrett too maintains that the cows of Bashan are the elite women of Samaria. Regarding the 3mp suffix on אדון "lord," he states, "Hebrew is not consistent about using the feminine plural pronominal suffixes for feminine antecedents (cf. Ruth 1:8)." Garrett, *Amos*, 108. Other scholars understand the feminine gender more broadly in the passage as a figure of speech. The mixture of masculine and feminine forms in 4:1–3 could be evidence that men are the target of the indictment throughout. In the Targum, all the forms are masculine. Scholars who view the "cows of Bashan" as women and men include Jason Blair Wilgus, "Judgment on Israel: Amos 3–6 Read as a Unity" (PhD diss., University of Edinburgh, 2012), 99–102, 105–8; Emmanuel O. Nwaoru, "A Fresh Look at Amos 4:1-3 and Its Imagery," *VT* 59 (2009): 460–74; Hans M. Barstad, "Die Basankühe in Am iv 1," *VT* 25 (1975): 286–97; Barstad, *The Religious Polemics of Amos*, 37–44.

51. Chapter 5 discusses 4:4-5 in more detail.

52. Kessler says of the plagues, "Although scholars dispute the precise referents of these catastrophes, few would see them as being imposed one directly on top of the other on the same group of people, with no intervals or relief between them." John Kessler, "Patterns of Descriptive Curse Formulae in the Hebrew Bible, with Special

Proverbs who does not abandon his folly though crushed in a mortar with pestle (Prov. 27:22).[53] Their rejection of YHWH's warning crescendos in the ominous threat in 4:12c: "prepare to meet your God, O Israel."[54]

In the first strophe (v. 6), YHWH sends a nationwide famine. This deprivation of food is ironically described as YHWH *giving* "cleanness of teeth" and "lack of bread."[55] The first of these phrases is found only here in the Hebrew Bible, but the meaning, nonetheless, is clear. Without food, one's teeth remain "clean."[56] Famine was a feared reality in agrarian societies and frequently leveled as a threat in the Prophets, appearing most commonly in Jeremiah.[57] Famines primarily resulted from either climatological disruptions, accompanied by plant disease and pestilence,

---

Attention to Leviticus 26 and Amos 4:6–12," in *The Formation of the Pentateuch: Bridging the Academic Cultures of Europe, Israel, and North America*, ed. J. C. Gertz et al., FAT 111 (Tübingen: Mohr Siebeck, 2016), 969. While this rightly orients the perception of the plagues in reference to each other, Wilgus is correct that these need not be plagues in rapid, or any, succession. Rather, "[The] progression in severity may indicate simply that Yahweh judged in the past to no avail." Wilgus, "Judgment on Israel," 124.

53. Kessler states, "[The] description of Israel's failure to learn from Yahweh's disciplinary measures is reminiscent of the fool who is smitten a hundred times to no avail (Prov 17:10)." Kessler, "Patterns of Descriptive Curse Formulae in the Hebrew Bible," 964–95.

54. This call has been understood as a hopeful occasion for repentance and restoration by some scholars. Brueggemann, for instance, understands this verse positively as an occasion for covenant renewal. The repentance YHWH desired from the people in 4:6-11, says Brueggemann, is still in view in v. 12. Thus, the threats of vv. 6-11 "are not to be taken in the form of a death sentence, but as elsewhere in the curse ritual, one of the options set before Israel" (Brueggemann, "Amos 4:4-13," 7). Also see Linville, *Amos and the Cosmic Imagination*, 116, 118; Carroll R., *Contexts for Amos*, 250; Soggin, *The Prophet Amos*, 97. Others, rightly note the contextual and interpretive aspects that favor a negative tone of judgment. See Möller, *A Prophet in Debate*, 282; Hayes, *Amos*, 148; Paul, *Amos*, 149–53. The reference to "your God" may function similarly to the phrase "my people Israel" in contexts of judgment (7:8, 15; 8:2). On "your God" in 4:12, see below.

55. So, Eidevall, *Amos*, 146.

56. Paul, *Amos*, 144.

57. The noun רעב, "famine," occurs over thirty times in Jeremiah. Cf. Jer. 5:12; 11:22; 14:12-13, 15-16, 18; 15:2; 16:4; 18:21; 21:7, 9; 24:10; 27:8, 13; 29:17-18; 32:24, 36; 34:17; 38:2, 9; 42:16-17, 22; 44:12-13, 18, 27; 52:6. This noun frequently occurs in a formula with "sword" (הרב) and "plague" (דבר). Hadjiev is likely correct that Amos is not dependent here on this formula since these plagues do not appear together, but are separated. Hadjiev, *Composition and Redaction of Amos*, 151 n. 50.

or destabilized sociopolitical conditions necessary for crop growth.[58] The Hebrew Bible connects famine at several points to the outworking of YHWH's greater purposes (cf. Gen. 45:6-8; 2 Sam. 21:1; 1 Kgs 17:1). In Amos, the famine was designed to evoke repentance; a call, however, that went unheeded. Unlike the scope of the second plague, which is selective, the famine struck *all* the cities and *all* the places. YHWH's comprehensive call to repentance exempted no one.

The second strophe (vv. 7-8) describes YHWH sending draught. These verses contain the most complex syntax in the series.[59] YHWH states that he withheld rain while there was yet three months until the harvest time, the results of which would be devastating. The conceptual effect of such a draught would produce famines like that of v. 6. The difference here involves those affected. YHWH singled out specific cities to receive rain while he allowed others to wither. These cities ("two or three cities") are said to wander to a city that supposedly has water. The text makes no indication that these cities were rebuffed in their attempt to secure water, but does specify that they were nevertheless unsatisfied. Moreover, the moral standing of the cities is not mentioned as a reason for rain or draught in the verses, but simply that YHWH is the ultimate source of disaster.[60]

The third strophe (v. 9) involves the destruction of crops and vegetation by blight, mildew, and locust. The first of these, blight (שדפון), is caused by the east wind known as the sirocco.[61] The hot east wind scorched the crops causing them to dry up and turn brown.[62] This plague, explicitly mentioned five times in the Old Testament (Deut. 28:22; 1 Kgs 8:37; Amos 4:9; Hag. 2:17; 2 Chron. 6:28), appears always in conjunction with ירקון ("mildew").[63] Both the gardens and vineyards are said to be affected

---

58. William H. Shea, "Famine," *ABD* 2:769-70.

59. Eidevall states that though the complexity of the verses has given rise to several hypotheses of textual expansion, the uncertainty involved makes it best to refrain from such speculation. Eidevall, *Amos*, 146. On the various proposals, see Jarl H. Ulrichsen, "Der Einschub Amos 4,7b-8a. sprachliche Erwägungen zu einem umstrittenen Text," *Orientalia Suecana* 41-42 (1992): 284-98.

60. Hayes, *Amos*, 146-7.

61. On the sirocco in the Hebrew Bible, see Aloysius Fitzgerald, *The Lord of the East Wind*, CBQMS 34 (Washington, DC: Catholic Biblical Association of America, 2002). Fitzgerald only references Amos 4:9 in a footnote of verses describing the harm to vegetation (109). Also see Philip J. King, *Amos, Hosea, Micah: An Archaeological Commentary* (Philadelphia: Westminster John Knox, 1988), 111.

62. Wolff, *Joel and Amos*, 223.

63. The noun ירקון appears alone in Jer. 30:6 but is clearly used in a different sense.

by the pair of plagues. The trees, however, were devoured by locusts (גזם).[64] In the third strophe, several agents of destruction are mentioned (blight, mildew, locusts), but the audience is reminded that it is YHWH who strikes the people. What may seem like a natural disaster is in a very real sense an act of God.

The fourth strophe (v. 10) contains a memory of pestilence and war sent by YHWH. The pestilence (דבר) that struck the people is likened to the pestilence that struck Egypt (בדרך מצרים, "in the manner of Egypt"), presumably prior to the exodus event.[65] The mention of Egypt's affliction here adds to the pointed polemic against the addressees in at least two ways. First, this reference puts the past and the present on the same plane. The legendary account of Egypt's affliction before the exodus was not a phenomenon simply reserved for the distant past. Rather, YHWH replayed this affliction in "recent history" for the sake of the addressees in the present. In other words, these great acts of judgment are not just something YHWH simply did "back then." Rather, there is continuity in YHWH's actions from then to now. Second, the reference to Egypt's affliction puts the addressees on par with those under the judgment of YHWH.[66] The distinction made between Israel and Egypt in the Exodus narrative (cf. Exod. 8:22; 9:4, 26; 10:23; 11:7) was no longer in effect. Israel's heart has become as obstinate as Pharaoh's, so YHWH afflicts them in like manner. In addition to the Egyptian-like pestilence, YHWH declares that he killed the young men (בחוריכם) with the sword and sent their horses into captivity.[67] There may be a wordplay with בחור, as it was the בכור, "firstborn," who were killed during the final plague in the exodus

---

64. Though locusts are a common threat in the Hebrew Bible, outside this verse, גָּזָם appears only in Joel 1:4 and 2:25. For a discussion of these terms, see Wolff, *Joel and Amos*, 27–8.

65. Some scholars prefer the emendation כְּדֶרֶךְ מִצְרָיִם, "like [the] manner of Egypt." For a discussion and defense of the MT reading, see Paul, *Amos*, 147 n. 75.

66. Scholars understand the comparison with Egypt in different ways. Does it allude to one or more specific Egyptian plague(s) in the Exodus narrative? Or does it refer to the affliction as a whole? Paul likens the pestilence here to the fifth and seventh plagues in Exod. 9:3-7 and 9:15. Paul, *Amos*, 147. Harper provides a succinct summary of the options, but argues that no one event is in view. Harper, *A Critical and Exegetical Commentary*, 100.

67. Some emend שְׁבִי, "captivity," to צְבִי, "beauty," because the former typically refers to people and not horses. Paul points to Zeijdner as an early proponent of this emendation. See H. Zeijdner, "Bijdragen der Tekstkritiek op het O. T.," *Theologische Studien* 4 (1886): 196–204; Paul, *Amos*, 148. While this usage is more common, שְׁבִי can include animals/property (cf. Num. 31:26; Dan. 11:8).

(cf. 12:29), while it is the בחור, "young men," who are put to the sword in Amos's memory.⁶⁸

This othering strategy in the fourth strophe—the collapse of time and conflation of people—reinforces what was discovered in Amos 3:1-2, namely that traditional boundary markers of ingroup identity (national identification, history of YHWH's kindness, etc.), are not determinative for social identity in the present. The behavior of the addressees warranted a judgment like that which fell upon a classic Other in their social memory. Here again readers are reminded that these events were not random or happenstance. It was YHWH himself who sent the affliction and killed the young men, causing a stench to rise from their camp.

In the fifth and final strophe (v. 11), YHWH recounts how he overthrew (הפך) the addressees ("you," plural). This memory is compared to when "God overthrew Sodom and Gomorrah."⁶⁹ Depending on their view of composition, some commentators interpret this overthrow in light of the fall of either the northern kingdom in 721 BCE or the southern kingdom in 586 BCE.⁷⁰ On the other hand, the majority of commentators interpret this overthrow as an earthquake.⁷¹ Andersen and Freedman claim, "[The]

---

68. So, Carroll R., *Contexts for Amos*, 213; W. Rudolph, "Amos 4, 6–13," in *Wort-Gebot-Glaube: Beiträge zur Theologie des Alten Testaments, Walter Eichrodt zum 80. Geburtstag*, ed. J. J. Stamm, E. Jenni, and H. J. Stoebe, Abhandlungen zur Theologie des Alten und Neuen Testaments 59 (Zurich: Zwingli, 1970), 33.

69. Paul states that the mention of אלהים increases the immensity of the catastrophe. Paul, *Amos*, 149. Some scholars view the third person here as evidence that this phrase was a well-known proverb for destruction. See, for instance, Weston Fields, *Sodom and Gomorrah: History and Motif in Biblical Narrative* (Sheffield: Sheffield Academic, 1997), 169. Contrary to some, Hadjiev maintains that this proverbial phrase was likely popular in the pre-exilic period. See Hadjiev, *Composition and Redaction of Amos*, 153.

70. Wolff views the overthrow with relation to 721 BCE. See Wolff, *Joel and Amos*, 221–2. Eidevall and Jeremias identify the events of 586 BCE as the referent. Eidevall, *Amos*, 147; Jeremias, *The Book of Amos*, 73–4.

71. Paul, *Amos*, 148–9; Hayes, *Amos*, 147; Andersen and Freedman, *Amos*, 417; Soggin, *The Prophet Amos*, 76; R. Reed Lessing, "Amos's Earthquake in the Book of the Twelve," *CTQ* 74 (2010): 244; Lessing, *Amos*, 281; Hadjiev, *Composition and Redaction of Amos*, 154–5; D. K. Ogden, "The Earthquake Motif in the Book of Amos," in *Goldene Äpfel in silbernen Schalen: Collected Communications to the XIIIth Congress of the International Organization for the Study of the Old Testament, Leuven 1989*, ed. K. D. Schunck and M. Augustin, Beiträge zur Erforschung des Alten Testaments und des antiken Judentums 20 (Frankfurt: Peter Lang, 1992), 73; David Noel Freedman and Andrew Welch, "Amos's Earthquake and Israelite Prophecy,"

conventional 'overthrow' connected with the traditions of Sodom and Gomorrah is often associated with seismic forces; but the cause named in Genesis 19 was 'fire from Heaven,' as in Amos 1–2."[72] Though the language may be metaphorical in the Genesis narrative, the description is not best explained by an earthquake.[73]

Rather than specifying the precise form of affliction in the fifth strophe, the parallel with Sodom and Gomorrah may function on an ethical level. The previous strophe (v. 10) described YHWH's treatment of the addressee like the Egyptians prior to the exodus (i.e., an outgroup). Here the memory of the judgment of Sodom and Gomorrah may imply that the addressees were no better than these infamous cities. YHWH dealt with the addressees like he dealt with the cities on the plain. This speaks not so much about the judgment itself as it does about the people involved.[74] Thomas Jemielity aptly states,

> [Drawing] on the hated role of Egypt and the despised place of Sodom and Gomorrah in their history, Amos, ironically, has Israel play the role of these three despised nations in experiencing like them the ineffectual chastisement of the LORD and soon to experience like them the doom of the LORD... *Israel is the new Egypt, the new Sodom and Gomorrah.*[75]

Together, all of these afflictions lead to an ominous encounter with YHWH (v. 12). The addressees had refused to return and thus must prepare themselves for battle with the Deity. Though the addressees are

---

in *Scripture and Other Artifacts: Essays on the Bible and Archaeology in Honor of Philip J. King*, ed. M. D. Coogan, J. C. Exum, and L. E. Stager (Louisville, KY: Westminster John Knox, 1994), 190.

72. Andersen and Freedman, *Amos*, 444.

73. Lot, for instance, is concerned about escaping to the mountain lest the disaster overtake him, preferring instead to find refuge in a nearby city (Gen. 19:19-20). If the destruction in view was an earthquake, it would make little sense for Lot to remain closer to the site of the coming disaster. It could be claimed that Lot was unaware of the exact form the destruction would take, but the messengers would not likely have granted this request if this was the case. On the Amos reference, see Katharine J. Dell, "Amos and the Earthquake: Judgment as Natural Disaster," in Hagedorn and Mein, eds., *Aspects of Amos*, 4 n. 11.

74. As Carroll R. notes, this "implies a correspondence not only of miraculous judgment but also of sinful character." Carroll R., *Contexts for Amos*, 214.

75. Thomas Jemielity, *Satire and the Hebrew Prophets*, Literary Currents in Biblical Interpretation (Louisville, KY: Westminster John Knox, 1992), 91 (emphasis added).

framed as an outgroup, Amos nevertheless refers here to YHWH as "your God." Though this identification may appear odd with reference to an outgroup, at least two points can be made. First, in light of the context of judgment, this phrase could hardly indicate a positive designation. The people's refusal to return to YHWH has brought them to this point and now they will face the consequences. Thus, "your God" does not afford any sense of positive ingroup identity. Second, similar to the description in 3:2, as well as the reference to outgroup Israel in Amos' confrontation with Amaziah (7:15), this designation can be explained in terms of the historic covenantal relationship with YHWH, who also exercises sovereignty over all the earth. It was not the gods of the nations who called for Israel to return, but YHWH himself. They are accountable to him, and to no other, for their violation of the terms of the covenant. This appellation, then, indicates the severity of the coming confrontation, as the past and present disobedience culminate in the future judgment. Though the people already claim that YHWH is with them (5:14), this meeting will entail not blessing, but ruin.

As shown above, more than merely recounting historical events, Amos employs these memories to say something about the identity of the implied audience. While they may not lack the innate ability to return to YHWH, their behavior evidences their outgroup status. They are defined, in a sense, by their lack of responsiveness to YHWH. The comparison with historic outgroups furthers the othering strategies of the text. Thus, the social identity of the implied ingroup is not derived merely from a past relationship with YHWH. The collapse of the past and present necessitates an ongoing relationship of listening and obeying. In this context, this would at minimum touch on issues of justice and religion.

5:25-26

Following a woe oracle, which counters the implied audience's optimistic view of the Day of YHWH, Amos turns to cultic matters and their relation to justice in 5:21-27.[76] YHWH voices his hatred for the cultic practices of the addressees, refusing to recognize their worship (vv. 21-22). In fact, their liturgy is nothing more than noise YHWH would rather be rid of (v. 23). The problem, as expressed throughout the book of Amos, is that justice and righteousness were absent (v. 24).

Amos 5:25 poses a question to the addressees invoking memory of the wilderness period: "Did you bring me sacrifices and offering 40 years in

---

76. Some scholars argue that 5:21-27 comprises a separate unit from vv. 18-20. So, Paul, *Amos*, 188 n. 1. Against this, Wilgus argues that the text should be read as a single unit. See Wilgus, "Judgment on Israel," 155–6.

the wilderness, House of Israel?"[77] While it would seem like this question would welcome a straightforward answer, there are in fact significant complications. Verse 26 itself is a notorious interpretive crux in Hebrew Bible scholarship. Hans Barstad asserts, "Without hesitation I would characterize Am 5, 26 as the most difficult passage in the whole Book of Amos."[78] The problems of vv. 25-26 lay at both the textual and historical/ theological levels.

The first problem that surfaces in v. 25 is the expected answer to the question, "Did you bring me sacrifices and offering in the wilderness." Some interpreters understand an implied negative response to the question ("No, we did not bring sacrifices in the wilderness"). There are two notable ways this is argued. In Wellhausen's classical formulation, the negative answer to Amos's question, namely that there were no sacrifices in the wilderness period, evidences the received belief in Amos's day that sacrificial worship was not Mosaic in origin.[79] Somewhat differently, Shalom Paul states that Amos relied on the traditions found in JE, which involved cultic activity prior to the exodus and at Sinai but not during the wilderness period.[80]

Apart from the issue of Pentateuchal sources available during the composition of Amos, some scholars argue, rather, that sacrifices simply were not required prior to entry into the land. Douglas Stuart, for example, says, "The sacrificial system was essentially predesigned for a coming era of normal food production…in a landed, settled situation. Though it began in an inaugural manner during the first year's encampment at Sinai (e.g., Lev. 9:8-24), sacrificing and its association with the three yearly festivals became regular only after the conquest."[81] This claim begs the

---

77. Though the ה on זבחים, "sacrifices," is pointed like a definite article, Garrett supports the consensus view that it is in fact an interrogative הֲ (cf. Num 13:19). If it were a definite article one would expect מנחה to have an article as well. Garrett, *Amos*, 173. Also, see Soggin, *The Prophet Amos*, 98; Paul, *Amos*, 193 n. 53.

78. Barstad, *The Religious Polemics of Amos*, 119.

79. Julius Wellhausen, *Prolegomena to the History of Ancient Israel: With a Reprint of the Article "Israel" from the Encyclopedia Britannica* (1885; repr., Atlanta, GA: Scholars Press, 1994), 56–7. Also, see Hywel Clifford, "Amos in Wellhausen's Prolegomena," in Hagedorn and Mein, eds., *Aspects of Amos*, 145–9.

80. Paul, *Amos*, 194. The dating of P continues to be debated in critical scholarship. See the various articles in Jan Christian Gertz et al., eds., *The Formation of the Pentateuch: Bridging the Academic Cultures of Europe, Israel, and North America*, FAT 111 (Tübingen: Mohr Siebeck, 2016). Also, Jean Louis Ska, *Introduction to Reading the Pentateuch* (Winona Lake, IN: Eisenbrauns, 2006), 159–61; G. J. Wenham, "The Priority of P," *VT* 49, no. 2 (1999): 240–58.

81. Stuart, *Hosea–Jonah*, 355. Similarly, Wolff, *Joel and Amos*, 265.

question of what degree of the cultic institution Amos intends in 5:25, as well as what Stuart means by "it began in an inaugural manner." If Amos is asking whether the people participated in an *established* cultic system, then Stuart's assertion that the prescription for the sacrificial system was yet in the future from the 40 years in the wilderness would have merit. If, however, what is intended is *ad hoc* sacrifice, Stuart's claim may be more problematic, a point indicated by Stuart's own citation of Lev. 9:8-24.[82] For if sacrifices did begin in "an inaugural manner" in the wilderness, it is doubtful whether Amos's question would achieve the desired negative response.

Jeremiah 7:22 seemingly supports the negation of Israel's cult during the wilderness period. The text reads, "For I [YHWH] did not speak with your fathers and I did not command them on the day I brought them out of the land of Egypt concerning matters of offering and sacrifice."[83] Jeremiah appears to say, with Amos, that YHWH did not expect, and Israel did not give, sacrifice during the stint in the wilderness.[84] This could contribute to the notion that the wilderness without sacrifice is viewed as an idealized period of Israel's history (cf. Hos. 3:4). This interpretation, however, fails to convince. The wilderness period is predominantly described as anything but ideal in the Old Testament. Indeed, the very reason for the 40 years in the wilderness was the people's rebellion against YHWH (cf. Num. 14:26-35).[85] Moreover, the wilderness generation commonly is

---

82. Some scholars state the lack of sacrifices was the result of limited resources. See W. Rudolph, *Joel, Amos, Obadja, Jona*, Kommentar zum Alten Testament 13/4 (Gütersloh: Gerd Mohn, 1971), 212; Eidevall, *Amos*, 171; Soggin, *The Prophet Amos*, 100.

83. Barton, for example, says that Amos 5:25 and Jer. 7:22 both indicate that YHWH had no thought of imposing cultic requirements after the exodus. Rather, the cultic system was a later development. John Barton, "The Prophets and the Cult," in *Temple and Worship in Biblical Israel: Proceedings of the Oxford Old Testament Seminar*, ed. John Day, LHBOTS 422 (London: T&T Clark, 2005), 120–1. Kraus states that these verses "[point] to a time when it was simply the Divine law that determined the relationship between God and his people." Hans-Joachim Kraus, *Worship in Israel: A Cultic History of the Old Testament*, trans. Geoffrey Buswell (Richmond, VA: John Knox, 1966), 112.

84. For a thorough analysis of all prophetic texts that speak of absence of sacrifice in the wilderness, see Göran Eidevall, *Sacrificial Rhetoric in the Prophetic Literature of the Hebrew Bible* (Lewiston, NY: Edwin Mellen, 2012), 137–71.

85. Similarly, Marvin A. Sweeney, *The Twelve Prophets*, vol. 1, Berit Olam (Collegeville, MN: Liturgical Press, 2000), 241; Eidevall, *Amos*, 170. Similarly, David Allan Hubbard, *Joel and Amos: An Introduction and Commentary*, TOTC 25 (1989; repr., Downers Grove, IL: IVP Academic, 2009), 195.

characterized as a grumbling, disobedient, and evil people (Num. 32:13; Josh. 5:6; Ps. 95:8). On a more practical level, in light of the contemporary understanding of religion in the ancient world, it is difficult to imagine that a generation would come and go in the wilderness without some form of sacrificial system.[86]

Some scholars argue that the point of Jer. 7:22 is not that sacrifices were wholly absent, but rather that *regulations* concerning sacrifice are what is in view.[87] In this view, Israel was not obligated to offer sacrifice according to a divine mandate during this period, but they were nevertheless free to do so. The regulations came into effect once the people entered the land. Though this could help explain the language of YHWH not speaking or instructing Israel concerning sacrifice, it introduces another problem. It is difficult to imagine a cultic system without a divine origin functioning among the people of Israel.[88] Furthermore, the specific prescriptions concerning various ordinances and rituals in the Priestly material often adds a warning that transgressors "will be cut off from the people" (Exod. 31:14; Lev. 7:20-21; 17:4; 19:8; Num. 9:13). One may wonder if a system of sacrifice essentially created by the people would have accomplished the intended purpose of maintaining their relationship with YHWH. In short, YHWH makes clear that he cannot be approached simply in any way the people choose. It is reasonable to expect some instruction regarding such matters.

Hayes attempts to resolve the issue by claiming that what Amos envisions as absent are the two specific forms of sacrifice named in Amos 5:25, namely זבח ("well-being offering") and מנחה ("cereal offering").[89] The response to the question would then be, "No, we did not bring *those* kinds of sacrifices, but we did bring other kinds." To distinguish these two sacrifices from the rest, says Hayes, would not be to quibble about minor details. For those who participated in the Israelite cult, this differentiation would have been meaningful. More likely, however, is Eidevall's

---

86. So, Soggin, *The Prophet Amos*, 99.

87. W. H. Schmidt, *Das Buch Jeremia: Kapitel 1–20*, Das Alte Testament Deutsch 20 (Göttingen: Vandenhoeck & Ruprecht, 2008), 185; Eidevall, *Sacrificial Rhetoric*, 150–1.

88. Watts states that few rituals actually claim divine authorship, and thus present difficulty. Without an explicit author specifying the meaning, a ritual is then open to various interpretations. Ritual texts that do make such a claim, Watts argues, function to persuade readers to perform the rites and interpret them in a certain way. James W. Watts, *Ritual and Rhetoric in Leviticus: From Sacrifice to Scripture* (Cambridge: Cambridge University Press, 2007), 30–1.

89. Hayes, *Amos*, 175.

suggestion that זבח and מנחה form a merism, representing the entire cultic system.⁹⁰ Thus, what seems to be in view in Amos 5:25 is the totality of sacrifice, though this need not imply the final form of the institution established in the land. It is necessary to first discuss v. 26 before drawing a conclusion regarding the expected answer to the question of v. 25.

Amos 5:26 contains a number of problems for interpretation. First, the translation of the initial verb ונשאתם is unclear with relation to time. Some take the verb in the future tense ("You will lift up"), which would be grammatically appropriate if connected with v. 27.⁹¹ This would envision whatever is described in v. 26 (see below) as part of the people's punishment, alongside exile announced in v. 27. Other interpreters, following most ancient versions, render the verb in a past tense, like v. 25. The past meaning here can take two forms: (1) v. 26 could introduce a separate but related question to the one in v. 25 ("Did you offer sacrifices and offerings... And did you lift up...?"); or, (2) v. 26 could serve as a single question with v. 25 ("Did you offer sacrifices and offerings...while you lifted up...?").⁹² Still other scholars propose that the verb constitutes

---

90. Eidevall, *Sacrificial Rhetoric*, 165.

91. Those who favor a future translation include Andersen and Freedman, *Amos*, 529; Carroll R., *Contexts for Amos*, 250; Linville, *Amos and the Cosmic Imagination*, 116, 118; Paul, *Amos*; Richard S. Cripps, *A Critical and Exegetical Commentary on the Book of Amos*, 2nd ed., ICC (London: SPCK, 1955), 198–200; Paul, *Amos*, 188; Lanchester and Driver, *The Books of Joel and Amos*, 192; Jan De Waard and William A. Smalley, *A Translator's Handbook on the Book of Amos* (New York: United Bible Societies, 1979), 123; Charles D. Isbell, "Another Look at Amos 5:26," *JBL* 97, no. 1 (1978): 97–9; Mays, *Amos*, 110; Michael B. Shepherd, *Commentary on Book of the Twelve: The Minor Prophets*, Kregel Exegetical Library (Grand Rapids: Kregel, 2018), 176; Gary V. Smith, *Amos*, Mentor Commentary (Fearn, Scotland: Christian Focus, 2015), 244; Soggin, *The Prophet Amos*, 97.

92. Proponents of a variation of the past tense include Barstad, *The Religious Polemics of Amos*, 58–22; Robert B. Coote, *Amos Among the Prophets: Composition and Theology* (Philadelphia: Fortress Press, 1981), 46–47, 85; Wolff, *Joel and Amos*, 259; Eidevall, *Amos*, 169–72; Garrett, *Amos*, 74–5, 133; Hadjiev, *Composition and Redaction of Amos*, 166–7; Hayes, *Amos*, 170–9; Hubbard, *Joel and Amos*, 194–9; Jeremias, *The Book of Amos*, 98; Lessing, *Amos*, 360; Stuart, *Hosea–Jonah*, 352. The LXX has καὶ ἀνελάβετε in v. 26, a reference to the carrying of idols during the forty-year wandering, though some manuscripts omit the phrase "in the wilderness." See W. Edward Glenny, *Amos: A Commentary Based on Amos in Codex Vaticanus*, Septuagint Commentary Series (Leiden: Brill, 2013), 107–9. For a thorough discussion of the ancient versions of this text and 9:11-15, see Aaron W. Park, *The Book of Amos as Composed and Read in Antiquity*, StBibLit 37 (New York: Peter Lang, 2001), 171–214.

a present idea, or suggest a different reading altogether.[93] The intent of the past and present interpretations could be to contrast the presumably favorable character of the wilderness generation with the unfavorable reality of the current generation.[94] But this interpretation is unlikely, as shown previously.

A second problem in Amos 5:26 is the identification of the objects carried by the people. The MT seemingly refers to two supposed astral deities: אֵת סִכּוּת מַלְכְּכֶם וְאֵת כִּיּוּן צַלְמֵיכֶם, "Sikkuth your king and Kiyyun your images."[95] This may be surprising since this would be the first explicit mention of foreign gods in the book of Amos (cf. 8:14).[96] The idea would

---

93. The present tense translation can be found in Harper, *Critical and Exegetical Commentary on Amos and Hosea*, 136–8; Stanley Gevirtz, "A New Look at an Old Crux: Amos 5:26," *JBL*, no. 87 (1968): 267–76; J. L. Berquist, "Dangerous Waters of Justice and Righteousness," *BTB* 23 (1993): 54–63. Though Sweeney does not include a translation, his comments lend themselves to a present understanding. Sweeney, *The Twelve Prophets*, 241–2. Radine appears to render the verb as an imperative, "Take up *sikkût* your king and *kiyyûn*…" Radine, *Book of Amos in Emergent Judah*, 60.

94. The contrast could still function without an idealized wilderness generation. The point of comparison could be that though the wilderness generation was bad, the current generation is worse. Eidevall, who views v. 26 as a late addition, states, "Through the addition of v. 26, the question in v. 25 takes on a new nuance. A sharp contrast is now being made between the wilderness generation and the addressees. It is implied that the sins of the latter are worse." Eidevall, *Amos*, 172.

95. On these deities, see Samuel A. Meier, "Sakkuth and Kaiwan (Deities)," *ABD* 5:904; M. Stol, "Sakkuth," *DDD* 722–3; M. Stol, "Kaiwan" *DDD* 478; Radine, *Book of Amos in Emergent Judah*, 60–7.

96. There is a debate as to the meaning of כזביהם, "lies," in 2:4, which led Judah astray. The phrase "those after which their fathers walked" may indicate that the "lies" (כזב) that caused the people to err are idols. The LXX adds the clause ἃ ἐποίησαν ("which they made") after τὰ μάταια αὐτῶν ("their vanities"), supporting an ancient iconic interpretation. See Mays, *Amos*, 41; Wolff, *Joel and Amos*, 164; Jeremias, *The Book of Amos*, 44; Joyce Rilett Wood, *Amos in Song and Book Culture*, JSOTSup 337 (London: Sheffield Academic, 2002), 205–6; Glenny, *Amos*, 54–5. Critics of this view note that כזב is nowhere else used with reference to an idol (Ps. 40:5 [Eng. 40:4] may be an exception). An alternative view is that the "lies" refer to false prophecy. So, Andersen and Freedman, *Amos*, 299–305. Brettler uses this interpretation to support his redactional framework. In his view, since false prophecy was not a major feature during the era of classical prophecy, such content would inevitably be a later addition. See Brettler, "Redaction, History, and Redaction-History," 109. Similarly, see Eberhard Bons, "Das Denotat von כזביהם 'ihre Lügen' im Judaspruch, Am 2,4-5," *ZAW* 108 (1996): 201–13. Linville, among others, understands both false prophecy and false gods to be in view here. See Linville, *Amos and the Cosmic Imagination*, 60. Yet even if idols were in view, they are still not specified as in 5:26.

be the notion of carrying the deities in sacred procession. If the wilderness period is in view in v. 26, this text may make the bold assertion that these gods, whether literally or metaphorically, were worshiped instead of YHWH.[97] Duane Garrett, on the other hand, argues that the mention of these deities shows the incompatibility of reverencing YHWH while simultaneously venerating other gods.[98] The implied negative answer to the singular question in vv. 25-26 ("No, we did not sacrifice in the wilderness while worshipping Sikkuth and Kiyyun") would then expose the incompatibility of participating in the cult (5:21-24) while engaging in behavior that is offensive to YHWH.[99] Within the broader argument of 5:21-27, this interpretation seems most compelling.

But while many understand astral deities to be the best reading of the terms in Amos 5:26, ancient textual witnesses provide other options. Instead of סִכּוּת, other evidence support a reading of סֻכָּה, "booth/tent," (LXX, Symmachus, Peshitta, Old Latin, Vulgate, CD 7.14b–15a, Acts 7:43).[100] According to John Hayes, this verse does not condemn Israel for idolatry or apostasy, but depicts a Yahwistic procession led by the king and bearing divine authority, likely during the fall festival.[101] The point

---

97. This is the line of reason in Stephen's speech in Acts 7:42-43, although the text reads "the tent of Moloch and the star of your god Rephan" (τὴν σκηνὴν τοῦ Μόλοχ καὶ τὸ ἄστρον τοῦ θεοῦ [ὑμῶν] Ῥαιφάν). See Ju-Won Kim, "Old Testament Quotations Within the Context of Stephen's Speech in Acts" (PhD diss., Pretoria University, 2007), 141–62; Michael B. Shepherd, *The Twelve Prophets in the New Testament*, StBibLit 140 (New York: Peter Lang, 2011), 38–40. Also, Huub van de Sandt, "The Minor Prophets in Luke–Acts," in *The Minor Prophets in the New Testament*, ed. Maarten J. J. Menken and Steve Moyise, LNTS 377 (New York: T&T Clark, 2009), 65–9; Hubertus W. van de Sandt, "Why Is Amos 5,25-27 Quoted in Acts 7,42f.?" *Zeitschrift für die neutestamentliche Wissenschaft und die Kunde der älteren Kirche* 82 (1991): 67–87; Gert J. Steyn, "Trajectories of Scripture Transmission: The Case of Amos 5:25-27 in Acts 7:42-43," *Hervormde Teologiese Studies* 69, no. 1 (2013): 1–9; Craig S. Keener, *Acts: An Exegetical Commentary*, vol. 2 (Grand Rapids: Baker Academic, 2013), 1408–12.

98. Garrett, *Amos*, 175.

99. Wilgus argues similarly. He paraphrases vv. 25-26 in context, "You would not mix worshipping me with worshipping other gods but you have mixed worshipping me with oppressing the poor." Wilgus, "Judgment on Israel," 161.

100. Scholars who read סֻכָּה include Hayes, *Amos*; Shepherd, *Commentary on Book of the Twelve*; Berquist, "Dangerous Waters of Justice and Righteousness"; Gevirtz, "A New Look at an Old Crux"; Harper, *Critical and Exegetical Commentary on Amos and Hosea*; Isbell, "Another Look at Amos 5."

101. Hayes appeals to later Persian to understand כּוֹכָב as a standard carried during the festival. While himself acknowledging that this may seem farfetched, he maintains that an earlier usage was preserved in later language. Hayes, *Amos*, 176–7.

would then be that Amos claims that the practices of the current generation was unknown in the wilderness period. It is not clear, however, how this would contribute to the broader indictment against the people. LXX, on the other hand, contains the phrase τὴν σκηνὴν τοῦ Μόλοχ ("the tent of Moloch"), which would render סֻכָּה, "booth/tent," but still with reference to a foreign god.[102] The people's lifting of the tent of Moloch would contrast with God's lifting of τὴν σκηνὴν Δαυιδ ("the tent of David") in Amos 9:11.[103] This could also fit if "the tent of your king" is the correct reading (Symmachus).[104]

In conclusion, Amos 5:25-26 present a number of complex textual and interpretive issues.[105] While the precise wording of the text may be lost to modern readers, it seems best in my view to understand these verses as a singular question referencing a hypothetical comparison of Israel's experience in the wilderness with their present behavior.[106] Regardless whether astral deities are intended, the point would be to show that the addressees act in a manner that would have been unthinkable in the past, even though the past itself was characterized by disobedience. While understanding the temporal orientation is not without difficulty, the historical analogy creates both continuity and discontinuity between the past and present. On the one hand, the outgroup status of the addressees is reaffirmed. There is no indication in the text that the wilderness period should be viewed as anything other than a time of rebellion. This memory of the past brings the past and the present into unison.[107] Yet now the degree of offense has reached a fever pitch for the addressees in the present. Their continual mixing of Yahwistic worship with injustice has exhausted the patience of the Deity. We may paraphrase Amos's intent

---

102. The rendering of מֹלֶךְ, "Moloch," is found in the LXX, the Old Greek, and the Vulgate. Aquila and the Peshitta support a reading of "Milcom." The Targums render מַלְכְּבֶם as פתכריכון, "your idols."

103. Glenny, *Amos*, 158.

104. There is more consensus on the name of the second deity, כִּיּוּן, although some versions read כּוֹכָב, "star" (Theodotian, Vulgate, CD). The LXX's Ῥαιφάν, "Raiphan," is surprising. Barstad suggests that this reading results from an early translator's confusion of R for K. Barstad, *The Religious Polemics of Amos*, 120. Also, Park, *Book of Amos as Composed and Read in Antiquity*, 173.

105. Barstad concludes his lengthy discussion by saying, "The only conclusion we may draw from this extremely difficult text is that the verse contains polemics against non-Yahwistic deities, and that these deities were of a planetary character." Barstad, *The Religious Polemics of Amos*, 126.

106. Garrett, *Amos*, 175; Wilgus, "Judgment on Israel," 161–2.

107. For the use of historical analogy as a tool for establishing continuity, see Zerubavel, *Time Maps*, 48–52.

as follows, "Mixing the worship of YHWH with offensive behavior was not acceptable even during your wilderness wandering [while you were under the judgment of God], what would make it acceptable now? In light of this, I will exile you." Together, these verses utilize memories of the past to frame an othering strategy that exposes the outgroup status of the addressees in the present.

9:7

Following the fifth vision in chs. 7–9 (9:1-4) and the third and final hymn fragment of the book (9:5-6), Amos asks a series of rhetorical questions in 9:7. The verse begins with the question, "Are you not like Cushites to me, Children of Israel?" (הלוא כבני כשיים אתם לי).[108] This comparison is unexpected for several reason. First, this is the first and only occurrence of the Cushites in the book of Amos. The singular mention appears to come from nowhere. As such, the only interpretive help comes from the immediate context, which presents its own difficulties, and other occurrences of Cush in the Old Testament as a whole.[109] Second, the question is worded in a way to evoke an affirmative response. The problem is that this would stand in tension with the exclusivist claims of the Israel–YHWH relationship referenced in 3:2, and elsewhere. Was Israel the only people known by YHWH? Or were they just like the other nations? As argued previously, the latter is precisely what Amos has in mind.

The question in 9:7a is followed by the rhetorical question again invoking the memory of the exodus: "Did I not bring up Israel from the land of Egypt?" The tension introduced in 9:7a notwithstanding, the question in 9:7b is more straightforward. Of course, YHWH brought them up from Egypt. This seems to be a central component to the addressees' sense of self. They were an "exodus people." Here again, Amos projects the addressees into the past as the direct participants in the formative exodus event. This event, in their minds, secured their ingroup status. Yet immediately this question is qualified by two more questions (9:7c): Did not YHWH bring the Philistines up from Caphtor and did he not bring the

---

108. This is the only place in the Hebrew Bible where the formula בני-X is used where the gentilic "X" is plural. Sadler takes this to indicate that this may be an unusual meaning matching the unusual form. Rodney Steven Sadler, *Can a Cushite Change His Skin? An Examination of Race, Ethnicity, and Othering in the Hebrew Bible*, LHBOTS 425 (New York: T&T Clark, 2005), 44.

109. The term "Cush" is also used in ancient Egyptian and Assyrian texts to refer to Africans both in a narrow and broad sense. For a summary, see David T. Adamo, *Africa and the Africans in the Old Testament* (1998; repr., Eugene, OR: Wipf & Stock, 2001), 11–15.

Arameans up from Kir? The exoduses of these other people are set right alongside Israel's own deliverance from Egypt. While it is clear that the questions relate to one another, the specific connection between them is debated by interpreters.[110] This connection, however, is largely determinative for the meaning of the initial comparison with Cush. Since our focus is Amos's use of the past, I will largely focus on the social memory of other exoduses akin to Israel's own deliverance from Egypt. I will argue that the past here functions similarly to Amos 3:2 to recategorize the boundaries of ingroup social identity. Just as the past kindness of YHWH was no magic talisman in Amos 3, so too here, YHWH's past action on behalf of the addressees no more defines their status than it does other nations who experienced similar actions.

The history of interpretation of the initial comparison with the Cushites has revealed the ugly prejudice of many interpreters. Some have assumed that the comparison engenders an inherently negative stereotype about the Cushites.[111] The parallel of the Cushites with Israel's enemies (Philistines and Arameans) in the following clauses, according to these interpreters, supports such an understanding. Thus, they claim that the Cushites are primitive, uncivilized, and, perhaps, frequently enslaved. Geographical distance often is added to these claims as a reason for comparison. The Cushites were those far off, thus amplifying the inherently negative defining characteristics of this people. The British Ethiopianist Edward Ullendorff is representative: "The climactic inference of [Amos's] words can only be fully appreciated if the Ethiopians serve, in the present context, as the epitome of a far-distant, uncivilized, and despised black race."[112]

---

110. Martin-Achard, for instance, views these as separate questions. Robert Martin-Achard, *Amos: l'homme, le message, l'influence*, Publications de la Faculté de Théologie de l'Université de Genéve 7 (Geneva: Labor et Fides, 1984), 125–6. Strawn argues at length for reading the verse as composed of a tricolon. Brent A. Strawn, "What Is Cush Doing in Amos 9:7? The Poetics of Exodus in the Plural," *VT* 63, no. 1 (2013): 107. Eidevall states, "It is reasonable to assume that these four assertions should be read together, as part of a (more or less) consistent argumentation." Eidevall, *Amos*, 234.

111. For a summary of the racial interpretations of the passage, see Sadler, *Can a Cushite Change His Skin?*, 40–6. Also, David M. Goldenberg, *The Curse of Ham: Race and Slavery in Early Judaism, Christianity, and Islam* (Princeton, NJ: Princeton University Press, 2003), 22–5; Gene Rice, "Was Amos a Racist?" *The Journal of Religious Thought* 35 (1978): 36.

112. Edward Ullendorff, *Ethiopia and the Bible* (Oxford: Oxford University Press, 1968), 9. Here he is following Harper, *Critical and Exegetical Commentary on Amos and Hosea*, 192.

Likewise, Wellhausen refers to the Cushites as *verachtetes schwarzes Sklavenfolk* ("despised black slavefolk").[113] Some have even linked the reference here to the so-called Curse of Ham in Genesis 9.[114] Carl F. Keil parallels the blackness of the Cushites' skin with the supposed darkness of their spiritual condition.[115] The common assumption with all of these views is that Cushite must embody an intrinsically negative conception for the audience. Not surprisingly, this verse (and many commentators!) was frequently cited in the nineteenth and twentieth centuries to support the deplorable practice of enslaving Africans.[116] The weight of evidence from the Hebrew Bible, however, stands against this.[117] Instances where the Cushites are portrayed negatively unfold much like other nations. Thus, there is nothing *uniquely* offensive about people from Cush in biblical literature. Thus, the reprehensible racialized view says more about an interpreter and their social context than it does about the meaning of Amos 9:7.[118]

Separate from the racialized view, many scholars understand the issue of geographic distance alone to be the basis for comparison. YHWH, in essence, asks, "Are you, Israel, not just like the people who are distant and far away to me?"[119] For the chosen people of YHWH, this comparison

---

113. Julius Wellhausen, *Die kleinen Propheten Übersetzt und erklärt* (Berlin: de Gruyter, 1963), 94.

114. See, for example, Robert F. Horton, *The Minor Prophets*, vol. 1 (Edinburgh: Oxford University Press, 1904), 172.

115. Carl F. Keil, *Biblischer Commentar über die zwölf kleinen Propheten*, BCAT 4 (Leipzig: Dörffling & Franke, 1866), 232.

116. Adamo notes the responsibility African biblical scholars have of "exposing and correcting such academic prejudice and sin." David T. Adamo, "Amos 9:7-8 in an African Perspective," *Orita* 24 (1992): 40. I would go further to suggest that the entire academic community, not simply our African colleagues, bears a responsibility of resisting dehumanizing (mis)interpretation of texts like this.

117. See an exhaustive treatment in Sadler, *Can a Cushite Change His Skin?*, esp. 147–51.

118. Though Brueggemann does not advocate a racist interpretation, he does remain open to racial considerations in the verse: "It is not clear that the contrast means to accent the matter of race, that is, the Ethiopians are blacks. If this dimension is intended, then of course the radicalness of the contrast is even more powerful." Walter Brueggemann, "Exodus in the Plural (Amos 9:7)," in *Texts That Linger, Words That Explode: Listening to Prophetic Voices*, ed. Patrick D. Miller (Minneapolis: Fortress, 2000), 127 n. 20.

119. See Paul, *Amos*, 282–3; Andersen and Freedman, *Amos*, 903; Hayes, *Amos*, 219; Rice, "Was Amos a Racist?" 42; Wolff, *Joel and Amos*, 347; Smith, "Continuity and Discontinuity in Amos' Use of Tradition," 39.

with an especially remote place would jeopardize their special status, much like the Oracles against the Nations (1:3–2:5).[120] The following clauses, which mention the exodus of Philistia and Aram, would further solidify this point. In this case, Amos would here too show that Israel is simply one of many nations under the sovereignty of YHWH.[121] One of the very events that was thought to make the addressees special, it turns out, was a common occurrence for YHWH. He brought out Israel from one place and the Philistines and Arameans from another.

Still other interpreters understand the point of comparison with the other nations in a positive sense. Knut Holter, for example, argues that the parallelism between Cush and Israel in 9:7a and 9:7b expresses YHWH's positive concern for all nations.[122] Thus, the verse illustrates the universalism found in many places throughout the Old Testament.[123] J. Daniel Hays argues that the verse points to the eschatological inclusion of foreign nations into the true people of God.[124] Rodney Sadler, Jr. views the Cushites not in terms of those far off, but as those who had migrated to the Levant. The point of comparison is that YHWH was kind not just towards far-away peoples, but to those in the midst of Israel.[125] Walter Brueggemann argues that the verse resists the ideological exclusivism of the audience, promoting instead a radical pluralism.[126] Brent Strawn, detecting a number of poetic devices as operative in the verse, argues

---

120. It is notable that the Philistines and Arameans coupled here in 9:7 also head the OAN collection (Aram, 1:3-5; Philistia, 1:6-8). Hadjiev views this connection in terms of the book's composition. He argues that 9:7-8a originally followed directly after 2:16, thus continuing the othering of Israel as simply one of the nations. Hadjiev, *Composition and Redaction of Amos*, 113–18.

121. Eidevall states that the text indicates that (1) Israel is like other people to YHWH; and (2) this equality before YHWH includes even geographically distant people like the Cushites. Eidevall, *Amos*, 236.

122. Knut Holter, *Yahweh in Africa: Essays on Africa and the Old Testament*, vol. 1, BTA (New York: Peter Lang, 2000), 120.

123. Adamo argues similarly, "The comparison demonstrates that Israel is as precious as Africans before Yahweh." Adamo, *Africa and the Africans in the Old Testament*, 100. Also, see Knut Holter, "Being Like the Cushites: Some Western and African Interpretations of Amos 9:7," in *New Perspectives on Old Testament Prophecy and History: Essays in Honour of Hans M. Barstad*, ed. Rannfrid I. Thelle, Terje Stordalen, and Mervyn E. J. Richardson, VTSup 168 (Leiden: Brill, 2015), 317.

124. J. Daniel Hays, *From Every People and Nation: A Biblical Theology of Race*, New Studies in Biblical Theology (Downers Grove, IL: InterVarsity, 2003), 116–19.

125. Sadler, *Can a Cushite Change His Skin?*, 44–5.

126. Brueggemann, "Exodus in the Plural (Amos 9:7)."

that the lines work together to emphasize YHWH's benevolent activity on behalf of several people groups.[127] As he states, "Yahweh is an exodus kind of God—not just for Israel, but also for others."[128] While all of these interpretations have various and notable strengths, a positive interpretation of this passage does not make best sense of the context. Perhaps the desire to avoid the racialized sins of past interpreters has caused the pendulum to swing too far the other way. Thus, Cush, and by necessity Philistia and Aram, are not viewed negatively, but positively. This, in my view, seems doubtful.

Leaving Cush aside for a moment, neither Philistia nor Aram are viewed positively in the book of Amos. As noted above, they are both included in the OAN collection. The Arameans are indicted for their threshing of Gilead (1:3) and the Philistines for exiling a whole people to Edom (1:6). Aram appears in the punishment of 5:27 where the addressees will be exiled "beyond Damascus." The Philistines are called, alongside Egypt, to gather on the Mountains of Samaria to witness the oppression of Israel (3:9). Both Aram and Philistia are included in 6:2, where the addressees are invited to reflect upon the downfall of Calneh, Hamath, and Gath. In all of these occurrences, with the "neutral" geographical exception in 5:27, the nations are framed as outgroups and invoked to exemplify the outgroup status of the implied audience. In short, Aram and Philistia are bad, but the addressees are worse. It is against this background that one must consider the function of these nations in 9:7. Moreover, the context of 9:1-10 is one of judgment. In 9:1-4, YHWH expresses his purpose to seek and destroy the sinful people when he "sets [his] eye on them for evil and not for good" (9:4). The following verses after the series of questions (9:8) continue the notion of YHWH directing his "eyes" for destruction upon "the sinful kingdom." Thus, it seems most appropriate to read 9:7 within this frame in view. Rather than celebrating YHWH's kindness to all these nations, Amos employs the past as an othering strategy to reiterate the addressees' outgroup identification.

In light of the above, the comparison with Cush may simply contribute to the othering strategy alongside Amos's use of the past. The mention of the three nations together represent a series of outgroups that relativize the social identification of the addressees. As has been stated, there is no basis

---

127. Strawn, "What Is Cush Doing in Amos 9." He situates this interpretation in the mid- to late eighth century BCE, specifically during the Twenty-fifth dynasty in Egypt, where a Cushite king rose to power.

128. Ibid., 122–3.

to assume racial animus as a factor motivating the reference to Cush. The remoteness hypothesis—that Cush is invoked due to their geographical distance from Israel—seems like the most plausible explanation, but this view is not essential to the interpretation. What matters the most is that the past is used here to expose the outgroup membership of the people. What is surprising is that the questions regarding other exoduses anticipate an affirmative answer from the implied audience.[129] The addressees are expected to know that YHWH brought these other people up from these lands.[130] This memory should have produced an honest assessment regarding group norms and boundaries. A singular past event does not afford security when group members depart from the ingroup values. Though social injustice is not explicit in the chapter, readers may assume that the remainder of the book provides the impetus for judgment. The link to the exodus theme in 3:2, suggests that YHWH again is prototypical. He showed kindness to those in need, even those who were considered outsiders, but the addressees have done the opposite. Amos once again utilizes the past as an othering strategy. Thus, those desiring a positive distinctiveness in the world of the text must look not to the past, but to the future for a satisfactory sense of self.

---

129. Brueggemann suggests that the mention of other exoduses requires some form of reconstructed "hidden history," which closely parallels Israel's deliverance from Egypt. He imagines that these other nations were oppressed like Israel, they cried out in pain, and were heard by YHWH who brought them up from their suffering. Though he acknowledges the speculative nature of this reconstruction, he extrapolates a pluralism that resists the notion of "God's elect people." Brueggemann, "Exodus in the Plural (Amos 9:7)," 96–7. Against this, see Robin Routledge, "Creation and Covenant: God's Direct Relationship with the Non-Israelite Nations in the Old Testament," in *Interreligious Relations: Biblical Perspectives; Proceedings from the Second Norwegian Summer Academy of Biblical Studies (NSABS), Ansgar University College, Kristiansand, Norway, August 2015*, ed. Hallvard Hagelia and Markus Zehnder (London: T&T Clark, 2017), 61.

130. These events would seem to fit Assmann's category of communicative memory. Assmann states that communicative memory has a "clear meaning" while cultural memory is in need of interpretation. Assmann, *Cultural Memory and Early Civilization*, 49. The assumption in Amos 9:7 is that the implied audience grasps the significance of the comparison with these other nations. This shared knowledge would seem to present a degree of chronological proximity between the editor(s) of the book and their target audience. Even when the precise interpersonal memory faded, the verse still functioned in the process of socialization. See Assmann, *Religion and Cultural Memory*, 4.

Conclusion

This chapter explored Amos's use of the past in service of identity formation. As seen, history is not presented as an objective series of linear events. Rather, Amos shapes the past in order to influence the audience's sense of self—their social identity. This was analyzed with the help of social memory as an additional heuristic tool. The memories of the past in Amos merge the past with the "present" as an othering strategy. The addressees are projected back in time as participants in events such as the exodus, as well as the prolonged history of rebellion and injustice. Each memory, albeit in different ways, exposes the outgroup status of the addressees. Though tension exists between their election and outgroup status, the addressees are indicted for twisting YHWH's kindness into a pledge of security. Though the implied audience presumably believed their history guaranteed a hopeful future, YHWH turns the table on their confidence. Their history itself is presented as continual disobedience and obstinance. Rather than guaranteeing security, YHWH's past kindness serves as a foil, exposing the outgroup behavior of the addressees. YHWH's ingroup prototypicality contrasts sharply with the values of the people. For unresisting readers and hearers entering the world of the text, the desire for positive distinctiveness will result in a rejection of the norms and values criticized in the book. They must negotiate their social group membership in light of the temporal orientation set by Amos. If the past was not sufficient to secure hope for the ingroup, the audience must then look to the future.

Chapter 5

ESCHATOLOGY AND SOCIAL IDENTITY IN AMOS

As was seen in the previous chapter, the book of Amos uses time as a discursive strategy of identity-formation. Our investigation revealed that Amos shapes the past for the sake of the "present." This chapter explores the future of Israel in Amos and its effect on the social identity of the audience.[1] In line with the goal of the present work, the analysis will not be concerned with the supposed "original proclamation" of Amos, but will focus rather on the received literary form of the book. From this perspective, there is certainly a future for the people (9:11-15). But how this future relates to Amos's words of complete destruction is another question. I will demonstrate how the tools of the Social Identity Approach aid the interpretation of Amos's conception of the future in relation to the construction of social identity. In short, this chapter addresses eschatology and identity-formation in Amos.[2]

---

1. The future envisaged in the book is, as Paul Noble states, one of the most controversial issues in Amos studies. Paul R. Noble, "Amos' Absolute 'No,'" *VT* 41 (1997): 329. Also, Hasel, *Understanding the Book of Amos*, 105.

2. Not all agree that "eschatology" is an appropriate term for the study of Amos. As Hasel notes, whether the future hope in Amos is deemed eschatological depends largely on one's definition of eschatology. I follow Hasel's broad definition of eschatology "in the sense of an end of the present world order which can either be within the flow of history or, in an absolute and final sense, at the end of all history." Gerhard F. Hasel, "The Alleged 'No' of Amos and Amos' Eschatology," *AUSS* 29 (1991): 3. Sang Hoon Park includes an extended discussion on terminology for the future in Amos, as well as various definitions of eschatology. Sang Hoon Park, "Eschatology in the Book of Amos: A Text-Linguistic Analysis" (PhD diss., Trinity Evangelical Divinity School, 1996), 77–103. Also, see Bill T. Arnold, "Old Testament Eschatology and the Rise of Apocalypticism," in *The Oxford Handbook of Eschatology*, ed. Jerry L. Walls (Oxford: Oxford University Press, 2008), 23–39.

This discussion of the future in Amos focuses on three specific topics: the Day of YHWH, the remnant motif, and the restoration in 9:11-15. Though these overlap at many points, separate analysis allows one to uncover their individual contributions to the future of Israel in the book. In particular, these features allow a reader to gain an understanding of the social identifiers of both those under judgment (i.e. the outgroup) as well as those who are delivered (i.e. the ingroup). Based upon the analysis of these three features, I briefly consider the process of identity-formation from a Social Identity Approach.

The Day of YHWH Motif

The Day of YHWH is a common motif in the Prophetic literature.[3] Though it appears frequently in various texts, the origin of the concept continues to be debated.[4] Nevertheless, the motif is an important piece of how the Prophets conceive of the future of Israel and the world. In Amos, the majority of instances describe a future disaster. Various expressions are used to this end throughout the book, including "day of battle" and "day of the whirlwind" (1:14), "that day" (2:16; 8:3, 9, 13), "the day" (3:14), "days are coming" (4:2; 8:11), "day of YHWH" (5:18-20), and "day of disaster" (6:3).[5] With regards to judgment, this Day entails the

---

3. House provides a broad survey of "The Day of the Lord" passages in the Hebrew Bible and New Testament. Paul R. House, "The Day of the Lord," in *Central Themes in Biblical Theology: Mapping Unity in Diversity*, ed. Scott J. Hafemann and Paul R. House (Grand Rapids: Baker Academic, 2007), 179–224. See also Barstad, *The Religious Polemics of Amos*, 89–108; Michael Ufok Udoekpo, *Re-Thinking the Day of YHWH and Restoration of Fortunes in the Prophet Zephaniah: An Exegetical and Theological Study of 1:14-18; 3:14-20* (Bern: Peter Lang, 2010), 43–79; Joel D. Barker, "Day of the Lord," *DOTP* 132–43.

4. The two primary claims for the origin of the motif are (1) the so-called Holy War tradition; and (2) the cult. See, for instance, Gerhard von Rad, "The Origin of the Concept of the Day of Yahweh," *Journal of Semitic Studies* 4 (1959): 97–108; F. C. Fensham, "A Possible Origin of the Concept of the Day of the Lord," *Neotestamentica* 1966, no. 1 (1966): 90–7; Meir Weiss, "The Origin of the 'Day of the Lord' Reconsidered," *HUCA* 37 (1966): 29–60; John Barton, "The Day of Yahweh in the Minor Prophets," in *Biblical and Near Eastern Essays: Studies in Honour of Kevin J. Cathcart*, ed. Carmel McCarthy and John F. Healey (London: T&T Clark, 2004), 68–94; Daniel E. Fleming, "The Day of Yahweh in the Book of Amos: A Rhetorical Response to Ritual Expectation," *RB* 117, no. 1 (2010): 20–38.

5. Barstad rightly notes that investigation of the concept should not be restricted exclusively to the phrase *expressis verbis*. Barstad, *The Religious Polemics of Amos*, 94.

destruction of the outgroup. This section briefly summarizes the distribution of the motif, exploring the individual contributions to the portrayal of the future. Of particular interest here is the object(s), nature, and justification of judgment on the Day of YHWH. This inevitable judgment cuts across traditional boundaries, resulting in the downfall of Israel's social and religious life. The characterization of the guilty further illustrates the outgroup status of the people. In other words, the Day of YHWH is a motif for universal judgment against the outgroup, though it manifests itself in various ways.

The first mention of the Day of YHWH, referred to as the "day of battle" and the "day of the whirlwind," occurs in the oracle against the Ammonites in 1:14.[6] Though all the nations in the OAN collection are condemned, the Ammonites' violence against pregnant women for the purpose of territory expansion especially warrants the destroying fire of YHWH.[7] The vocabulary suggests a theophanic event. This is not mitigated by the mention of the Ammonite king's exile in Amos 1:15, which places the judgment within human history.[8] The theophanic element increases the severity of the judgment. Thus, the Day of YHWH in view here involves a foreign nation under the judgment of YHWH, resulting in the exile of its leadership. Similar threats are made against outgroup Israel throughout Amos (cf. 4:2-3; 6:7; 7:11, 17). The specification of exile for the Ammonites indicates that the nation is not brought to utter end. YHWH's judgment is complete, but not exhaustive. This first instance may alert the audience that the Day of YHWH does not simply affect Israel, but may have a global dimension. As shown in Chapter 3, Israel is framed as one among the nations in the OAN collection. Though they are assimilated among the nations, as Paul Noble states, they are also differentiated.[9] Nevertheless, the rhetorical structure of the first two chapters of

---

6. The phrase "day of battle" (יום מלחמה) occurs four times in the Hebrew Bible (1 Sam. 13:22; Hos. 10:14; Amos 1:14; Prov. 21:31). The reference in Hosea illustrates that the "day of battle" need not refer exclusively to future events. The phrase "day of a whirlwind," though occurring only here in the Hebrew Bible, has parallels in Isa. 29:6 and 66:15, which both use the noun סופה in conjunction with fire.

7. While this Day is not specified in the other oracles against the nations, the formulaic pattern lends weight to the judgments (1:4-5, 7-8, 10, 12, 14-15; 2:2-3, 5) all occurring in coordination.

8. Linville, *Amos and the Cosmic Imagination*, 57–8. Linville mistakenly cites Jer. 29:6 as a theophanic text, where he intends Isa. 29:6.

9. Noble, "Israel Among the Nations," 69–70. One example of the differentiation is the definitive declaration of judgment by fire. The conditional exhortation to seek YHWH contains a warning that a failure to do so would result in him breaking out

the book, as well as the inclusion of non-Israelite nations at various points (e.g., 3:9; 9:7), may signal the future effect of the Day on both groups of peoples.

The mention of "that day" in 2:16 occurs within the larger unit of vv. 13-16.[10] In response to the spurning of his kindness, YHWH pronounces judgment upon the addressees, identified by the second-person suffix כֶם ("you"). What follows is a series of effects of the judgment involving the swift, the strong, the bowman, the horseman, and the stout-hearted. In each case, their respective skills and abilities prove useless to escape the coming judgment that will occur on "that day." Though these heroes are singled out, the judgment will certainly affect the entire nation. The justification for the judgment is described in 2:6-12, which details their oppression and failure to follow the pattern of mercy embodied by YHWH. Thus, the Day of YHWH here is shown to be both inevitable and terrible for the nation. Like the mighty Amorites who were destroyed by YHWH (2:9), Israel's mighty one's would be brought down.

Another reference to the Day of YHWH is described as the "day I [YHWH] visit the transgressions of Israel upon him" in Amos 3:14. The punishment in vv. 14-15 results in the downfall of the cultic life of the people as well as their economic grandeur. M. Daniel Carroll R. notes that the judgment upon the altars of Bethel and the destruction of the luxurious houses of those in power reveal the intermingling role of sacred and royal interests in Amos.[11] Since Bethel was a national sanctuary frequented by the people, the Day of YHWH described in these verses must affect all of Israel. Here again we see the far-reaching destruction to come on the Day of YHWH. The mention of Bethel furthers the outgroup characterization present throughout the book (4:4; 5:4; 7:13). The basis of YHWH's judgment is the people's great transgressions (v. 14a). Though the judgment is inevitable, the exact nature is not specified. While YHWH

---

like fire in the house of Joseph (5:6). This judgment, however, is not certain, as the people have occasion to repent. The second vision (7:4-6) also involves a devouring fire conjured by YHWH, but this judgment is averted by Amos's intercession. Though the end does come upon the people, its specific manifestation is different than that in the OAN collection.

10. Göran Eidevall seems correct in suggesting that this section serves a similar function to the formal pronouncement of judgment by fire in the OAN collection. Eidevall, *Amos*, 118.

11. Carroll R., *Contexts for Amos*, 199–200. Paul says that the wealthy residents of Samaria followed the example of the monarchy in constructing pleasure estates according to the local climate. Shalom M. Paul, "Amos III 15—Winter and Summer Mansions," *VT* 28, no. 3 (1978): 358–60.

may employ an earthquake to bring about this destruction, a foreign military is perhaps more plausible when read alongside the coming military destruction in v. 11.

The Day of YHWH is mentioned in 4:2 in the phrase "the days are coming upon you." The "you" of this oracle is specified as the cows of Bashan who oppress and crush the poor and needy (4:1).[12] Judgment is the result of the exorbitant lifestyle of the elite in Samaria at the expense of the poor and needy, a judgment that will take place in the coming days. The exact nature of the punishment is unclear due to the lexical difficulty of the passage.[13] The imagery could refer to the exile of the elites, taking the noun צן as "ropes," "(fish)hooks," or "baskets," or to the exposure of their corpses on pikes or meat hooks. While exile was part of the judgment for the Ammonites on the Day of YHWH (1:14-15), this expression could function similarly to 3:12 where a piece of meat is evidence that YHWH has mauled the people. Though the elites are targeted, a military invasion would not differentiate social class. Thus, in some sense, the judgment upon the elites involves all of the people. We see here again that the Day of YHWH is a time of severe destruction upon Israel, especially the elites, that is yet to come.

The next Day of YHWH text is 5:18-20, where the phrase occurs three times. This passage has been the focus of intense study related to the nature of the Day itself.[14] The lamentation sounded in 5:1 becomes a woe oracle in 5:18. The pronouncement is directed at those who desire the Day of YHWH, addressed in the second person. The assumption is that the implied audience believed, presumably because of their religious observance, that they would experience the Day as a time of ultimate blessing

---

12. On the cows of Bashan, see Chapter 3.
13. For a survey of options, see Paul, *Amos*, 130–5; Garrett, *Amos*, 111–13.
14. See Cornelius Van Leeuwen, "The Prophecy of the *Yom Yahweh* in Amos V 18–20," in *Language and Meaning, Studies in Hebrew Language and Biblical Exegesis*, ed. A. S. van der Woude, OtSt 19 (Leiden: Brill, 1974), 113–34. Interpreters such as Everson and Hoffman, and many who have followed, begin their analysis of the Day of the Lord with 5:18-20 since it comprises, in their view, the earliest appearance of the concept. A. Joseph Everson, "The Days of Yahweh," *JBL* 93, no. 3 (1974): 329–37; Yair Hoffmann, "The Day of the Lord as a Concept and a Term in the Prophetic Literature," *ZAW* 93, no. 1 (1981): 37–50. Von Rad criticized this view, claiming that this passage is "not sufficiently unequivocal to be used as a suitable starting point for the examination." Von Rad, "The Origin of the Concept of the Day of Yahweh," 105. Cathcart rejects von Rad's claim, stating that just because Amos 5:18 is difficult, it cannot be conveniently ignored. K. J. Cathcart, "Day of Yahweh," *ABD* 2:84–5.

and vindication. Indeed, v. 14 indicates that they believed YHWH to already be on their side. But the opposite is in fact the case: YHWH is against them and the great Day will bring ruin and judgment. It will be darkness and not light. YHWH, who according to the hymn fragment in 5:8 turns deep darkness into morning and darkens the day into night, will bring utter darkness upon the addressees in the future. Though the specific calamity of the Day is not detailed in 5:18-20, the reality of disaster is illustrated in a series of similes. The Day of YHWH will be like a man who escapes a lion only to then meet a bear; or a man who returns to the comfort of his own home only to be bitten by a serpent (v. 19). The point is that the Day of YHWH will not be safe for the addressees. The mention of the lion, bear, and serpent supports the view that death is the outcome of this encounter (cf. 3:12; 9:3). The woe oracle is followed directly by a criticism of the cult (vv. 21-23), as well as a call for an outpouring of justice (v. 24). As elsewhere in Amos, religion and justice form two poles between which a straight line should run. The addressees appear to have inverted the desired order of things. Rather than justice being upheld by the religious life of the people, their religion legitimated injustice. Thus, the Day of YHWH would bring devastation upon the outgroup.

The Day of YHWH reference in 6:1-3 follows a similar outgroup characterization of 5:18-23. The addressees are those who are at ease in Zion and those who feel secure in Samaria (6:1).[15] Like those in 5:18 who desire the Day of YHWH, these elites "put far the day of disaster" (6:3). This collocation attributes an inherently destructive element to the Day. This will not be a day of deliverance, but a day of disaster. The justification for this destruction is given in vv. 1-7, which likely describe a *marzēaḥ* banquet.[16]

---

15. The supposed intrusion of Zion into a book primarily oriented towards the northern kingdom has led many to emend 6:1a or label it as a later redactional insertion. So, Polley, *Amos and the Davidic Empire*, 94–5. Hadjiev supports the reference as an addition but on different grounds. Hadjiev, *Composition and Redaction of Amos*, 174–5. But see, Radine, *Book of Amos in Emergent Judah*, 31–6; Paul, *Amos*, 199–200; Andersen and Freedman, *Amos*, 559; Hayes, *Amos*, 182–3.

16. The literature on the *marzēaḥ* is voluminous. See John L. McLaughlin, *The Marzēaḥ in the Prophetic Literature: References and Allusions in Light of the Extra-Biblical Evidence* (Leiden: Brill, 2001); Mark S. Smith, *The Ugaritic Baal Cycle: Introduction with Text, Translation, and Commentary of Ktu 1.1.–1.2.*, vol. 1 (Leiden: Brill, 1994), 140–4; Barstad, *The Religious Polemics of Amos*, 128–42. See also Sharon Moughtin-Mumby, "'A Man and His Father Go to Naarah in Order to Defile My Holy Name!': Rereading Amos 2:6-8," in Hagedorn and Mein, eds., *Aspects of Amos*, 77–82; Greer, "A Marzea and a Mizraq," 243–61.

In v. 3, the addressees not only "put far the day of disaster," but also "bring near the reign of violence."[17] Violence is not unknown to the elites, as illustrated in 3:10, where the oppressors in Samaria are said to store up "violence and robbery."[18] Here again we see the characterization of the outgroup in terms of injustice. The oppression in Amos 6, in addition to their pride, results in a military invasion and exile (vv. 7-8). The following verse states that if ten people remain in one house, they will die. Like other Day of YHWH references (cf. 5:19), this instance shows the inevitability and horror of the coming judgment. The events on that day are comprehensive. Although the elites are singled out as responsible for YHWH's judgment, the rest of the nation is not unaffected. The day of disaster will be an equal opportunity catastrophe. Joseph has been fractured within (v. 6), but YHWH will bring an outside force to execute his punishment.

The Day of YHWH is mentioned several times in Amos's fourth vision (8:1-14), contributing to coming judgment of the outgroup. After seeing and identifying a basket of summer fruit (קָיִץ), YHWH announces that "the end (קֵץ) has come upon his people; I will never again pass by them" (v. 2). This judgment takes places "on that day," when the songs of the temple become wailing (v. 3). The result in Amos 8 is a litter of corpses thrown everywhere. The injustice of the elites is again specified as the justification for the judgment (vv. 4-6). The same phrase "on that day" also occurs in vv. 9 and 13. In the former, YHWH eclipses the sun at noon, turning the day into darkness.[19] The cosmological phenomena match the sobriety of the occasion, as mourning and lament overtake the people

---

17. The phrase שבת חמס is enigmatic, giving rise to a number of interpretations. See Wolff, *Joel and Amos*, 272 n. h. Nevertheless, as Wittenberg argues, the phrase most likely refers to violence seated upon the throne, i.e., a rule/reign of violence. G. H. Wittenberg, "Amos 6:1-7: 'They Dismiss the Day of Disaster but You Bring Near the Rule of Violence,'" *Journal of Theology for Southern Africa* 58 (1987): 62. Also, J. J. M. Roberts, "Amos 6:1-7," in *Understanding the Word: Essays in Honor of Bernhard W. Anderson*, ed. James T. Butler, Edgar W. Conrad, and Ben C. Ollenburger, JSOTSup 37 (Sheffield: JSOT, 1987), 159–60.

18. Houston rightly interprets this as a hendiadys "implying violent, ruthless oppression and exploitation." Houston, *Contending for Justice*, 68. His survey of violence in Amos, however, omits treatment of 6:3. Carroll R. maintains that the unit attacks not simply political and economic matters, but a sense of nationalistic pride with a deeply theological ideology. Carroll R., *Contexts for Amos*, 257–9.

19. The first two hymn fragments both express similar ideas, as the Deity converts light to darkness (4:13–5:8). Susan Gillingham draws attention to the paradoxical nature of YHWH's portrayal as both creator and destroyer in Amos. Susan Gillingham, "'Who Makes the Morning Darkness': God and Creation in the Book of Amos," *SJT* 45, no. 2 (1992): 166. The first two hymns (4:13; 5:8-9) present YHWH

(v. 10). Further, the "on that day" formula in 8:13 describes the fainting of beautiful maidens and young men because of thirst. The preceding unit (vv. 11-12), which begin with the phrase "the days are coming," describe the deprivation of YHWH's words from the land. People wander from sea to sea seeking instruction, but do not find satisfaction. The irony in light of the outgroup's behavior elsewhere is stark. The people have sought to silence the prophets (2:12; 5:13; 7:12-13), who were conduits of YHWH's message (3:7), so here they reap what they have sown. This is not a temporary condition. Those who experience this divine famine are those who swear by the "Guilt of Samaria" in v. 14.[20] Their religious devotion will result in their fall, never again to rise (v. 14; also cf. 5:2). The definitive nature of their collapse is not specified in military terms in this unit, but the cosmic effects upon the earth (8:8-9) may support such interpretation.[21] The collective sense of the Day of YHWH in ch. 8 is that disaster will be complete. Both injustice and religious defection are to blame. Due to either physical death or spiritual starvation, the people would be no more. YHWH will never forget their deeds (8:7).

The above survey of the Day of YHWH motif with reference to judgment reveals particular facets about the anticipated future of the outgroup in Amos. While more will be said below about how this relates to identity-formation, there are two noteworthy aspects here. First, while the primary focus is on Israel, 1:14 suggests that the Day may affect other nations.[22] Ironically, the addressees, perhaps, expected the Day to mean

---

as bringing harmony and order as well as chaos, while the third (9:5-6) focuses more on his destructive power. The one who commands the day and night will bring deep darkness upon the people.

20. Some understand "the Guilt of Samaria," "Dan," and "the Way of Beersheba" to refer to non-Yahwistic deities. See Barstad, *The Religious Polemics of Amos*, 143–201. Against this, Carroll R., "'For So You Love to Do'," 179–81.

21. While this is not always the case, warfare and cosmology are often correlated in the ancient Near Eastern literature. See Crouch, *War and Ethics in the Ancient Near East*, 12–32. She denies, however, that cosmology plays any role in Amos's message (98). The rising and sinking of the Nile mentioned in 8:8 parallels the same phrasing, with minor adjustment, in the final hymn fragment (9:5). This puts more direct agency on YHWH in acting upon the earth.

22. As stated above, while the Day is mentioned only in relation to the Ammonites, the organization and structure of the OAN collection suggests that the fiery destruction announced against the other nations occurs in conjunction with the judgment of the Ammonites. The oracle against Ammon includes other unique features in the collection, such as the reference to kindling a fire (הצתי אש) instead of the typical sending of fire (שלחתי אש), and the explicit reference to the exile of the king's officials (1:15).

the downfall of their enemies (5:18), but the distribution of the motif shows that they themselves are in the crosshairs of divine judgment. The Day is overwhelmingly dark for Israel. But the coming judgment of exile and death is one common to all groups who are enemies of YHWH. As seen in Chapter 3, the book of Amos puts outgroup Israel on par with the surrounding peoples. Thus, readers may then expect the future of Israel to be in some way intertwined with the future of the nations.

Second, the justifications for Israel's judgment on the Day of YHWH include both the religious and social spheres. Though the elites are often identified as the culprits, the Day of YHWH, in some sense, implicates the nation as a whole. This is evident in the destruction of the national cult (3:14; 8:3), which legitimated the state government (7:13).[23] Thus, the complex web of social dynamics that characterize the outgroup cuts across socio-religious lines. The import of this for the formation of the audience's social identity will be discussed below.

The Remnant Motif

Alongside the pervasive destruction depicted by the Day of YHWH motif, the notion of a remnant appears in a number of texts.[24] This motif contributes to the conception of the future in that it may function positively or negatively. Is the motif used to instill hope for the future after destruction? Or, does it contribute to the severity of the inevitable judgment?[25] As will be shown, though several instances function negatively, the motif provides positive motivation for the audience to pursue membership in the ingroup.

The noun שארית, "remnant," occurs three times in Amos, twice referring to non-Israelite nations (Philistines, 1:8; Edomites, 9:12) and once regarding Israel (5:15). Other common remnant vocabulary is used for the motif in the book, such as שאר, "to remain" (5:3), יתר, "to be left"

---

23. Carroll R., *Contexts for Amos*, 200. Houston expresses reservations about the widespread participation of the people in the state cult, which legitimated injustice. He limits the guilt to the Samaria-based ruling class. Houston, *Amos*, 34–5. However, the diversity of expressions for Amos's indictment appears to expand the culpability more broadly.

24. For a thorough treatment of the remnant motif, see G. F. Hasel, *The Remnant: The History and Theology of the Remnant Idea from Genesis to Isaiah*, 2nd ed., AUM 5 (Berrien Springs, MI: Andrews University Press, 1974).

25. For a study that assesses the positive and negative function of the remnant in Isaiah, see Andrew M. King, "A Remnant Will Return: An Analysis of the Literary Function of the Remnant Motif in Isaiah," *JESOT* 4, no. 2 (2015): 145–69.

(6:9), נצל, "to deliver" (3:12), מלט, "to escape" (2:14-15; 9:1), and פליט, "survivor" (9:1). Most scholars recognize the negative function of some of these instances. In Amos 3:12, for instance, YHWH follows the declaration in v. 11 that an "adversary" would plunder Israel with an analogy of a shepherd who "delivers" (נצל) from the lion's mouth a few scraps of a sheep. In like manner, those who dwell in Samaria would be "delivered" (נצל) after the coming invasion. Clearly, the analogy does not engender hope. As Reed Lessing states, "This is one of the most commonly recognized examples of irony in Amos. Death is death, no matter what leftover body parts remain."[26] Though a remnant remains, the function of the motif here is clearly to amplify the judgment. Other widely accepted examples of the negative usage of the motif include the reduction of the population in 5:3 and the extermination of remaining people after judgment in 6:9 and 9:1-4.[27] More disputed is the function of the "remnant of Joseph" in 5:15 and the sieve metaphor in 9:8-10.

The mention of the "remnant of Joseph" (5:15) occurs within a generally recognized chiastic structure spanning 5:1-17.[28] To comprehend the meaning of the remnant here, one must turn attention first to the literary structure of the unit, in particular the exhortations in vv. 14-15 in which it occurs. The chiasm unfolds as follows:[29]

---

26. Lessing, *Amos*, 237. So too, Alison Lo, "Remnant Motif in Amos, Micah, and Zephaniah," in *A God of Faithfulness: Essays in Honour of J. Gordon McConville on His 60th Birthday*, ed. Jamie A. Grant, Alison Lo, and Gordon J. Wenham (New York: T&T Clark, 2011), 132–3; Garrett, *Amos*, 97; Hayes, *Amos*, 135; Wolff, *Joel and Amos*, 198; Mays, *Amos*, 67. Andersen and Freedman retain a place for hope in this passage. Andersen and Freedman, *Amos*, 410.

27. Barstad, perhaps, goes too far by claiming that the reduction is "simply a means of describing the total annihilation of the Israelite people." Barstad, *The Religious Polemics of Amos*, 77. See Paul R. Noble, "The Remnant in Amos 3–6: A Prophetic Paradox," *HBT* 19, no. 2 (1997): 143 n. 22.

28. Jan de Waard, "Chiastic Structure of Amos 5:1-17," *VT* 27, no. 2 (1977): 170–7; N. J. Tromp, "Amos 5:1-17: Towards a Stylistic and Rhetorical Analysis," in *Prophets, Worship and Theodicy*, OTS 23 (Leiden: Brill, 1984), 56–84; Houston, *Amos*, 21–2. Wilgus slightly modifies the central section of the chiasm. Wilgus, "Judgment on Israel," 147–54. For a defense of the section as a single discourse unit more broadly, see David A. Dorsey, "Literary Architecture and Aural Structuring Techniques in Amos," *Bib* 73 (1992): 312–14; Jeremias, *The Book of Amos*, 84–5; Möller, *A Prophet in Debate*, 68–9; Paul, *Amos*, 158–9.

29. This structure follows Eidevall, *Amos*, 152; Jeremias, *The Book of Amos*, 84–5; Wilgus, "Judgment on Israel," 148; Linville, *Amos and the Cosmic Imagination*, 105–6; Möller, *A Prophet in Debate*, 68.

A. Lamentation (5:1-3)
   B. Exhortation to seek YHWH (5:4-6)
      C. Description of unjust Israel (5:7)
         D. Doxology (5:8-9)
      C'. Description of unjust Israel (5:10-13)
   B'. Exhortation to seek YHWH (5:14-15)
A'. Lamentation (5:16-17)

The opening verses of the unit introduces a funeral lamentation (קִינָה) taken up over the nation (vv. 1-3).[30] Verse 2 describes Israel's fallen state as a present reality.[31] They are fallen without hope of resuscitation. Though their death was already asserted, there would be a whittling judgment ahead (v. 3).[32] The corresponding section of the chiasm repeats the theme of mourning. The lament in the opening verses will be amplified in the future when YHWH passes through their midst (vv. 16-17).

The next pair of verses in the chiasm (5:4-6, 14-15) exhort the addressees to "seek YHWH" (vv. 5, 6), and to "seek good" (v. 14), in order that they may live.[33] The former unit divides into two exhortations (vv. 4b-5 and v. 6). The first call to seek YHWH is contrasted with the charge not to seek Bethel, enter Gilgal, or cross over to Beersheba. The juxtaposition of the exhortation with the prohibitions of these cult places

---

30. The noun קִינָה occurs 18 times in the Hebrew Bible, most notably in Jeremiah and Ezekiel (e.g., 2 Sam. 1:17; Jer. 7:29; 9:10; Ezek. 19:1; 26:17; 27:2; 28:12; 32:2; 2 Chron. 35:25). The only other instance of the noun in Amos is in 8:10, where YHWH converts the songs of the people into lament on the Day of YHWH.

31. Note the use of perfect verbs in 5:2. Israel is said to be forsaken in her land (5:2c), indicating that exile has not yet occurred.

32. The lamentation in prophetic literature can be used to express the certainty of future judgment (cf. Isa. 14; Ezek. 27–28). This would supplement the definitive pronouncement expressed through the Day of YHWH motif. Greg Schmidt Goering, "Proleptic Fulfillment of the Prophetic Word: Ezekiel's Dirges Over Tyre and Its Ruler," *JSOT* 36, no. 4 (2012): 483–505; Gale A. Yee, "The Anatomy of Biblical Parody: The Dirge Form in 2 Samuel 1 and Isaiah 14," *CBQ* 50, no. 4 (1988): 565–86. Also see Paul, *Amos*, 160. Andersen and Freedman understand the fallen state in Amos to be a hyperbolic statement of the coming military defeat described in v. 3. Andersen and Freedman, *Amos*, 474.

33. On proposals for the meaning of "seek YWHW," see Johan Lust, "Remarks on the Redaction of Amos V 4–6, 14–15," in *Remembering All the Way: A Collection of Old Testament Studies Published on the Occasion of the Fortieth Anniversary of the Oudtestamentisch Werkgezelschap in Nederland*, ed. A. S. van der Woude, OtSt 21 (Leiden: Brill, 1981), 137–40.

seems to indicate that the issue is worship. The people are instructed not to seek YHWH at these cult sites, but seemingly to approach him another way. The reason for the exhortation is that the cult places will be destroyed (v. 5d-e). The second exhortation to "seek YHWH and live" (v. 6) describes the results of failing to do so: "lest he rush upon the House of Joseph like fire." This clause appears to indicate that the judgment is conditional. If the people seek YHWH, then he will not rush upon them like fire. Though the altars of the popular cult places are doomed, there may yet be hope for those who seek YHWH.

The parallel section of the chiasm, B', exhorts the people to "seek good and not evil" (v. 14) and to "hate evil, and love good, and establish justice in the gate" (v. 15). This expands the notion of worship to the realm of ethics. The people are not simply restricted in where they worship, but how they are supposed to behave. Seeking YHWH necessarily entails loving good and maintaining justice as a way of life. Though the exhortations in B appended judgment clauses to show YHWH's way as the rational choice, B' employs positive motivators. A favorable response to the exhortations in vv. 14-15 results in YHWH's presence with the people (v. 14) and his gracious dealings with the remnant of Joseph (v. 15).

The call to seek YHWH and pursue justice stands opposite the moral corruption of the people described in C and C'. They poison justice and cast down righteousness (v. 7),[34] oppressing the poor and silencing those who would advocate for justice (vv. 10-11b). This characterization of the people contrasts sharply with that of YHWH in the doxology at the center of the chiasm (5:8).[35] Whereas they are those who turn (הַהֹפְכִים) justice into poison, YHWH turns (הֹפֵךְ) the night into day. YHWH exhibits his creative power in the manipulation of the natural elements, sustaining order in the world. The people, on the other hand, manipulate and exploit

---

34. Though many English translations insert a second-person address in 5:7, the Hebrew lacks a second-person verb or suffix. Some interpreters view the referent of the participle ההפכים, "those who turn [justice into wormwood]," as the same addressees of the exhortation in v. 6a (masculine plural imperative). See Paul, *Amos*, 166–7; Carroll R., *Contexts for Amos*, 235; Jeremias, *The Book of Amos*, 82, 90; Hayes, *Amos*, 160; De Waard and Smalley, *A Translator's Handbook*, 104. Duane Garrett argues that the referent is the priests and officials at Bethel mentioned in v. 6. Garrett, *Amos*, 143–4.

35. Some commentators, including Shalom Paul, view 5:7 // 5:10-12, 13 to be the center of the chiasm. Paul, *Amos*, 159. Yet apart from mentioning the intrusive nature of the doxology in vv. 8-9, Paul does not explain how it fits the chiastic structure. Also see Hadjiev, *Composition and Redaction of the Book of Amos*, 129–32.

the weak in their society, inverting the natural order of things.³⁶ Though Amos does not emphasize the prototypicality of YHWH, as in 2:9-11 (see Chapter 4), this contrast shows where true power lies.

In light of the overall structure, the remnant of Joseph, as part of the exhortations, contributes to a degree of tension in 5:1-17. Both A and A' frame the destruction as unconditional realities.³⁷ This is warranted by the perpetuation of systemic injustice. The people are described as hostile (צררי) to the righteous and takers (לקחי) of bribes (v. 12c). Other finite verbs generalize their other activities: they hate the arbiter in the gate; they abhor the speaker of truth; they tread upon the poor and impose taxes upon them (v. 11). Thus, it may appear odd to have seemingly hopeful exhortations to seek YHWH and live in a context of announced death. Hans Walter Wolff goes so far as to say, "The attached promise of life actually stands in contradiction to that which precedes, as well as to the total message of the prophet."³⁸ The series of afflictions in 4:6-11 revealed that in spite of YHWH's repeated summons to return, the people are completely unresponsive. What purpose then would a further exhortation to repent have in this circumstance? Scholars have dealt with these issues in several ways, from questioning the genuine nature of the exhortations,³⁹ to reading the lament as entirely conditional upon the people's response.⁴⁰ The latter does not seem likely when viewed within the book as a whole. For, the people are consistently viewed as an outgroup (see Chapter 4). They love to frequent the cults at Bethel and Gilgal, enough so that YHWH sarcastically invites them to come and sin there (cf. 4:4-5). The violence and robbery of Samaria have invited an adversary who will

---

36. Carroll R. states, "The impression that arises is of a 'world' of perverse values which are incarnated in social life and structures, and never questioned by (and perhaps are even perpetuated by) the nation's religion." Carroll R., *Contexts for Amos*, 234.

37. Noble, "The Remnant in Amos 3–6," 135.

38. Wolff, *Joel and Amos*, 237.

39. A. Vanlier Hunter, "Seek the Lord! A Study of the Meaning and Function of the Exhortations in Amos, Hosea, Isaiah, Micah, and Zephaniah" (ThD diss., Universität Basel, 1982), 122. Also, Donald E. Gowan, *Theology of the Prophetic Books: The Death and Resurrection of Israel* (Louisville, KY: Westminster John Knox, 1998), 35; Thomas M. Raitt, "Prophetic Summons to Repentance," *ZAW* 83, no. 1 (1971): 30–49.

40. Paul, *Amos*, 161–2; Lessing, *Amos*, 320. Wood views the exhortation as an opportunity rejected by the northern kingdom, but subsequently offered to Judah. Joyce Rilett Wood, *Amos in Song and Book Culture*, JSOTSup 337 (London: Sheffield Academic, 2002), 113.

plunder their strongholds (3:9-11). Exile has been announced for those at ease in Zion (6:7-9). Though the prophet was able to intercede successfully on behalf of the people in the first two visions (7:2-3, 5-6), he no longer has occasion to do so in the third and following visions. YHWH states that the end has come upon the people (8:2). Thus, judgment is stated everywhere else as unconditional (cf. 9:1-4). Claiming that this sentence could entirely be commuted if the people repent appears to blunt the sharp edge of the book's message.[41]

Questioning the genuine nature of the oracles, as ironic statements, is equally implausible in light of the rhetorical shape of the verses. If the exhortation to seek YHWH in 5:5b is understood to be ironic, what are readers to make of the warning to avoid Bethel, Gilgal, and Beersheba? Additionally, this would also be the only instance I am aware of in the Hebrew Bible where a call to seek YHWH would in fact mean the opposite. How should one resolve this issue of unconditional judgment juxtaposed with exhortations that would mitigate disaster? I would suggest that the remnant motif in v. 15 provides a way forward.[42]

The phrase itself, "remnant of Joseph," has been interpreted in several ways.[43] Some relate it to the present condition of the people, whether resulting from the previous plagues of 4:6-11,[44] military defeats,[45] or to supposed popular cultic expressions identifying Israel with the patriarchs.[46] More commonly, the expression is understood to refer to survivors after the coming judgment.[47] This view fits the context, as the unit began by

---

41. So, Carroll R., *Contexts for Amos*, 240; Noble, "The Remnant in Amos 3–6," 135. Against Michael Ufok Udoekpo, *Rethinking the Prophetic Critique of Worship in Amos 5 for Contemporary Nigeria and the USA* (Eugene, OR: Pickwick, 2017), 80–1. Möller, through the lens of Speech-Act Theory, views Amos's judgment speeches as a summons to repent. Karl Möller, "Words of (In-)Evitable Certitude? Reflections on the Interpretation of Prophetic Oracles of Judgment," in Bartholomew, Greene, and Möller, eds., *After Pentecost*, 352–86; Möller, *A Prophet in Debate*, 141–4. Also see Houston, "What Did the Prophets Think They Were Doing?" 167–88.

42. So, Smith, *Amos*, 209; Hasel, *The Remnant*, 101.

43. Tchavdar Hadjiev identifies six different interpretations of "the remnant of Joseph" in this passage. Hadjiev, *Composition and Redaction of the Book of Amos*, 186 n. 17. See also Park, "Eschatology in the Book of Amos," 166–9; Carroll R., *Contexts for Amos*, 227 n. 1, 236 n. 3.

44. Hubbard, *Joel and Amos*, 184; Andersen and Freedman, *Amos*, 509–10; Harper, *A Critical and Exegetical Commentary*, 125–6.

45. Hayes, *Amos*, 167; Soggin, *The Prophet Amos*, 87–8.

46. Hunter, "Seek the Lord!" 85–94.

47. Noble, "The Remnant in Amos 3-6," 131; Jeremias, *The Book of Amos*, 96; Mays, *Amos*, 102.

detailing the reduction of the population that would soon occur (5:3).⁴⁸ In contrast to this negative use of the remnant, which serves to illustrate the severity of judgment of the people's transgressions (cf. 3:12), the remnant of Joseph in 5:15 is connected to ingroup identifiers, such as YHWH's presence and the establishment of justice. In other words, the remnant that receives divine favor acts according to the norms and values of YHWH. In addition to the dominant outgroup of Israel, these behaviors are an indication of another group present, namely the ingroup. That there is an ingroup alongside the outgroup is further supported by the fact that there are those who are righteous and wise (vv. 12-13), in addition to those who arbitrate for justice in the gate (5:10). Though this ingroup is only glimpsed in passing at this point in the book, it is central to Amos's conception of the future. YHWH's dealings with both groups could not be more different. The same "YHWH, the God of hosts, the Lord" who brings wailing upon the land when he passes through their midst (vv. 16-17), is the same "YHWH, the God of hosts" who will be gracious to the remnant of Joseph (v. 15).⁴⁹ Though judgment is inevitable for the nation, hope is held out for those who live differently.⁵⁰

Whereas the remnant in 5:15 contains a subtler differentiation between the ingroup and the outgroup and their respective futures, the motif surfacing in 9:8–10 is more explicit. The beginning of the fifth vision (9:1-4) describes YHWH's relentless and deadly pursuit of the people when he fixes his "eyes upon them for evil and not for good" (v. 4c). After

---

48. Barstad argues that the reduction in 5:3 does not connote a surviving remnant, but functions to express the total annihilation of the people. Barstad, *The Religious Polemics of Amos*, 77. Against this, Noble states that if total destruction were in view, there would be many easier and clearer ways to express such an idea. Noble, "The Remnant in Amos 3-6," 143 n. 22.

49. The use of אולי, "perhaps," in the clause describing YHWH's gracious behavior towards the remnant does not detract from the sincerity of the exhortation. Wolff claims that the semantic range of the word does not include guilt and forgiveness. Wolff, *Joel and Amos*, 251. But Jeremiah attests to such usage (cf. Jer. 36:7). A parallel call to seek YHWH (בקשו את יהוה) occurs in conjunction with אולי in Zeph. 2:3. A similar idea is found in Jon. 3:9: מי יודע ישוב ונחם האלהים ושב מחרון אפו ולא נאבד ("Who knows? God may turn and relent and turn from his fierce anger, so that we may not perish").

50. Noble states, "In Amos 5:4-6, 14-15, then, there is not only a reaffirmation of unconditional judgment but also the possibility of a better future for the remnant that survives the judgment." Noble, "The Remnant in Amos 3–6," 135. Carroll R. notes the role that those in positions of influence maintain in the pursuit of a just society. They must remake the system according to YHWH's demands. Carroll R., *Contexts for Amos*, 237.

pledging to annihilate the "sinful kingdom," YHWH strikingly states, "except I will not completely destroy the house of Jacob" (v. 8b). The unexpected and sudden note of restraint has led many scholars to view v. 8b as a redactional insertion, correcting the unmitigated declaration of complete judgment.[51] Others argue that there is a qualitative distinction between the "sinful kingdom" (v. 8a) and the "house of Jacob" (v. 8b), whether in terms of identification (i.e., political entity versus general population) or morality (i.e., sinful versus righteous).[52] Verse 9 then employs the imagery of a sieve.[53] Though the exact action portrayed is not completely clear, the idea appears to be one of scattering and separation. At YHWH's command, the "house of Israel" would be shaken among the nations as with a sieve.

The sieve metaphor is further specified in v. 10, when YHWH states, "by the sword all the sinners of my people shall die."[54] The identification of "sinners" here introduces an ethical component to the judgment. While the "sinners" die, presumably those not included in this group live. These sinners are "those who say, 'disaster will not overtake or meet us'" (v. 10b). As seen throughout the book, outgroup Israel clings to tradition (3:2; 9:7), wealth (4:1; 6:1), and religion (4:4-5; 5:18; 7:12-13) for security, all of which prove to be no help on the day of judgment.[55] YHWH's destruction of the sinners in 9:8-10, carrying on the distinction between the ingroup and the outgroup with the remnant motif, sets the stage for the transition to the hopeful restoration in vv. 11-15.[56] The fact that repentance is not mentioned in the epilogue could indicate that what

---

51. See Nogalski, *Literary Precursors to the Book of the Twelve*, 103–4. Also, Lo, "Remnant Motif in Amos, Micah, and Zephaniah," 135–6; Hadjiev, *Composition and Redaction of Amos*, 115.

52. For a helpful summary of views, see Mark E. Biddle, "Sinners Only? Amos 9:8-10 and the Problem of Targeted Justice in Amos," *Perspectives in Religious Studies* 43, no. 2 (2016): 163–5.

53. The word כברה, "sieve," occurs only here in the Hebrew Bible. See Paul, *Amos*, 286 n. 39. Garrett is skeptical regarding the common notion of sifting in this verse. Garrett, *Amos*, 277–9.

54. This translation understands חטאי as a noun ("sinners"). Noble interprets the word as an adjective ("sinful"), rendering the verse, "every one of my exceedingly sinful people shall die." Noble, "Amos' Absolute 'No,'" 337–8. In his view, Amos announces the total destruction of Israel, down to the last person. But v. 10b identifies the people put to the sword as those who claim that disaster will not overtake them. This appears to differentiate a specific subgroup of people.

55. Möller takes 9:10 as a kind of hermeneutical key to understand the absolute rhetoric of destruction. Möller, *A Prophet in Debate*, 145.

56. See, for example, Hasel, *The Remnant*, 207.

is in view is a future ingroup not counted among the "sinners." Thus, the remnant motif provides a bridge between the negative portrayal of Israel who will be destroyed and people who will experience a hopeful restoration in the final verses.

The Restoration of Israel

The final issue for this chapter's assessment of Israel's future in Amos is the epilogue of 9:11-15.[57] After the transition framed by the remnant motif in vv. 8-10, YHWH announces his purposes to restore his people "on that day." The Day of YHWH motif, mentioned twice in this unit (vv. 11, 13), breaks from the negative function elsewhere in the book. No more does the Day portend disaster for the outgroup, but here spells blessing and hope for the ingroup. But how does this utopian future comport with the rest of the book? The questions prompted by a Social Identity Approach, I suggest, provide helpful tools for answering this question, especially as it relates to the social identity of the audience. This section explores Amos's epilogue for its conception of the future.

The unit opens with YHWH's raising up "the booth of David" (v. 11).[58] The lament of 5:2 stated that Israel was fallen "with none to raise her up." In a grand reversal, YHWH himself raises the ruins that remain. The "booth of David" most likely refers to the Davidic empire, paralleling the similar phrase, אהל דוד ("tent of David") in Isa. 16:5.[59] Its humble state is the result of the winnowing judgment in vv. 8-10. The mention

---

57. The authenticity of this passage is much debated. For a discussion, see Thang, *The Theology of the Land in Amos 7–9*, 181–7. Also, see Marvin A. Sweeney, "The Dystopianization of Utopian Prophetic Literature: The Case of Amos 9:11-15," in *Utopia and Dystopia in Prophetic Literature*, ed. Ehud Ben Zvi, Publications of the Finnish Exegetical Society 92 (Göttingen: Vandenhoeck & Ruprecht, 2006), 175–85.

58. David is mentioned explicitly only here and with reference to his musical abilities in 6:5.

59. The exact meaning of the "booth of David" continues to be debated. Among other options, scholars argue that it represents the Davidic empire (Paul, Hayes), the city of Jerusalem (Pomykala, Eidevall, Wolff), the city of Succoth (Stuart, Richardson), and the Jerusalem Temple (Goswell, Dunne, Radine). Paul, *Amos*, 290; Hayes, *Amos*, 223–4; Kenneth E. Pomykala, "Jerusalem as the Fallen Booth of David in Amos 9:11," in *God's Word for Our World: Biblical Studies in Honor of Simon John De Vries*, vol. 1, ed. J. Harold Ellens et al., JSOTSup 338 (London: T&T Clark International, 2004), 275–93; Eidevall, *Amos*, 240–1; Wolff, *Joel and Amos*, 353; Stuart, *Hosea–Jonah*, 398; H. Neil Richardson, "SKT (Amos 9:11): 'Booth' or 'Succoth'?" *JBL* 92, no. 3 (1973): 375–81; Greg Goswell, "David in the Prophecy of Amos," *VT* 61, no.

of David here would be a potent memory for a nation that has seen the depths of moral/spiritual ruin. YHWH states that he will rebuild David's booth "as in the days of old." Since the "sinners" were separated from the ingroup in vv. 8-10, the generalized continuity with the past here takes on a different form than what was seen in Chapter 4. When applied to the outgroup, the past is employed to highlight their perpetuation of wickedness. But the epilogue establishes continuity in terms of blessing. David's booth emerges as the remnant ingroup seen previously.[60] Though there is continuity with the Davidic empire of the past, Amos develops the understanding of this group in the future.

The restoration of David's booth is "so that they may possess the remnant of Edom and all the nations who are called by my [YHWH's] name" (v. 12). The verb ירש ("possess") commonly indicates possession by force (cf. Exod. 34:24; Num. 21:35; Deut. 2:12; Judg. 3:13),[61] while the following phrase, "all the nations who are called by my [YHWH's] name," indicates ownership.[62] The later phrase, however, does not necessarily entail the negative connotation implied by ירש.[63] In Deut. 28:10, YHWH states that all the peoples of the earth will see that his name has been called over Israel and they will be afraid. This act of possession is favorable towards Israel, resulting in fertility and blessing (Deut. 28:11-12). Those left in Edom, perhaps representative of the nations judged in the OAN collection, are once again subjected to the restored Davidic empire "as in the days of old."[64] Thus, 9:12 embodies the eschatological

---

2 (2011): 243–57; John Anthony Dunne, "David's Tent as Temple in Amos 9:11-15: Understanding the Epilogue of Amos and Considering Implications for the Unity of the Book," *WTJ* 73, no. 2 (2011): 363–74. For an exhaustive analysis of views until the mid-nineteenth century, see Sabine Nägele, *Laubhütte Davids und Wolkensohn: Eine auslegungsgeschichtliche Studie zu Amos 9,11 in der jüdischen und christlichen Exegese* (Leiden: Brill, 1995). Nägele concludes that the booth of David refers to the Jerusalem Temple. Also, see Radine, *The Book of Amos in Emergent Judah*, 194–205.

60. Eviatar Zerubavel details the role of discursive continuity in forming a continuous biography of identity. This process involves the playing up of aspects of the past that are consistent with, or somehow prefigure, the present identity. See Zerubavel, *Time Maps*, 52–4.

61. It occurs especially in various stereotypical formulae involving the conquest of the land. See H. H. Schmid, "ירש," *TLOT* 2:578–81.

62. Paul, *Amos*, 292.

63. Against Harper, *Critical and Exegetical Commentary on Amos and Hosea*, 198; Cripps, *A Critical and Exegetical Commentary on the Book of Amos*, 273.

64. Timmer argues that the possession of the remnant of Edom and all the nations over whom YHWH's name is called should be understood "as the non-violent establishment of relationship dependent upon some sort of divine initiative...rather than

tension often discovered in the Hebrew Bible between Israel conquering the nations and the more peaceful incorporation of the nations into the true Israelite community (Mic. 4:1-5).[65]

Amos 9:13-15 details the secure and prosperous life in the land when David's booth is restored. No longer will exploitation of the poor be the means of prosperity for the elites, but the fruitfulness of the land will consistently yield enough for all. The normal dormant periods in the annual agricultural cycle will be abolished. The land will be perpetually fertile and the conditions continually favorable. More than that, when YHWH "rebuilds" the booth of David (v. 11), the people will "rebuild" their ruined cities (v. 14). This reverses the judgment of 5:11, which was linked to the outgroup characterization of the people as those who hate the one arbitrating justice in the gate (5:10), trample the poor (5:11), and silence the righteous (5:13). YHWH's judgment caused the farmers to mourn and brought wailing in all the vineyards (5:16-17), but the future would see farmers cultivating their land securely. YHWH's final and definitive declaration is that he will plant the people in their land and they shall never be uprooted. The stability of creation in the restoration of the people shows that this is the way the world ought to be.[66] No longer is the world in disarray because of injustice and oppression (cf. 8:4-10). When the ingroup is settled in the land, creation attests to its proper order.[67]

The Future and Identity-Formation

As with the last chapter, the focus on time is central to the identity-forming potential of Amos. This is especially true when it comes to the future and social identity. In a much-cited article, Marco Cinnirella explores the role of "possible social identities" (PSI) in group processes

---

YHWH making these nations his own through violent conquest." Timmer, *The Non-Israelite Nations in the Book of the Twelve*, 61. While a peaceful inclusion of Edom, perhaps representative of the nations, may be signified by the calling of YHWH's name over them, the possession of Edom proves more difficult. David's early victory of Edom in 2 Samuel involved the striking down of 18,000 Edomites, after which Edom became a servant of David (2 Sam. 8:13-14). If the rule of the Davidic kingdom is in view in Amos 9:12, *pace* Timmer, a peaceful solution appears difficult.

65. Timmer, *Non-Israelite Nations in Book of the Twelve*, 58; Garrett, *Amos*, 284. Also, see Thang, *Theology of the Land in Amos 7–9*, 196–7.

66. This unit fulfills many aspects of the covenant blessings of Lev. 26:3-13 and Deut. 28:1-14.

67. Thang, *Theology of the Land in Amos 7–9*, 200.

and identity maintenance.⁶⁸ He demonstrates how perceptions of possible group membership may serve as a motivating factor for non-group members to join the ingroup. As has been argued, the book of Amos exposes the outgroup status of the addressees in various ways. Audience members searching for positive distinctiveness in the world of the text have seen only glimpses of the ingroup, primarily through prototypical members (YHWH, Amos) and the exhortations. But in the final resolution of the epilogue, the audience is able to see a vision of blessings that lay ahead for YHWH's people. They will enjoy prosperity and dwell securely in the land. This possible future may provide the necessary motivation for non-group members to pursue membership in the ingroup.

Cinnirella suggests eight key properties of a "possible social identity," namely:

> (1) *Diffusion*. i.e. degree to which awareness of the possible social identity has diffused within both the ingroup and relevant outgroups. (2) *Degree of acceptance/validity within the ingroup*. (3) *Affect* i.e. whether is desired/feared/neutral. (4) *Perceived likelihood of realization*—(for future-oriented) possible social identities. (5) *Perceived source* e.g. ingroup versus outgroup. (6) *Salience and inherent accessibility*. (7) *Temporal focus*—whether it focuses on past, present, future, or some combination of these. (8) *Qualitative content of possible social identity*—for example, a description of the specific past or future scenario(s) involved, including on the discourses and rhetoric employed by ingroups.⁶⁹

While some of these are difficult to ascertain through a textual medium, Amos's epilogue (9:11-15) specifically supports a number of these key properties. The qualitative content of the PSI (#8) in Amos's epilogue, for instance, describes the prosperous life to come (#7) in the land for ingroup members. The affect of such portrayal (#3) is clearly positive for those who will experience it. The source of this future social identity (#5) is YHWH himself, thus guaranteeing its likelihood of realization (#4). The one who exercises sovereign control over creation is the one will raise up David's booth (Amos 9:11a). It is he, YHWH, "who does this" (v. 12c). The very last clause of the book reiterates who pronounces this future: "says YHWH your God" (v. 15d). The God who judges nations and manipulates the cosmos is the one who will bring the blessing for the

---

68. Cinnirella, "Exploring Temporal Aspects of Social Identity," 227–48. His article seeks to rectify the underdeveloped notion of "cognitive alternatives" in the work of Tajfel and Turner.

69. Ibid., 234.

ingroup. Thus, the epilogue of Amos meets the criteria for an effective "possible social identity" as outlined by Cinnirella. This increases the motivation potential for the audience to pursue ingroup membership.

Moreover, the perceived impermeable boundaries that may be thought to make social mobility impossible (shared history, prior experience with YHWH, socio-economic status, etc.) have been systematically dismantled throughout the book of Amos.[70] The defining features of the ingroup are not simply in the past. The future-orientation of ingroup Israel's destiny invites audience members to be shaped in the present by the values of the group. This process of self-stereotyping leads individuals to define the group in terms of what it means to be "us" and then seek to conform to these norms.[71] Amos's audience has witnessed at length what it means to be "them." The outgroup norms of oppression, social injustice, and state religion are set against what it means to be an ingroup member. The hopeful future for the ingroup creates a sense of responsibility for maintaining and changing one's self in anticipation of the future.[72] As Jonathan Cohen states, "Without a tacit belief in tomorrow nearly everything we do today would be pointless."[73] For audience members, meaning, as well as social cohesion, are the results of conformity to group norms in light of the hopeful future that awaits them "on that day."

Conclusion

This chapter has continued the exploration of time and social identity in the book of Amos. It was shown that the Day of YHWH, the remnant motif, and the final restoration of the book each contribute to the nature of the future envisioned in Amos, whether to amplify judgment or proclaim hope.[74] For audiences entering the world of the text who desire a positive social identity, the hopeful call sounded by the remnant and the utopian vision in Amos 9:11-15 provide motivation to pursue ingroup membership.

---

70. As Carol Sharp notes, "The audience of Amos gradually loses its grasp on its identity as the prophet destroys piece after piece of Israel's tradition history." Sharp, *Irony and Meaning in the Hebrew Bible*, 129.

71. Haslam, Reicher, and Platow, *The New Psychology of Leadership*, 143.

72. Condor, "Social Identity and Time," 305.

73. Jonathan Cohen, cited in ibid.

74. As stated above, whether an interpreter will label these future events as eschatological will largely depend on one's definition of eschatology. Hasel, *Understanding the Book of Amos*, 111. Our broader definition includes events both within and beyond the realm of human history.

It was shown that the tools of the Social Identity Approach are suitable to uncover these dynamics. Thus, wherever the audience is socially located, this hopeful future, centered on the restoration of the Davidic empire, can be their hopeful future; and membership in the ingroup will influence their behavior in the present.

Chapter 6

Conclusion

In his recent book on identity, Klyne Snodgrass quotes the Mexican proverb, "Tell me who you are with and I will tell you who you are."[1] This adage gets to the heart of the view of what it means to be "us." Humans, as social beings, commonly derive a sense of self from their respective social groups. The dynamics of these groups can span significant time and space. Members of certain religious movements, for instance, may trace the history of their faith to the creation of the world. Thus, they view themselves as a part of a continuous narrative group that gives meaning to group members in the present. The values of the group may be inscribed in rituals, traditions, memories, and texts. These tell group members who they are and who they are not.

This book has attempted to discover various strategies for social identity formation in the book of Amos. The Social Identity Approach (SIA), composed of Social Identity Theory and Self Categorization Theory, was adopted as the specific heuristic tool for the analysis. This method was detailed in Chapter 2. The theoretical foundation for SIA is that categorization as a member of a particular group both leads to social comparison and produces the desire for a positive distinctiveness of one's own group. Naturally, people tend to seek membership in groups that give them a positive sense of self. As they negotiate what it means to be "us," they also often define the group in contradistinction to what it means to be "them." This process is facilitated by group prototypes—ideal embodiments of the essence of the group—who provide a standard to which group members seek conformity. The value of the Social Identity Approach in biblical studies was seen in the survey of its application in New Testament and Hebrew Bible scholarship. Special focus was given to the textual construction of identity.

---

1. Snodgrass, *Who God Says You Are*, 13.

Chapter 3 looked at intergroup conflict in the Oracles against the Nations (1:3–2:4) and the confrontation between Amos and Amaziah (7:10-17). The formulaic oracles, it was argued, function to cast Israel as simply one among the nations. Whereas the audience may anticipate the historic people of God to be the ingroup, the collection of oracles destabilizes this expectation. On the contrary, Israel is framed as another outgroup. The Bethel narrative showed that both Amos and Amaziah are presented not simply as individuals, but representatives of their respective groups. More than this, both figures take on a degree of prototypicality. Here, norms and values can be seen that characterize the ingroup as presented in the world of the text. The dynamics of conflict intensify these group boundaries.

Chapters 4 and 5 explored the temporal nature of social identity in Amos. Chapter 4 analyzed the use of history in Amos as a mechanism for identity formation, with the additional help of social memory studies. It was argued that Amos establishes continuity between the past and "present." From this perspective the past is weaponized as an othering strategy against the outgroup. Traditional markers of ingroup identity (election, history with YHWH, the cult, etc.) are relegated to a peripheral role in light of the norms and values of outgroup Israel. Rather than conforming to the prototypical behavior of YHWH, showing kindness to the needy, Israel perpetuated a long history of oppression. This use of history allows the audience to associate injustice with outgroup behavior.

Chapter 5 turned to the identity-forming potential of the future in Amos. The eschatological nature of the Day of YHWH motif, the remnant motif, and the utopian epilogue of the book each contribute to the identity constructed in the text. On the one hand, the future judgment expressed by the Day of YHWH and remnant motifs, specifically, further exposes the social identifiers of the outgroup. On the other hand, the remnant motif was shown to have another function in presenting a hopeful future for the ingroup. Though the exhortations to the remnant of Joseph provide an initial impetus to join the ingroup (i.e., they will live and not die), the future is realized in the final restoration of the Davidic empire in 9:11-15. For audiences entering the world of the text, this hopeful future provides motivation to pursue membership in the ingroup. When set in conjunction with the numerous othering strategies of the book, this vision presents the kind of future that would provide a positive sense of self for an unresisting reader.[2]

---

2. As has been stated, an audience may resist the identity construct of the text. This, however, in no way nullifies a Social Identity Approach. In fact, it may be best explained by SIA. Audiences, for instance, who benefit from mass exploitation of the

In addition to the motivation to join the ingroup, Amos also provides social identifiers characterizing group members.[3] This identity involves both a particular relationship with the Deity and with other people. The choice between death and life lies in the decision to seek YHWH. For Amos, however, seeking YHWH cannot be reduced merely to religious ritual. It involves not only proper worship, but conformity to ingroup prototypes (YHWH, Amos). YHWH's kindness towards helpless Israel is paradigmatic for ingroup members. Since YHWH led the people out of Egypt and destroyed their enemies before them, in addition to giving them leaders in their midst, they are expected not to trample the poor or afflict the needy (2:6-12). This sharpens the demands of the text upon the audience. They are not simply to pursue justice in a generic sense. Rather, they are to conform to the character of Israel's God. Amos makes clear that justice is not tertiary for the people of God. For, as Walter Brueggemann states, "There is a general commitment in Israel's testimony to justice as a primary agenda of Yahweh."[4] Thus, membership in the ingroup necessitates adopting the norms and values of YHWH.

Ingroup membership equally involves obedience to YHWH, as modeled by the prophet Amos. When YHWH says to speak, ingroup members open their mouths. In the confrontation with the priest at Bethel, Amos served as a representative of the ingroup, leaving behind his profession to obey the voice of YHWH (7:14-16). These social identity norms are not limited to a particular social location, but they do involve certain kinds of worshippers. Those who claim to be part of God's people while mistreating their neighbors are, according to Amos, not a part of the ingroup. The book excoriates forms of religion that legitimate injustice and oppression.

Beyond ingroup norms, the social identifiers of the outgroup are most visible in the book. This is not incidental. For a group to have a sense of who they are, they must have a notion of who they are not. The attribution

---

poor would likely resist the egalitarian social identity norms in the text. In this case, their elite social group membership governs the values that they believe will give them a positive sense of self. Other audiences may reject the very notion of divine activity altogether. From this perspective, the world of the text itself is unintelligible. The present work, however, explores the process with respect to unresisting audiences.

3. The question of group identity, however, cannot simply be reduced to discerning who is in and who is out. For, this inevitably oversimplifies both the variable boundaries of groups as well as the context-dependent nature of social identity. The principles of "accessibility" and "fit" (see Chapter 2), in particular, contribute to the salience of a particular social identity in a specific circumstance.

4. Brueggemann, *Theology of the Old Testament*, 738.

of outgroups characteristics to the Other (i.e., stereotyping) function to reify one's sense of identity. As Michael Billig states, "[stereotypes] are often means of distinguishing 'them' from 'us,' thereby contributing to 'our' claims of a unique identity."[5] The attributes of the outgroup involve insensitivity to divine communication and the perpetuation of injustice and oppression. Those entering the world of the text must put these outgroup social identifiers in conversation with their own social context. What does it look like, for instance, for audience members socially located in an oppressive majority cultural context to pursue membership in Amos's ingroup? At a minimum, it would result in a community established upon the principles of generosity and justice.[6] Yet how this will relate to audiences in various social locations will differ due to the fact that social identity salience is contextually dependent.[7] Nevertheless, for an individual to pursue membership in the ingroup is to claim the heritage of the Davidic empire as one's own. YHWH's past dealing with Israel becomes a part of their past. In short, he will be their God and they will be his people.

This investigation has inevitably involved a hermeneutical quest for the embedded sense of identity in the final form book. Though this approach is particular, one must recognize that any statement about identity, whether regarding an individual or group, necessarily involves and presupposes an act of interpretation.[8] Since identity is not static, one would expect this process to involve some level of negotiation.[9] This is especially relevant in light of the claim that the book of Amos contains a transtemporal construct of identity.[10] Audiences in various social locations must discover how their own history, norms, and values relate to that of the ingroup in the text. Though I have pulled on some of these threads, the elaborate tapestry of identity doubtlessly leaves much more to be said. Even with a helpful tool, the scope of analysis remains limited. Indeed, as Christian Smith observes, "Any theory is descriptively simpler than what

---

5. Michael Billig, *Banal Nationalism* (London: Sage, 1995), 81.

6. Perhaps a glimpse of this is evident at the Jerusalem counsel in Acts 15, where Amos 9:11-12 LXX is quoted to show the inclusion of a historic outgroup into the people of God (Acts 15:16-18). See Kuecker, *The Spirit and the "Other"*, 205–7.

7. Abrams and Hogg, *Social Identifications*, 22.

8. Filtvedt, *The Identity of God's People*, 39.

9. Jonker, *Defining All-Israel in Chronicles*, 13 n. 42.

10. James Linville describes the trap of the book of Amos as a beautifully crafted condemnation of Israel's sins. The sting of the trap, he states, "is its universality, timelessness, and demands for a personal engagement... The word of doom in not constrained by the limits of the text." Linville, *Amos and the Cosmic Imagination*, 8.

it theorizes."[11] This approach to social identity formation by means of the biblical text has provided but one line of inquiry. The stakes of these questions are high. In a world rife with oppression, violence, and social division, the kind of ingroup community envisioned in Amos can display what it means to be the people of God. The hope of the text, as articulated by a Social Identity Approach, is that audiences located anywhere at any time can seek YHWH and live.

---

11. Christian Smith, *Religion: What It Is, How It Works, and Why It Matters* (Princeton, NJ: Princeton University Press, 2017), 61.

Bibliography

Abrams, Dominic, and Michael A. Hogg. *Social Identifications: A Social Psychology of Intergroup Relations and Group Processes*. London: Routledge, 1998.
Ackroyd, P. R. "Amos 7:14." *ExpTim* 68, no. 3 (1956): 94.
Adamo, David T. *Africa and the Africans in the Old Testament*. 1998. Reprint, Eugene, OR: Wipf & Stock, 2001.
Adamo, David T. "Amos 9:7-8 in an African Perspective." *Orita* 24 (1992): 76–84.
Adams, Jim W. *The Performative Nature and Function of Isaiah 40–55*. LHBOTS 448. New York: T&T Clark, 2006.
Alter, Robert. *The Art of Biblical Poetry*. New York: Basic, 1985.
Andersen, Francis I., and David Noel Freedman. *Amos*. AYB 24A. New York: Doubleday, 1989.
Arnold, Bill T. "Old Testament Eschatology and the Rise of Apocalypticism." In *The Oxford Handbook of Eschatology*, edited by Jerry L. Walls, 23–39. Oxford: Oxford University Press, 2008.
Assmann, Jan. *Cultural Memory and Early Civilization: Writing, Remembrance, and Political Imagination*. New York: Cambridge University Press, 2011.
Assmann, Jan. *Das kulturelle Gedächtnis: Schrift, Erinnerung und politische Identität in frühen Hochkulturen*. Munich: Beck, 1992.
Assmann, Jan. *Religion and Cultural Memory: Ten Studies*. Translated by R. Livingstone. Stanford, CA: Stanford University Press, 2006.
Assmann, Jan. *Religion und kulturelles Gedächtnis. zehn Studien*. Munich: Beck, 2000.
Bach, R. "Erwägungen Zu Amos 7,14." In *Die Botschaft und die Boten: Festschrift für Hans Walter Wolff zum 70. Geburtstag*, edited by J. Jeremias and L. Perlitt, 203–16. Neukirchen-Vluyn: Neukirchener Verlag, 1981.
Baker, Coleman A. *Identity, Memory, and Narrative in Early Christianity: Peter, Paul, and Recategorization in the Book of Acts*. Eugene, OR: Pickwick, 2011.
Barentsen, Jack. *Emerging Leadership in the Pauline Mission: A Social Identity Perspective of Local Leadership Development in Corinth and Ephesus*. Princeton Theological Monograph 168. Eugene, OR: Pickwick, 2011.
Barker, Joel D. "Day of the Lord." *DOTP* 132–43.
Barsalou, L. W., and D. R. Sewell. *Constructing Representations of Categories from Different Points of View*. Emory Cognition Projects Report 2. Atlanta, GA: Emory University, 1984.
Barstad, Hans M. "Die Basankühe in Am Iv 1." *VT* 25 (1975): 286–97.
Barstad, Hans M. "History and Memory: Some Reflections on the 'Memory Debate' in Relation to the Hebrew Bible." In *The Historian and the Bible: Essays in Honour of Lester L. Grabbe*, edited by Philip R. Davies and Diana V. Edelman, 1–10. LHBOTS 530. London: T&T Clark, 2010.

Barstad, Hans M. *The Religious Polemics of Amos: Studies in the Preaching of Am 2,7b-8; 4,1-13; 5,1-27; 6,4-7; 8,14*. Supplements to VTSup 34. Leiden: Brill, 1984.
Bartelmus, Rüdiger. *HYH: Bedeutung und Funktion eines hebräischen "Allerweltwortes."* St. Ottilien: Eos, 1982.
Barton, John. "Covenant in Old Testament Theology." In *Covenant as Context: Essays in Honour of E. W. Nicholson*, edited by A. D. H. Mayes and R. B. Salters, 23–38. Oxford: Oxford University Press, 2003.
Barton, John. "The Day of Yahweh in the Minor Prophets." In *Biblical and Near Eastern Essays: Studies in Honour of Kevin J. Cathcart*, edited by Carmel McCarthy and John F. Healey, 68–94. London: T&T Clark, 2004.
Barton, John. "The Prophets and the Cult." In *Temple and Worship in Biblical Israel: Proceedings of the Oxford Old Testament Seminar*, edited by John Day, 111–22. LHBOTS 422. London: T&T Clark, 2005.
Barton, John. *The Theology of the Book of Amos*. New York: Cambridge University Press, 2012.
Barton, John. "Thinking about Reader-Response Criticism." *ExpTim* 113, no. 5 (2002): 147–51.
Barton, John. *Understanding Old Testament Ethics: Approaches and Explorations*. Louisville, KY: Westminster John Knox, 2003.
Bell, Robert D. "The Theology of Amos." *Biblical Viewpoint* 27, no. 2 (1993): 47–54.
Bentzen, Aage. "The Ritual Background of Amos i 2-Ii 16." *OtSt* 8 (1950): 85–99.
Ben Zvi, Ehud. *Hosea*. Forms of the Old Testament Literature 21A/1. Grand Rapids: Eerdmans, 2005.
Ben Zvi, Ehud. "Introduction: Writings, Speeches, and the Prophetic Books—Setting an Agenda." In *Writings and Speech in Israelite and Ancient Near Eastern Prophecy*, edited by Ehud Ben Zvi and Michael H. Floyd, 1–29. Symposium 10. Atlanta, GA: SBL, 2000.
Ben Zvi, Ehud. "On Social Memory and Identity Formation in Late Persian Yehud: A Historian's Viewpoint with a Focus on Prophetic Literature, Chronicles and the Deuteronomistic Historical Collection." In *Texts, Contexts and Readings in Postexilic Literature: Explorations into Historiography and Identity Negotiation in Hebrew Bible and Related Texts*, edited by Louis C. Jonker, 95–148. FAT 2 53. Tübingen: Mohr Siebeck, 2011.
Ben Zvi, Ehud. "Remembering the Prophets through the Reading and Rereading of a Collection of Prophetic Books in Yehud: Methodological Considerations and Explorations." In *Remembering and Forgetting in Early Second Temple Judah*, edited by Christoph Levin and Ehud Ben Zvi, 17–44. FAT 85. Tübingen: Mohr Siebeck, 2012.
Ben Zvi, Ehud. *Social Memory among the Literati of Yehud*. BZAW 509. Berlin: de Gruyter, 2019.
Ben Zvi, Ehud. "Studying Prophetic Texts against Their Original Backgrounds: Pre-Ordained Scripts and Alternative Horizons of Research." In *Prophets and Paradigms: Essays in Honor of Gene M. Tucker*, edited by Stephen Breck Reid, 125–35. JSOTSup 229. Sheffield: Sheffield Academic, 1996.
Berger, Peter L., and Thomas Luckmann. *The Social Construction of Reality: A Treatise in the Sociology of Knowledge*. New York: Doubleday, 1966.
Berquist, J. L. "Dangerous Waters of Justice and Righteousness." *BTB* 23 (1993): 54–63.
Biddle, Mark E. "Sinners Only? Amos 9:8-10 and the Problem of Targeted Justice in Amos." *Perspectives in Religious Studies* 43, no. 2 (2016): 161–75.
Billig, Michael. *Banal Nationalism*. London: Sage, 1995.

Bird, Phyllis A. "Poor Man or Poor Woman? Gendering the Poor in Prophetic Texts." In *Missing Persons and Mistaken Identities: Women and Gender in Ancient Israel*, 67–78. OBT. Minneapolis: Fortress, 1997.

Blanz, Mathias. "Accessibility and Fit as Determinants of the Salience of Social Categorizations." *EJSP* 29, no. 1 (1999): 43–74.

Blenkinsopp, Joseph. *A History of Prophecy in Israel*. Rev. ed. Louisville, KY: Westminster John Knox, 1996.

Blenkinsopp, Joseph. *Sage, Priest, Prophet: Religious and Intellectual Leadership in Ancient Israel*. Library of Ancient Israel. Louisville, KY: Westminster John Knox, 1995.

Bons, Eberhard. "Das Denotat von מהיכזב 'ihre Lügen' im Judaspruch, Am 2,4-5." *ZAW* 108 (1996): 201–13.

Bosman, Jan Petrus. *Social Identity in Nahum: A Theological-Ethical Enquiry*. Piscataway, NJ: Gorgias, 2008.

Bosman, Jan Petrus. "Social Identity in Nahum: A Theological-Ethical Enquiry." ThD diss., University of Stellenbosch, 2005.

Botha, J. Eugene. "Speech Act Theory and Biblical Interpretation." *Neotestamentica* 41 (2007): 274–94.

Boyle, Marjorie O'Rourke. "Covenant Lawsuit of the Prophet Amos: 3:1-4:13." *VT* 21, no. 3 (1971): 338–62.

Branscombe, Nyla R., Naomi Ellemers, Russell Spears, and E. J. Doosje. "The Context and Content of Social Identity Threat." In *Social Identity: Context, Commitment, Content*, edited by N. Ellemers, R. Spears, and B. Doosje, 35–58. Oxford: Blackwell, 1999.

Brettler, Marc Zvi. "Redaction, History, and Redaction-History of Amos in Recent Scholarship." In *Israel's Prophets and Israel's Past: Essays on the Relationship of Prophetic Texts and Israelite History in Honor of John H. Hayes*, edited by Brad E. Kelle and Megan Bishop Moore, 103–12. New York: T&T Clark, 2006.

Briggs, R. S. "The Uses of Speech-Act Theory in Biblical Interpretation." *CRBS* 9 (2001): 229–76.

Brinthaupt, Thomas M. "Identity." In *International Encyclopedia of the Social Sciences*, edited by William A. Darity, Jr., 55155. New York: Macmillan, 2008.

Brueggemann, W. "Amos 4:4-13 and Israel's Covenant Worship." *VT* 15, no. 1 (1965): 1–15.

Brueggemann, W. "Exodus in the Plural (Amos 9:7)." In *Texts That Linger, Words That Explode: Listening to Prophetic Voices*, edited by Patrick D. Miller, 89–103. Minneapolis: Fortress, 2000.

Brueggemann, W. *A Social Reading of the Old Testament: Prophetic Approaches to Israel's Communal Life*. Edited by Patrick D. Miller. Minneapolis: Fortress, 1994.

Brueggemann, W. *Theology of the Old Testament: Testimony, Dispute, Advocacy*. Minneapolis: Fortress, 1997.

Buss, M. J. "The Social Psychology of Prophecy." In *Prophecy: Essays Presented to Georg Fohrer on His 65th Birthday, 6 Sept 1980*, 1–11. BZAW 150. Berlin: de Gruyter, 1980.

Byrskog, Samuel. "Philosophical Aspects on Memory: Aristotle, Augustine and Bultmann." In *Social Memory and Social Identity in the Study of Early Judaism and Early Christianity*, edited by Samuel Byrskog, Raimo Hakola, and Jutta Jokiranta, 23–47. NTOA/SUNT 116. Göttingen: Vandenhoeck & Ruprecht, 2016.

Byrskog, Samuel, Raimo Hakola, and Jutta Jokiranta, eds. *Social Memory and Social Identity in the Study of Early Judaism and Early Christianity*. NTOA/SUNT 116. Göttingen: Vandenhoeck & Ruprecht, 2016.
Campos, Martha E. "Structure and Meaning in the Third Vision of Amos (7:7-17)." *Journal of Hebrew Scriptures* 11 (2011): 2–28.
Carroll R., M. Daniel. *Amos, the Prophet and His Oracles: Research on the Book of Amos*. Louisville, KY: Westminster John Knox, 2002.
Carroll R., M. Daniel. *Contexts for Amos: Prophetic Poetics in Latin American Perspective*. JSOTSup 132. Sheffield: JSOT, 1992.
Carroll R., M. Daniel. "'For So You Love to Do': Probing Popular Religion in the Book of Amos." In *Rethinking Contexts, Rereading Texts: Contributions from the Social Sciences to Biblical Interpretation*, 168–89. JSOTSup 299. Sheffield: Sheffield Academic, 2000.
Carroll R., M. Daniel. "God and His People in the Nations' History: A Contextualised Reading of Amos 1–2." *TynBul* 47 (1996): 39–70.
Carroll R., M. Daniel. "'I Will Send Fire:' Reflections on the Violence of God in Amos." In *Wrestling with the Violence of God: Soundings in the Old Testament*, edited by M. Daniel Carroll R. and J. Blair Wilgus, 113–32. BBRSup 10. Winona Lake, IN: Eisenbrauns, 2015.
Carroll R., M. Daniel. "Seek Yahweh, Establish Justice: Probing Prophetic Ethics: An Orientation from Amos 5:1-17." In *The Bible and Social Justice: Old Testament and New Testament Foundations for the Church's Urgent Call*, edited by Cynthia L. Westfall and Bryan R. Dyer, 64–83. McMaster New Testament Studies. Eugene, OR: Wipf & Stock, 2015.
Carroll R., M. Daniel, and J. Blair Wilgus, eds. *Wrestling with the Violence of God: Soundings in the Old Testament*. BBRSup 10. Winona Lake, IN: Eisenbrauns, 2015.
Cathcart, K. J. "Day of Yahweh." *ABD* 2:84–5.
Childs, Brevard S. "Speech-Act Theory and Biblical Interpretation." *SJT* 58 (2005): 375–92.
Chisholm, Robert B., Jr. "'For Three Sins…Even for Four': The Numerical Sayings in Amos." *Bibliotheca Sacra* 147, no. 586 (1990): 188–97.
Christensen, Duane L. "Prosodic Structure of Amos 1-2." *Harvard Theological Review* 67, no. 4 (1974): 427–36.
Christensen, Duane L. *Transformations of the War Oracle in Old Testament Prophecy: Studies in the Oracles Against the Nations*. Missoula, MT: Scholars Press, 1975.
Cinnirella, Marco. "Exploring Temporal Aspects of Social Identity: The Concept of Possible Social Identities." *EJSP* 28, no. 2 (1998): 227–48.
Claassens, L. Julia. "God and Violence in the Prophets." In *The Oxford Handbook of The Prophets*, edited by Carolyn J. Sharp, 334–49. Oxford: Oxford University Press, 2016.
Clements, R. E. *Prophecy and Covenant*. Studies in Biblical Theology 43. London: SCM, 1965.
Clements, R. E. *Prophecy and Tradition*. Atlanta, GA: Westminster John Knox, 1975.
Clifford, Hywel. "Amos in Wellhausen's Prolegomena." In *Aspects of Amos: Exegesis and Interpretation*, edited by Anselm C. Hagedorn and Andrew Mein, 141–56. New York: T&T Clark, 2011.
Cohen, Simon. "Amos Was a Navi." *HUCA* 32 (1961): 175–8.
Coleman, Janet. *Ancient and Medieval Memories: Studies in the Reconstruction of the Past*. Cambridge: Cambridge University Press, 1992.

Collins, John J. "History and Tradition in the Prophet Amos." *Irish Theological Quarterly* 41, no. 2 (1974): 120–33.
Condor, Susan. "Social Identity and Time." In *Social Groups and Identities: Developing the Legacy of Henri Tajfel*, edited by W. Peter Robinson, 285–315. International Series in Social Psychology. Oxford: Butterworth-Heinemann, 1996.
Condor, Susan, and Rupert Brown. "Psychological Processes in Intergroup Conflict." In *The Social Psychology of Intergroup Conflict: Theory, Research and Applications*, edited by Wolfgang Stroebe, Arie W. Kruglanski, Daniel Bar-Tal, and Miles Hewstone, 3–26. New York: Springer, 1988.
Coote, Robert B. *Amos Among the Prophets: Composition and Theology*. Philadelphia: Fortress, 1981.
Coser, Lewis A. Introduction to *On Collective Memory*, by Maurice Halbwachs, 1–34. Translated by Lewis A. Coser. Chicago: University of Chicago Press, 1992.
Cripps, Richard S. *A Critical and Exegetical Commentary on the Book of Amos*. 2nd ed. ICC. London: SPCK, 1955.
Crouch, C. L. *War and Ethics in the Ancient Near East: Military Violence in Light of Cosmology and History*. BZAW 407. Berlin: de Gruyter, 2009.
Davies, Eryl W. "Reader-Response Criticism and Old Testament Studies." In *Honouring the Past and Shaping the Future: Religious and Biblical Studies in Wales: Essays in Honour of Gareth Lloyd Jones*, edited by Robert Pope, 20–37. Leominster, UK: Gracewing, 2003.
Davis, A. R. *Tel Dan in Its Northern Cultic Context*. Archaeology and Biblical Studies 20. Atlanta, GA: SBL, 2013.
Dearman, J. Andrew. *Property Rights in the Eighth-Century Prophets: The Conflict and Its Background*. SBLDS 106. Atlanta, GA: Scholars Press, 1988.
De Fina, A., D. Schiffrin, and M. Bamberg, eds. *Discourse and Identity*. Cambridge: Cambridge University Press, 2006.
De Hulster, Izaak J. *Iconographic Exegesis and Third Isaiah*. FAT 2/36. Tübingen: Mohr Siebeck, 2009.
Dell, Katharine J. "Amos and the Earthquake: Judgment as Natural Disaster." In *Aspects of Amos: Exegesis and Interpretation*, edited by Anselm C. Hagedorn and Andrew Mein, 1–14. New York: T&T Clark, 2011.
Dicou, Bert. *Edom, Israel's Brother and Antagonist: The Role of Edom in Biblical Prophecy and Story*. JSOTSup 169. Sheffield: Sheffield Academic, 1994.
Dorsey, David A. "Literary Architecture and Aural Structuring Techniques in Amos." *Bib* 73 (1992): 305–30.
Driver, G. R. "Affirmation by Exclamatory Negation." *JNES* 5 (1973): 107–14.
Dunne, John Anthony. "David's Tent as Temple in Amos 9:11-15: Understanding the Epilogue of Amos and Considering Implications for the Unity of the Book." *WTJ* 73, no. 2 (2011): 363–74.
Edelman, Diana V. "YHWH's Othering of Israel." In *Imagining the Other and Constructing Israelite Identity in the Early Second Temple Period*, edited by Ehud Ben Zvi and Diana V. Edelman, 41–69. LHBOTS 591. New York: T&T Clark, 2014.
Eidevall, Göran. *Amos*. AYB 24G. New Haven, CT: Yale University Press, 2017.
Eidevall, Göran. "A Farewell to the Anticultic Prophet: Attitudes towards the Cult in the Book of Amos." In *Priests and Cults in the Book of the Twelve*, edited by Lena-Sofia Tiemeyer, 99–114. ANEM 14. Atlanta, GA: SBL, 2016.

Eidevall, Göran. *Sacrificial Rhetoric in the Prophetic Literature of the Hebrew Bible*. Lewiston, NY: Edwin Mellen, 2012.
Ellemers, Naomi, and Ad Van Knippenberg. "Stereotyping in Social Context." In *The Social Psychology of Stereotyping and Group Life*, edited by R. Spears, P. J. Oakes, N. Ellemers, and S. A. Haslam, 208–35. Cambridge, MA: Blackwell, 1997.
Ellemers, Naomi, Ad Van Knippenberg, Nanne de Vries, and Henk Wilke. "Social Identification and Permeability of Group Boundaries." *EJSP* 18, no. 6 (1988): 497–513.
Emerson, Michael O., and Christian Smith. *Divided by Faith: Evangelical Religion and the Problem of Race in America*. Oxford: Oxford University Press, 2000.
Erikson, Erik H. *Identity and the Life Cycle*. New York: W. W. Norton, 1994.
Erikson, Erik H. *Identity: Youth and Crisis*. New York: W. W. Norton, 1968.
Escobar, Donoso S. "Social Justice in the Book of Amos." *Review & Expositor* 92, no. 2 (1995): 169–74.
Esler, Philip F. *Conflict and Identity in Romans: The Social Setting of Paul's Letter*. Minneapolis: Fortress, 2003.
Esler, Philip F. "Group Norms and Prototypes in Matthew 5.3-12: A Social Identity Interpretation of the Matthaean Beatitudes." In *T&T Clark Handbook to Social Identity in the New Testament*, edited by J. Brian Tucker and Coleman Baker, 147–71. London: Bloomsbury, 2016.
Esler, Philip F., and Ronald A. Piper. *Lazarus, Mary and Martha: Social-Scientific Approaches to the Gospel of John*. Minneapolis: Fortress, 2006.
Everson, A. Joseph. "The Days of Yahweh." *JBL* 93, no. 3 (1974): 329–37.
Fensham, F. C. "Common Trends in Curses of the Near Eastern Treaties and Kudurru-Inscriptions Compared with Maledictions of Amos and Isaiah." *ZAW* 75 (1963): 155–75.
Fensham, F. C. "A Possible Origin of the Concept of the Day of the Lord." *Neotestamentica* 1966, no. 1 (1966): 90–7.
Ferguson, Neil, and Shelley McKeown. "Social Identity Theory and Intergroup Conflict in Northern Ireland." In *Understanding Peace and Conflict through Social Identity Theory: Contemporary Global Perspectives*, edited by S. McKeown, R. Haji, and N. Ferguson, 215–27. New York: Springer, 2016.
Fields, Weston. *Sodom and Gomorrah: History and Motif in Biblical Narrative*. Sheffield: Sheffield Academic, 1997.
Filtvedt, Ole Jakob. *The Identity of God's People and the Paradox of Hebrews*. WUNT 2/400. Tübingen: Mohr Siebeck, 2015.
Fitzgerald, Aloysius. *The Lord of the East Wind*. CBQMS 34. Washington, DC: Catholic Biblical Association of America, 2002.
Fleming, Daniel E. "The Day of Yahweh in the Book of Amos: A Rhetorical Response to Ritual Expectation." *RB* 117, no. 1 (2010): 20–38.
Freedman David Noel. "Deliberate Deviation from an Established Pattern of Repetition in Hebrew Poetry as a Rhetorical Device." In *Divine Commitment and Human Obligation: Selected Writings of David Noel Freedman*, edited by John R. Huddlestun, 2:205–12. Grand Rapids: Eerdmans, 1997,
Freedman, David Noel, and Andrew Welch. "Amos's Earthquake and Israelite Prophecy." In *Scripture and Other Artifacts: Essays on the Bible and Archaeology in Honor of Philip J. King*, edited by M. D. Coogan, J. C. Exum, and L. E. Stager, 188–98. Louisville, KY: Westminster John Knox, 1994.

Fuligni, A. J., G. J. Rivera, and A. Leininger. "Family Identity and the Educational Persistence of Students with Latin American and Asian Backgrounds." In *Contesting Stereotypes and Creating Identities: Social Categories, Social Identities and Educational Participation*, edited by A. J. Fuligni, 239–63. New York: Russell Sage Foundation Publications, 2007.

García-Treto, F. O. "A Reader-Response Approach to Prophetic Conflict: The Case of Amos 7:10-17." In *The New Literary Criticism and the Hebrew Bible*, edited by J. C. Exum and D. J. A. Clines, 114–24. JSOTSup 143. Sheffield: JSOT, 1993.

Garrett, Duane A. *Amos: A Handbook on the Hebrew Text*. Baylor Handbook on the Hebrew Bible. Waco, TX: Baylor University Press, 2008.

Garton, Roy E. "Rattling the Bones of the Twelve: Wilderness Reflections in the Formation of the Book of the Twelve." In *Perspectives on the Formation of the Book of the Twelve: Methodological Foundations, Redactional Processes, Historical Insights*, edited by R. Albertz, J. D. Nogalski, and J. Wöhrle, 237–51. BZAW 433. Berlin: de Gruyter, 2012.

Gass, E. "'Kein Prophet bin ich und kein Prophetenschüler bin ich': Zum Selbstverständnis des Propheten Amos in Am 7,14." *TZ* 68 (2012): 1–24.

Geertz, Clifford. *The Interpretation of Cultures: Selected Essays*. New York: Basic, 1973.

Gertz, Jan Christian, Bernard M. Levinson, Dalit Rom-Shiloni, and Konrad Schmid, eds. *The Formation of the Pentateuch: Bridging the Academic Cultures of Europe, Israel, and North America*. FAT 111. Tübingen: Mohr Siebeck, 2016.

Gevirtz, Stanley. "A New Look at an Old Crux: Amos 5:26." *JBL*, no. 87 (1968): 267–76.

Giffone, Benjamin D. *"Sit At My Right Hand": The Chronicler's Portrait of the Tribe of Benjamin in the Social Context of Yehud*. New York: T&T Clark, 2016.

Gillingham, Susan. "'Who Makes the Morning Darkness'? God and Creation in the Book of Amos." *SJT* 45, no. 2 (1992): 165–84.

Glenny, W. Edward. *Amos: A Commentary Based on Amos in Codex Vaticanus*. Septuagint Commentary Series. Leiden: Brill, 2013.

Goffman, Erving. *The Presentation of Self in Everyday Life*. Anchor Books ed. Garden City, NY: Doubleday, 1959.

Goldenberg, David M. *The Curse of Ham: Race and Slavery in Early Judaism, Christianity, and Islam*. Princeton, NJ: Princeton University Press, 2003.

Goering, Greg Schmidt. "Proleptic Fulfillment of the Prophetic Word: Ezekiel's Dirges Over Tyre and Its Ruler." *JSOT* 36, no. 4 (2012): 483–505.

Goswell, Greg. "David in the Prophecy of Amos." *VT* 61, no. 2 (2011): 243–57.

Gottwald, Norman K. *All the Kingdoms of the Earth*. New York: Harper & Row, 1964.

Gowan, Donald E. *Theology of the Prophetic Books: The Death and Resurrection of Israel*. Louisville, KY: Westminster John Knox, 1998.

Greer, Jonathan S. "A Marzea and a Mizraq: A Prophet's Mêlée with Religious Diversity in Amos 6.4-7." *JSOT* 32 (2007): 243–61.

Hadjiev, Tchavdar S. *The Composition and Redaction of the Book of Amos*. Berlin: de Gruyter, 2009.

Halbwachs, Maurice. *Les Cadres Sociaux de La Memoire*. Paris: Librarie Felix Alcan, 1925.

Halbwachs, Maurice. *On Collective Memory*. Translated by Lewis A. Coser. Chicago: University of Chicago Press, 1992.

Harper, William R. *A Critical and Exegetical Commentary on Amos and Hosea*. ICC 23. Edinburgh: T&T Clark, 1936.

Harper, William R. "The Utterances of Amos Arranged Strophically." *Biblical World* 12, no. 3 (1898): 179–82.
Hasel, G. F. "The Alleged 'No' of Amos and Amos' Eschatology." *AUSS* 29 (1991): 3–18.
Hasel, G. F. *The Remnant: The History and Theology of the Remnant Idea from Genesis to Isaiah*. 2nd ed. AUM 5. Berrien Springs, MI: Andrews University Press, 1974.
Hasel, G. F. *Understanding the Book of Amos: Basic Issues in Current Interpretations*. Grand Rapids: Baker, 1991.
Haslam, S. Alexander. *Psychology in Organizations: The Social Identity Approach*. 2nd ed. London: Sage, 2004.
Haslam, S. Alexander, Naomi Ellemers, Stephen D. Reicher, Katherine J. Reynolds, and Michael T. Schmitt. "The Social Identity Perspective Today: An Overview of Its Defining Ideas." In *Rediscovering Social Identity: Key Readings*, edited by Tom Postmes and Nyla R. Branscombe, 341–56. New York: Psychology Press, 2010.
Haslam, S. Alexander, Naomi Ellemers, Stephen D. Reicher, Katherine J. Reynolds, and Michael T. Schmitt. "The Social Identity Perspective Tomorrow: Opportunities and Avenues for Advance." In *Rediscovering Social Identity: Key Readings*, edited by Tom Postmes and Nyla R. Branscombe, 357–79. New York: Psychology Press, 2010.
Haslam, S. Alexander, and Penelope J. Oakes. "How Context-Independent Is the Outgroup Homogeneity Effect? A Response to Bartsch and Judd." *EJSP* 25, no. 4 (1995): 469–75.
Haslam, S. Alexander, Stephen D. Reicher, and Michael J. Platow. *The New Psychology of Leadership: Identity, Influence, and Power*. New York: Psychology Press, 2011.
Hayes, John H. *Amos: The Eighth-Century Prophet; His Times and His Preaching*. Nashville: Abingdon, 1988.
Hays, J. Daniel. *From Every People and Nation: A Biblical Theology of Race*. New Studies in Biblical Theology. Downers Grove, IL: InterVarsity, 2003.
Hendel, Ronald S. "The Exodus in Biblical Memory." *JBL* 120, no. 4 (2001): 601–22.
Hjelm, Titus. *Social Constructionisms: Approaches to the Study of the Human World*. New York: Macmillan, 2014.
Hoffmann, Yair. "The Day of the Lord as a Concept and a Term in the Prophetic Literature." *ZAW* 93, no. 1 (1981): 37–50.
Hoffmeier, James K. "Once Again the 'Plumb Line' Vision of Amos 7:7-9: An Interpretive Clue from Egypt." In *Boundaries of the Ancient Near Eastern World: A Tribute to Cyrus H. Gordon*, edited by Meir Lubetski, Claire Gottlieb, and Sharon Keller, 305–19. JSOTSup 273. Sheffield: Sheffield Academic, 1998.
Hogg, M. A. "Social Identity Theory." In *Contemporary Social Psychological Theories*, edited by Peter J. Burke, 111–36. Stanford, CA: Stanford University Press, 2006.
Hogg, M. A. "Social Identity Theory." In *Encyclopedia of Social Psychology*, edited by R. F. Baumeister and K. D. Vohs, 2:901–3. Thousand Oaks, CA: Sage, 2007.
Hogg, Michael A., Elizabeth A. Hardie, and Katherine J. Reynolds. "Prototypical Similarity, Self-Categorization, and Depersonalized Attraction: A Perspective on Group Cohesiveness." *EJSP* 25, no. 2 (1995): 159–77.
Hogg, M. A., J. C. Turner, and B. Davidson. "Polarized Norms and Social Frames of Reference: A Test of the Self-Categorization Theory of Group Polarization." *BASP* 11, no. 1 (1990): 77–100.
Holladay, William L. *Jeremiah 1: A Commentary on the Book of the Prophet Jeremiah, Chapters 1–25*. Hermeneia. Minneapolis: Fortress, 1986.

Holter, Knut. "Being Like the Cushites: Some Western and African Interpretations of Amos 9:7." In *New Perspectives on Old Testament Prophecy and History: Essays in Honour of Hans M. Barstad*, edited by Rannfrid I. Thelle, Terje Stordalen, and Mervyn E. J. Richardson, 306–18. VTSup 168. Leiden: Brill, 2015.

Holter, Knut. *Yahweh in Africa: Essays on Africa and the Old Testament*. Vol. 1. BTA. New York: Peter Lang, 2000.

Horrell, David G. "'Becoming Christian': Solidifying Christian Identity and Content." In *Handbook of Early Christianity: Social Science Approaches*, edited by Anthony J. Blasi, Jean Duhaime, and Paul-André Turcotte, 309–35. Walnut Creek, CA: AltaMira, 2002.

Horton, Robert F. *The Minor Prophets*. Vol. 1. Edinburgh: Oxford University Press, 1904.

House, Paul R. "The Day of the Lord." In *Central Themes in Biblical Theology: Mapping Unity in Diversity*, edited by Scott J. Hafemann and Paul R. House, 179–224. Grand Rapids: Baker Academic, 2007.

Houston, Walter J. *Amos: Justice and Violence*. T&T Clark Study Guides to the Old Testament. London: T&T Clark, 2017.

Houston, Walter J. *Contending for Justice: Ideologies and Theologies of Social Justice in the Old Testament*. London: T&T Clark, 2006.

Houston, Walter J. "Was There a Social Crisis in the Eighth Century?" In *Search of Pre-Exilic Israel*, edited by John Day, 130–49. JSOTSup 406. London: T&T Clark, 2004.

Houston, Walter J. "What Did the Prophets Think They Were Doing? Speech Acts and Prophetic Discourse in the Old Testament." *BibInt* 1 (1993): 167–88.

Hubbard, David Allan. *Joel and Amos: An Introduction and Commentary*. Tyndale Old Testament Commentaries 25. 1989. Reprint, Downers Grove, IL: IVP Academic, 2009.

Hübenthal, Sandra. "Social and Cultural Memory in Biblical Exegesis: The Quest for an Adequate Application." In *Cultural Memory in Biblical Exegesis*, edited by Pernille Carstens, Trine B. Hasselbalch, and Niels P. Lemche, 175–99. Perspectives on Hebrew Scriptures and Its Contexts 17. Piscataway, NJ: Gorgias, 2012.

Huffmon, Herbert B. "The Treaty Background of Hebrew Yāda'." *BASOR* 181 (1966): 31–7.

Huffmon, Herbert B., and Simon B. Parker. "A Further Note on the Treaty Background of Hebrew Yāda'." *BASOR*, no. 184 (1966): 36–8.

Hunter, A. Vanlier. "Seek the Lord! A Study of the Meaning and Function of the Exhortations in Amos, Hosea, Isaiah, Micah, and Zephaniah." ThD diss., Universität Basel, 1982.

Hutton, Jeremy M. "Amos 1:3–2:8 and the International Economy of Iron Age II Israel." *Harvard Theological Review* 107 (2014): 81–113.

Iggers, Georg G. Introduction to *The Theory and Practice of History*, by Leopold von Ranke, xi–xlv. Edited by Georg G. Iggers. New York: Routledge, 2011.

Irudayaraj, Dominic S. *Violence, Otherness and Identity in Isaiah 63:1–6: The Trampling One Coming from Edom*. LHBOTS 633. New York: T&T Clark, 2017.

Irwin, Brian. "Amos 4:1 and the Cows of Bashan on Mount Samaria: A Reappraisal." *CBQ* 74, no. 2 (2012): 231–46.

Isbell, Charles D. "Another Look at Amos 5:26." *JBL* 97, no. 1 (1978): 97–9.

Jackson, Jared J. "Amos 5:13 Contextually Understood." *ZAW* 98, no. 3 (1986): 434–5.

Jackson, Linda A., Linda A. Sullivan, Richard Harnish, and Carole N. Hodge. "Achieving Positive Social Identity: Social Mobility, Social Creativity, and Permeability of Group Boundaries." *JPSP* 70, no. 2 (1996): 241–54.

Jackson, Ronald L., ed. *Encyclopedia of Identity*. 2 vols. Thousand Oaks, CA: Sage, 2010.
Jaruzelska, Izabela. "Amasyah—prêtre de Béthel—fonctionnaire royal (essai socio-économique préliminaire)." *Folia Orientalia* 31 (1995): 53–69.
Jaruzelska, Izabela. "Social Structure in the Kingdom of Israel in the Eighth Century B.C. as Reflected in the Book of Amos." *Folia Orientalia* 29 (1992–1993): 91–117.
Jemielity, Thomas. *Satire and the Hebrew Prophets*. Literary Currents in Biblical Interpretation. Louisville, KY: Westminster John Knox, 1992.
Jenkins, R. *Social Identity*. 4th ed. London: Routledge, 2014.
Jeremias, Jörg. *The Book of Amos: A Commentary*. Translated by Douglas W. Stott. Louisville, KY: Westminster John Knox, 1998.
Jeremias, Jörg. *Die Reue Gottes: Aspekte alttestamentlicher Gottesvorstellung*. Biblische Studien 65. Neukirchen-Vluyn, Germany: Neukirchener Verlag, 1975.
Jokiranta, Jutta. "Black Sheep, Outsiders, and the Qumran Movement: Social-Psychological Perspectives on Norm-Deviant Behaviour." In *Social Memory and Social Identity in the Study of Early Judaism and Early Christianity*, edited by Samuel Byrskog, Raimo Hakola, and Jutta Jokiranta, 151–73. NTOA/SUNT 116. Göttingen: Vandenhoeck & Ruprecht, 2016.
Jokiranta, Jutta. "Prototypical Teacher in the Qumran Pesharim: A Social Identity Approach." In *Ancient Israel: The Old Testament in Its Social Context*, edited by Philip F. Esler, 254–63. Minneapolis: Fortress, 2006.
Jokiranta, Jutta. *Social Identity and Sectarianism in the Qumran Movement*. STDJ 105. Leiden: Brill, 2013.
Jokiranta, Jutta. "Social Identity Approach: Identity-Constructing Elements in the Psalms Pesher." In *Defining Identities: Who Is the Other? We, You, and the Others in the Dead Sea Scrolls. Proceedings of the Fifth Meeting of the IOQS in Groningen*, edited by Florentino García Martínez and Mladen Popović, 85–109. STDJ 70. Leiden: Brill, 2008.
Jokiranta, Jutta. "Social-Scientific Approaches to the Dead Sea Scrolls." In *Rediscovering the Dead Sea Scrolls: An Assessment of Old and New Approaches and Methods*, edited by Maxine L. Grossman, 246–63. Grand Rapids: Eerdmans, 2010.
Jonker, Louis C. *Defining All-Israel in Chronicles: Multi-Levelled Identity Negotiation in Late Persian-Period Yehud*. FAT 106. Tübingen: Mohr Siebeck, 2016.
Jonker, Louis C. "Human Dignity and the Construction of Identity in the Old Testament." *Scriptura* 105 (2010): 594–607.
Jonker, Louis C. "Refocusing the Battle Accounts of the Kings: Identity Formation in the Books of Chronicles." In *Behutsames Lesen: alttestamentliche Exegese im interdisziplinären Methodendiskurs: Christof Hardmeier zum 65. Geburtstag*, edited by Louis C. Jonker, Sylke Lubs, Andreas Ruwe, and Uwe Weise, 245–75. Arbeiten zur Bibel und ihrer Geschichte 28. Leipzig: Evangelische Verlagsanstalt, 2007.
Jonker, Louis C. "The Rhetorics of Finding a New Identity in a Multi-Cultural and Multi-Religious Society." *Verbum et Ecclesia* 24, no. 2 (2003): 396–416.
Jonker, Louis C. "Textual Identities in the Books of Chronicles: The Case of Jehoram's History." In *Community Identity in Judean Historiography*, edited by Gary N. Knoppers and Kenneth A. Ritsau, 197–217. Winona Lake, IN: Eisenbrauns, 2009.
Joyce, Paul M. "The Book of Amos and Psychological Interpretation." In *Aspects of Amos: Exegesis and Interpretation*, edited by Anselm C. Hagedorn and Andrew Mein, 105–16. LHBOTS 536. New York: T&T Clark, 2011.
Kakkanattu, J. P. *God's Enduring Love in the Book of Hosea: A Synchronic and Diachronic Analysis of Hosea 11:1–11*. FAT 2/14. Tübingen: Mohr Siebeck, 2006.

Kapelrud, Arvid S. *Central Ideas in Amos*. Oslo: Aschehoug, 1956.
Keener, Craig S. *Acts: An Exegetical Commentary*. Vol. 2. Grand Rapids: Baker Academic, 2013.
Keil, Carl F. *Biblischer Commentar über die Zwölf Kleinen Propheten*. BCAT 4. Leipzig: Dörffling & Franke, 1866.
Kelle, Brad E. *Hosea 2: Metaphor and Rhetoric in Historical Perspective*. Academia Biblica 20. Atlanta, GA: SBL, 2005.
Kellermann, Ulrich. "Der Amosschluss als Stimme deuteronomistischer Heilschoffnung." *EvT* 29 (1969): 169–83.
Kessler, John. "Patterns of Descriptive Curse Formulae in the Hebrew Bible, with Special Attention to Leviticus 26 and Amos 4:6–12." In *The Formation of the Pentateuch: Bridging the Academic Cultures of Europe, Israel, and North America*, edited by J. C. Gertz, B. M. Levinson, D. Rom-Shiloni, and K. Schmid. FAT 111. Tübingen: Mohr Siebeck, 2016.
Kim, Ju-Won. "Old Testament Quotations within the Context of Stephen's Speech in Acts." PhD diss., Pretoria University, 2007.
King, Andrew M. "Did Jehu Destroy Baal from Israel? A Contextual Reading of Jehu's Revolt." *BBR* 27, no. 3 (2017): 309–32.
King, Andrew M. "A Remnant Will Return: An Analysis of the Literary Function of the Remnant Motif in Isaiah." *JESOT* 4, no. 2 (2015): 145–69.
King, Philip J. *Amos, Hosea, Micah: An Archaeological Commentary*. Philadelphia: Westminster John Knox, 1988.
Kleven, Terence. "The Cows of Bashan: A Single Metaphor at Amos 4:1-3." *CBQ* 58 (1996): 215–27.
Kraus, Hans-Joachim. *Worship in Israel: A Cultic History of the Old Testament*. Translated by Geoffrey Buswell. Richmond, VA: John Knox, 1966.
Kuecker, Aaron. *The Spirit and the "Other": Social Identity, Ethnicity and Intergroup Reconciliation in Luke–Acts*. LNTS 444. New York: T&T Clark International, 2011.
Lacoviello, Vincenzo, Jacques Berent, Natasha S. Frederic, and Andrea Pereira. "The Impact of Ingroup Favoritism on Self-Esteem: A Normative Perspective." *JESP* 71 (2017): 31–41.
Lam, Joseph. *Patterns of Sin in the Hebrew Bible: Metaphor, Culture, and the Making of a Religious Concept*. Oxford: Oxford University Press, 2016.
Lanchester, H. C. O., and S. R. Driver. *The Books of Joel and Amos*. 2nd ed. CBSC. Cambridge: University Press, 1915.
Lau, P. H. W. *Identity and Ethics in the Book of Ruth: A Social Identity Approach*. BZAW 416. Berlin: de Gruyter, 2011.
Lehming, Sigo. "Erwägungen zu Amos." *ZTK* 55, no. 2 (1958): 145–69.
Lemaine, Gérard. "Inégalité, comparaison et incomparabilité: Esquisse d'une théorie de l'originalité sociale." *Bulletin de Psychologie* 20 (1966): 24–32.
Lemaine, Gérard. "Social Differentiation in the Scientific Community." In *The Social Dimension: European Developments in Social Psychology*, edited by Henri Tajfel, 1:338–59. ESSP. Cambridge: Cambridge University Press, 1984.
Lemos, T. M. *Violence and Personhood in Ancient Israel and Comparative Contexts*. Oxford: Oxford University Press, 2017.
Lessing, R. Reed. *Amos*. St. Louis: Concordia, 2009.
Lessing, R. Reed. "Amos's Earthquake in the Book of the Twelve." *Concordia Theological Quarterly* 74 (2010): 243–59.

Levin, Christoph. "Das Amosbuch der Anawim." *ZTK* 94 (1997): 407–36.
Levin, Christoph. *Re-Reading the Scriptures: Essays on the Literary History of the Old Testament*. FAT 87. Tübingen: Mohr Siebeck, 2013.
Levine, John M., and Michael A. Hogg, eds. *Encyclopedia of Group Processes and Intergroup Relations*. Vols. 1 and 2. Thousand Oaks, CA: Sage, 2010.
Lieu, Judith M. *Christian Identity in the Jewish and Graeco-Roman World*. Oxford: Oxford University Press, 2004.
Lim, Kar Yong. *Metaphors and Social Identity Formation in Paul's Letters to the Corinthians*. Eugene, OR: Wipf & Stock, 2017.
Linville, James R. *Amos and the Cosmic Imagination*. Society for Old Testament Study Monographs. Burlington, VT: Ashgate, 2008.
Linville, James R. "What Does 'It' Mean? Interpretation at the Point of No Return in Amos 1–2." *BibInt* 8 (2000): 400
Liu, James H., and Denis J. Hilton. "How the Past Weighs on the Present: Social Representations of History and Their Role in Identity Politics." *BJSP* 44, no. 4 (2005): 537–56.
Lo, Alison. "Remnant Motif in Amos, Micah, and Zephaniah." In *A God of Faithfulness: Essays in Honour of J. Gordon McConville on His 60th Birthday*, edited by Jamie A. Grant, Alison Lo, and Gordon J. Wenham, 130–48. New York: T&T Clark, 2011.
Lohfink, Norbert. "Was There a Deuteronomistic Movement?" In *Those Elusive Deuteronomists: The Phenomenon of Pan-Deuteronomism*, edited by Linda S. Schearing and Steven L. McKenzie, 36–66. JSOTSup 268. Sheffield: Sheffield Academic, 1999.
Luomanen, Petri. "The Sociology of Knowledge, the Social Identity Approach and the Cognitive Science of Religion." In *Explaining Christian Origins and Early Judaism: Contributions from Cognitive and Social Science*, edited by P. Luomanen, I. Pyysiäinen, and R. Uro, 199–229. Biblical Interpretation Series 89. Leiden: Brill, 2007.
Lust, Johan. "Remarks on the Redaction of Amos V 4–6, 14–15." In *Remembering All the Way: A Collection of Old Testament Studies Published on the Occasion of the Fortieth Anniversary of the Oudtestamentisch Werkgezelschap in Nederland*, edited by A. S. van der Woude, 129–54. OtSt 21. Leiden: Brill, 1981.
Marohl, Matthew J. *Faithfulness and the Purpose of Hebrews: A Social Identity Approach*. Princeton Theological Monographs 82. Eugene, OR: Pickwick, 2008.
Martin-Achard, Robert. *Amos: l'homme, le message, l'influence*. Publications de la Faculté de Théologie de l'Université de Genéve 7. Geneva: Labor et Fides, 1984.
Mays, James Luther. *Amos: A Commentary*. OTL. Philadelphia: Westminster John Knox, 1969.
Mays, James Luther. "Words about the Words of Amos: Recent Study of the Book of Amos." *Int* 13, no. 3 (1959): 259–72.
McConville, J. Gordon. "How Can Jacob Stand? He Is so Small!" In *Israel's Prophets and Israel's Past: Essays on the Relationship of Prophetic Texts and Israelite History in Honor of John H. Hayes*, edited by Brad E. Kelle and Megan Bishop Moore, 132–51. New York: T&T Clark, 2006.
McLaughlin, John L. *The Marzēaḥ in the Prophetic Literature: References and Allusions in Light of the Extra-Biblical Evidence*. Leiden: Brill, 2001.
McNally, Richard J. *Remembering Trauma*. Cambridge, MA: Harvard University Press, 2005.
Meier, Samuel A. "Sakkuth and Kaiwan (Deities)." *ABD* 5:904.
Melugin, Roy F. "Amos in Recent Research." *CRBS* 6 (1998): 65–101.

Melugin, Roy F. "Prophetic Books and Historical Reconstruction." In *Prophets and Paradigms: Essays in Honor of Gene M. Tucker*, edited by Stephen Breck Reid, 63–78. Sheffield: Sheffield Academic, 1996.

Miller, Cynthia L. "Pivotal Issues in Analyzing the Verbless Clause." In *The Verbless Clause in Biblical Hebrew: Linguistic Approaches*, edited by M. O'Connor and Cynthia L. Miller, 3–17. Linguistic Studies in Ancient West Semitic 1. Winona Lake, IN: Eisenbrauns, 1999.

Miller, Patrick D. "The Prophetic Critique of Kings." *Ex Auditu* 2 (1986): 82–95.

Miller, Patrick D. *The Religion of Ancient Israel*. Library of Ancient Israel. Louisville, KY: Westminster John Knox, 2000.

Miller, Patrick D. "What Do You Do with the God You Have? The First Commandment as Political Axiom." In *Shaking Heaven and Earth: Essays in Honor of Walter Brueggemann and Charles B. Cousar*, edited by C. R. Yoder, K. M. O'Connor, E. E. Johnson, and S. P. Saunders. Louisville, KY: Westminster John Knox, 2005.

Möller, Karl. "'Hear This Word Against You': A Fresh Look at the Arrangement and the Rhetorical Strategy of the Book of Amos." *VT* 50 (2000): 499–518.

Möller, Karl. *A Prophet in Debate: The Rhetoric of Persuasion in the Book of Amos*. New York: Sheffield Academic, 2003.

Möller, Karl. "Words of (In-)Evitable Certitude? Reflections on the Interpretation of Prophetic Oracles of Judgment." In *After Pentecost: Language and Biblical Interpretation*, edited by C. Bartholomew, C. Greene, and K. Möller, 352–86. Scripture and Hermeneutics 2. Grand Rapids: Zondervan, 2001.

Moore, Megan Bishop. *Philosophy and Practice in Writing a History of Ancient Israel*. LHBOTS 435. London: T&T Clark, 2006.

Moore, Megan Bishop, and Brad E. Kelle. *Biblical History and Israel's Past: The Changing Study of the Bible and History*. Grand Rapids: Eerdmans, 2011.

Moughtin-Mumby, Sharon. "'A Man and His Father Go to Naarah in Order to Defile My Holy Name!': Rereading Amos 2:6-8." In *Aspects of Amos: Exegesis and Interpretation*, edited by Anselm C. Hagedorn and Andrew Mein, 59–82. LHBOTS 536. New York: T&T Clark, 2011.

Nägele, Sabine. *Laubhütte Davids und Wolkensohn: Eine auslegungsgeschichtliche Studie zu Amos 9,11 in der jüdischen und christlichen Exegese*. Leiden: Brill, 1995.

Nam, Roger S. *Portrayals of Economic Exchange in the Book of Kings*. Leiden: Brill, 2012.

Nicholson, Ernest W. *God and His People: Covenant and Theology in the Old Testament*. Oxford: Clarendon, 1986.

Noble, Paul. "Amos' Absolute 'No.'" *VT* 41 (1997): 329–40.

Noble, Paul. "Amos and Amaziah in Context: Synchronic and Diachronic Approaches to Amos 7–8." *CBQ* 60, no. 3 (1998): 423–39.

Noble, Paul. "Israel Among the Nations." *HBT* 15 (1993): 56–82.

Noble, Paul. "The Remnant in Amos 3-6: A Prophetic Paradox." *HBT* 19, no. 2 (1997): 122–47.

Nogalski, James D. *Literary Precursors to the Book of the Twelve*. BZAW 217. Berlin: de Gruyter, 1993.

Nwaoru, Emmanuel O. "A Fresh Look at Amos 4:1-3 and Its Imagery." *VT* 59 (2009): 460–74.

Oakes, Penelope. "The Salience of Social Categories." In *Rediscovering the Social Group: A Self-Categorization Theory*, edited by John C. Turner, 117–41. New York: Blackwell, 1987.

Oakes, Penelope, S. A. Haslam, and J. C. Turner. "The Role of Prototypicality in Group Influence and Cohesion: Contextual Variation in the Graded Structure of Social Categories." In *Social Identity: International Perspectives*, edited by Stephen Worchel, J. Francisco Morales, Darío Páez, and Jean-Claude Deschamps, 75–92. London: Sage, 1998.

Oakes, Penelope, S. A. Haslam, and J. C. Turner. *Stereotyping and Social Reality*. Oxford: Blackwell, 1994.

Oakes, Penelope, John C. Turner, and S. Alexander Haslam. "Perceiving People as Group Members: The Role of Fit in the Salience of Social Categorizations." *BJSP* 30, no. 2 (1991): 125–44.

O'Brien, Julia M., and Chris Franke, eds. *The Aesthetics of Violence in the Prophets*. LHBOTS 517. London: T&T Clark, 2010.

O'Connell, Robert H. "Telescoping N + 1 Patterns in the Book of Amos." *VT* 46 (1996): 56–73.

Ogden, D. K. "The Earthquake Motif in the Book of Amos." In *Goldene Äpfel in silbernen Schalen: Collected Communications to the XIIIth Congress of the International Organization for the Study of the Old Testament, Leuven 1989*, edited by K. D. Schunck and M. Augustin, 69–80. Beiträge zur Erforschung des Alten Testaments und des antiken Judentums 20. Frankfurt: Peter Lang, 1992.

Olick, Jeffrey K., Vered Vinitzky-Seroussi, and Daniel Levy, eds. Introduction to *The Collective Memory Reader*, 9–62. Oxford: Oxford University Press, 2011.

Park, Aaron W. *The Book of Amos as Composed and Read in Antiquity*. StBibLit 37. New York: Peter Lang, 2001.

Park, Sang Hoon. "Eschatology in the Book of Amos: A Text-Linguistic Analysis." PhD diss., Trinity Evangelical Divinity School, 1996.

Paul, Shalom M. *Amos*. Hermeneia. Minneapolis: Fortress, 1991.

Paul, Shalom M. "Amos 1:3–2:3: A Concatenous Literary Pattern." *JBL* 90, no. 4 (1971): 397–403.

Paul, Shalom M. "Amos III 15–Winter and Summer Mansions." *VT* 28, no. 3 (1978): 358–60.

Peters, Richard S., and Henri Tajfel. "Hobbes and Hull—Metaphysicians of Behavior." *British Journal for the Philosophy of Science* 8 (1957): 30–44.

Pfeifer, Gerhard. "Das Ja des Amos." *VT* 39, no. 4 (1989): 497–503.

Pfeifer, Gerhard. *Die Theologie Des Propheten Amos*. Frankfurt: Peter Lang, 1995.

Polley, Max E. *Amos and the Davidic Empire: A Socio-Historical Approach*. New York: Oxford University Press, 1989.

Pomykala, Kenneth E. "Jerusalem as the Fallen Booth of David in Amos 9:11." In *God's Word for Our World: Biblical Studies in Honor of Simon John De Vries*, edited by J. Harold Ellens, Deborah L. Ellens, Rolf P. Knierim, and Isaac Kalimi, 1:275–93. JSOTSup 338. London: T&T Clark International, 2004.

Postmes, Tom. "Deindividuation." In *Encyclopedia of Social Psychology*, edited by R. F. Baumeister and K. D. Vohs, 1:233–5. Thousand Oaks, CA: Sage, 2007.

Raabe, Paul R. "Why Prophetic Oracles Against the Nations?" In *Fortunate the Eyes That See: Essays in Honor of David Noel Freedman in Celebration of His Seventieth Birthday*, edited by Astrid B. Beck, 236–57. Grand Rapids: Eerdmans, 1995.

Rad, Gerhard von. "The Origin of the Concept of the Day of Yahweh." *Journal of Semitic Studies* 4 (1959): 97–108.

Radine, Jason. *The Book of Amos in Emergent Judah*. FAT 45. Tübingen: Mohr Siebeck, 2010.

Raitt, Thomas M. "Prophetic Summons to Repentance." *ZAW* 83, no. 1 (1971): 30–49.
Ranke, Leopold von. *The Theory and Practice of History*. Edited by Georg G. Iggers. New York: Routledge, 2011.
Reicher, Stephen D. "The Determination of Collective Behaviour." In *Social Identity and Intergroup Relations*, edited by Henri Tajfel, 41–83. ESSP 7. Cambridge: Cambridge University Press, 2010.
Reicher, Stephen D. "Social Identity and Social Change: Rethinking the Context of Social Psychology." In *Social Groups and Identities: Developing the Legacy of Henri Tajfel*, edited by W. Peter Robinson, 317–36. International Series in Social Psychology. Oxford: Butterworth-Heinemann, 1996.
Reimer, H. "Agentes y Mecanismos de Opresión y Explotación en Amos." *Revista de Interpretación Bíblica Latinoamericana* 12 (1992): 69–81.
Reventlow, Henning Graf. *Das Amt des Propheten bei Amos*. Forschungen zur Religion und Literatur des Alten und Neuen Testaments 80. Göttingen: Vandenhoeck & Ruprecht, 1962.
Rice, Gene. "Was Amos a Racist?" *Journal of Religious Thought* 35 (1978): 35–44.
Richardson, H. Neil. "Critical Note on Amos 7:14." *JBL* 85, no. 1 (1966): 89.
Richardson, H. Neil. "SKT (Amos 9:11): 'Booth' or 'Succoth'?" *JBL* 92, no. 3 (1973): 375–81.
Ridge, David B. "On the Possible Interpretation of Amos 7:14." *VT* 68 (2018): 1–23.
Rilett Wood, Joyce. *Amos in Song and Book Culture*. JSOTSup 337. London: Sheffield Academic, 2002.
Roberts, H. C. "La Época de Amós y La Justicia Social." *BT* 50 (1993): 95–106.
Roberts, J. J. M. "Amos 6:1–7." In *Understanding the Word: Essays in Honor of Bernhard W. Anderson*, edited by James T. Butler, Edgar W. Conrad, and Ben C. Ollenburger, 155–66. JSOTSup 37. Sheffield: JSOT, 1987.
Rosch, Eleanor. "Principles of Categorization." In *Concepts: Core Readings*, edited by E. Margolis and S. Laurence, 189–206. Cambridge, MA: MIT, 1978.
Rottzoll, Dirk U. "II Sam 14,5—Eine Parallele Zu Am 7,14f." *ZAW* 100 (1988): 413–15.
Rottzoll, Dirk U. *Studien zur Redaktion und Komposition des Amosbuches*. BZAW 243. Berlin: de Gruyter, 1996.
Routledge, Robin. "Creation and Covenant: God's Direct Relationship with the Non-Israelite Nations in the Old Testament." In *Interreligious Relations: Biblical Perspectives. Proceedings from the Second Norwegian Summer Academy of Biblical Studies (NSABS), Ansgar University College, Kristiansand, Norway, August 2015*, edited by Hallvard Hagelia and Markus Zehnder, 52–69. London: T&T Clark, 2017.
Rowley, H. H. *The Biblical Doctrine of Election*. London: Lutterworth Press, 1948.
Rowley, H. H. "Was Amos a Nabi?" In *Festschrift Otto Eissfeldt zum 60. Geburtstag, 1. September 1947*, edited by Johann Fück, 191–8. Halle: Max Niemeyer, 1947.
Rudolph, W. "Amos 4, 6-13." In *Wort-Gebot-Glaube: Beiträge zur Theologie des Alten Testaments, Walter Eichrodt zum 80. Geburtstag*, edited by J. J. Stamm, E. Jenni, and H. J. Stoebe, 27–38. Abhandlungen zur Theologie des Alten und Neuen Testaments 59. Zurich: Zwingli, 1970.
Rudolph, W. *Joel, Amos, Obadja, Jona*. Kommentar zum Alten Testament 13/4. Gütersloh, Germany: Gerd Mohn, 1971.
Ryou, Daniel H. *Zephaniah's Oracles Against the Nations: A Synchronic and Diachronic Study of Zephaniah 2:1–3:8*. Biblical Interpretation 13. Leiden: Brill, 1995.

Sadler, Rodney Steven. *Can a Cushite Change His Skin? An Examination of Race, Ethnicity, and Othering in the Hebrew Bible*. LHBOTS 425. New York: T&T Clark, 2005.
Sandt, Huub van de. "The Minor Prophets in Luke–Acts." In *The Minor Prophets in the New Testament*, edited by Maarten J. J. Menken and Steve Moyise, 57–77. LNTS 377. New York: T&T Clark, 2009.
Sandt, Huub van de. "Why Is Amos 5,25-27 Quoted in Acts 7,42f.?" *Zeitschrift für die neutestamentliche Wissenschaft und die Kunde der älteren Kirche* 82 (1991): 67–87.
Schart, Aaron. *Die Entstehung des Zwölfprophetenbuchs: Neubearbeitungen von Amos im Rahmen schriftenübergreifender Redaktionsprozesse*. BZAW 260. Berlin: de Gruyter, 1998.
Schmid, H. "ירש." In *Theological Lexicon of the Old Testament*. Edited by E. Jenni and C. Westermann. Peabody, MA: Hendrickson, 1997.
Schmidt, W. H. *Das Buch Jeremia: Kapitel 1–20*. Das Alte Testament Deutsch 20. Göttingen: Vandenhoeck & Ruprecht, 2008.
Schmidt, W. H. "Die deuteronomistische Redaktion des Amosbuches." *ZAW* 77, no. 2 (1965): 168–93.
Scholz, Susanne, and Pablo R. Andiñach, eds. *La Violencia and the Hebrew Bible: The Politics and Histories of Biblical Hermeneutics on the American Continent*. Atlanta, GA: SBL, 2016.
Seibert, Eric A. *The Violence of Scripture: Overcoming the Old Testament's Troubling Legacy*. Minneapolis: Fortress, 2012.
Seitz, Christopher R. *Prophecy and Hermeneutics: Toward a New Introduction to the Prophets*. Studies in Theological Interpretation. Grand Rapids: Baker, 2007.
Seleznev, Michael. "Amos 7:14 and the Prophetic Rhetoric." In *Babel und Bibel*, edited by L. Kogan, N. Koslova, S. Loesov, and S. Tishchenko, 1:251–8. Ancient Near Eastern, Old Testament and Semitic Studies, Orentalia et Classica 5. Moscow: Russian State University of the Humanities, 2004.
Sharp, Carolyn J. *Irony and Meaning in the Hebrew Bible*. Bloomington: Indiana University Press, 2009.
Shea, William H. "Famine." *ABD* 2:769–73.
Shepherd, Michael B. *A Commentary on the Book of the Twelve: The Minor Prophets*. Kregel Exegetical Library. Grand Rapids: Kregel, 2018.
Shepherd, Michael B. *The Twelve Prophets in the New Testament*. StBibLit 40. New York: Peter Lang, 2011.
Shirer, William L. *The Rise and Fall of the Third Reich: A History of Nazi Germany*. New York: Simon & Schuster, 1988.
Shulman, David. *The Presentation of Self in Contemporary Social Life*. Thousand Oaks, CA: Sage, 2017.
Ska, Jean Louis. *Introduction to Reading the Pentateuch*. Winona Lake, IN: Eisenbrauns, 2006.
Smend, Rudolf. "Das Nein des Amos." *EvT* 23, no. 8 (1963): 404–23.
Smith, Christian. *Religion: What It Is, How It Works, and Why It Matters*. Princeton, NJ: Princeton University Press, 2017.
Smith, Gary V. *Amos*. Mentor Commentary. Fearn, Scotland: Christian Focus Publications, 2015.
Smith, Gary V. "Amos 5:13: The Deadly Silence of the Prosperous." *JBL* 107, no. 2 (1988): 289–91.

Smith, Gary V. "Continuity and Discontinuity in Amos' Use of Tradition." *JETS* 34, no. 1 (1991): 33–42.
Smith, Mark S. *The Ugaritic Baal Cycle: Introduction with Text, Translation, and Commentary of Ktu 1.1.–1.2*. Vol. 1. Leiden: Brill, 1994.
Snodgrass, Klyne. "Introduction to a Hermeneutics of Identity." *Bibliotheca Sacra* 168, no. 669 (2011): 3–19.
Snodgrass, Klyne. *Who God Says You Are: A Christian Understanding of Identity*. Grand Rapids: Eerdmans, 2018.
Soggin, J. Alberto. *The Prophet Amos: A Translation and Commentary*. Translated by John Bowden. London: SCM, 1987.
Sohn, Seock-Tae. *The Divine Election of Israel*. Grand Rapids: Eerdmans, 1991.
Stargel, Linda M. *The Construction of Exodus Identity in Ancient Israel: A Social Identity Approach*. Eugene, OR: Wipf & Stock, 2018.
Stavrakopoulou, F. "'Popular' Religion and 'Official' Religion: Practice, Perception, Portrayal." In *Religious Diversity in Ancient Israel and Judah*, edited by J. Barton and F. Stavrakopoulou, 37–58. London: T&T Clark, 2010.
Steinmann, Andrew E. "The Order of Amos's Oracles Against the Nations: 1:3–2:16." *JBL* 111 (1992): 683–9.
Stets, Jan E. "Identity Theory." In *Contemporary Social Psychological Theories*, edited by Peter J. Burke, 88–110. Stanford, CA: Stanford University Press, 2006.
Steyn, Gert J. "Trajectories of Scripture Transmission: The Case of Amos 5:25-27 in Acts 7:42-43." *Hervormde Teologiese Studies* 69, no. 1 (2013): 1–9.
Stol, M. "Kaiwan." In *Dictionary of Deities and Demons in the Bible*. Edited by K. van der Toorn, B. Becking, and P. W. van der Horst. Grand Rapids: Eerdmans, 1999.
Stol, M. "Sakkuth." In *Dictionary of Deities and Demons in the Bible*. Edited by K. van der Toorn, B. Becking, and P. W. van der Horst. Grand Rapids: Eerdmans, 1999.
Strawn, Brent A. "What Is Cush Doing in Amos 9:7? The Poetics of Exodus in the Plural." *VT* 63, no. 1 (2013): 99–123.
Stuart, Douglas K. *Hosea–Jonah*. WBC 31. Waco, TX: Word, 1987.
Sweeney, Marvin A. "The Dystopianization of Utopian Prophetic Literature: The Case of Amos 9:11-15." In *Utopia and Dystopia in Prophetic Literature*, edited by Ehud Ben Zvi, 175–85. Publications of the Finnish Exegetical Society 92. Göttingen: Vandenhoeck & Ruprecht, 2006.
Sweeney, Marvin A. "The Oracles Concerning the Nations in the Prophetic Literature." In *Concerning the Nations: Essays on the Oracles Against the Nations in Isaiah, Jeremiah and Ezekiel*, edited by Andrew Mein, Else K. Holt, and Hyun Chul Paul Kim, xvii–xx. New York: Bloomsbury, 2015.
Sweeney, Marvin A. *The Twelve Prophets*. Vol. 1. Berit Olam. Collegeville, MN: Liturgical, 2000.
Tajfel, Henri. "Cognitive Aspects of Prejudice." *JSI* 25, no.4 (1969): 79–97.
Tajfel, Henri. *Human Groups and Social Categories: Studies in Social Psychology*. Cambridge: Cambridge University Press, 1981.
Tajfel, Henri. "Individuals and Groups in Social Psychology." *British Journal of Social and Clinical Psychology* 18 (1979): 183–90.
Tajfel, Henri. "Interindividual Behaviour and Intergroup Behaviour." In *Differentiation between Groups: Studies in the Social Psychology of Intergroup Relations*, ed. Henri Tajfel, 27–60. London: Academic, 1978.
Tajfel, Henri. "La catégorisation sociale." In *Introduction Á La Psychologie Sociale*, edited by S. Moscovici, 272–302. Paris: Larousse, 1972.

Tajfel, Henri. "Quantitative Judgement in Social Perception." *BJSP* 50 (1959): 16–29.
Tajfel, Henri. "Social Categorization, Social Identity and Social Comparison." In *Differentiation between Groups: Studies in the Social Psychology of Intergroup Relations*, edited by Henri Tajfel, 61–76. London: Academic, 1978.
Tajfel, Henri. "Social Identity and Intergroup Behavior." *SSI* 13 (1974): 65–93.
Tajfel, Henri. "Value and the Perceptual Judgement of Magnitude." *Psychological Review* 64 (1957): 192–203.
Tajfel, Henri, and S. D. Cawasjee. "Value and the Accentuation of Judged Differences." *JASP* 59 (1959): 436–9.
Tajfel, Henri, and John C. Turner. "An Integrative Theory of Intergroup Conflict." In *The Social Psychology of Intergroup Relations*, 33–47. Monterey, CA: Brooks Cole, 1979.
Tal-Or, Nurit, and Jonathan Cohen. "Understanding Audience Involvement: Conceptualizing and Manipulating Identification and Transportation." *Poetics* 38 (2010): 402–18.
Taylor, Donald M., and Rupert J. Brown. "Towards a More Social Social Psychology?" *British Journal of Social and Clinical Psychology* 18 (1979): 173–80.
Taylor, Gary, and Steve Spencer. Introduction to *Social Identities: Multidisciplinary Approaches*, edited by Gary Taylor and Steve Spencer, 1–13. London: Routledge, 2004.
Thang, Robert Khua Hnin. *The Theology of the Land in Amos 7–9*. Cumbria, CA: Langham Monographs, 2014.
Thompson, Henry O. *The Book of Amos: An Annotated Bibliography*. American Theological Library Association Bibliographies 42. Lanham, MD: Scarecrow, 1997.
Thompson, Suzanne C., Jeffrey C. Kohles, Teresa A. Otsuki, and Douglas R. Kent. "Perceptions of Attitudinal Similarity in Ethnic Groups in the U.S.: Ingroup and Outgroup Homogeneity Effects." *EJSP* 27, no. 2 (1997): 209–20.
Timmer, Daniel. *The Non-Israelite Nations in the Book of the Twelve: Thematic Coherence and the Diachronic–Synchronic Relationship in the Minor Prophets*. Leiden: Brill, 2015.
Timmer, Daniel. "The Use and Abuse of Power in Amos: Identity and Ideology." *JSOT* 39, no. 1 (2014): 101–18.
Triandis, Harry C. "Collectivism and Individualism as Cultural Syndromes." *Cross-Cultural Research* 27, nos. 3–4 (1993): 155–80.
Triandis, Harry C. *Individualism and Collectivism*. New Directions in Social Psychology. New York: Routledge, 2018.
Tromp, N. J. "Amos 5:1–17: Towards a Stylistic and Rhetorical Analysis." In *Prophets, Worship and Theodicy*, 56–84. Old Testament Studies 23. Leiden: Brill, 1984.
Tsevat, Matitiahu. "Amos 7:14—Present or Preterit?" In *The Tablet and the Scroll: Near Eastern Studies in Honor of William W. Hallo*, edited by Mark E. Cohen, Daniel C. Snell, and David B. Weisberg, 256–8. Bethesda, MD: CDL, 1993.
Tucker, Gene M. "Amos the Prophet and Amos the Book: Historical Framework." In *Israel's Prophets and Israel's Past: Essays on the Relationship of Prophetic Texts and Israelite History in Honor of John H. Hayes*, edited by Brad E. Kelle and Megan Bishop Moore, 85–102. New York: T&T Clark, 2006.
Tucker, Gene M. "Prophetic Authenticity: A Form-Critical Study of Amos 7:10-17." *Int* 27, no. 4 (1973): 423–34.
Tucker, Gene M. "The Social Location(s) of Amos: Amos 1:3–2:16." In *Thus Says the Lord: Essays on the Former and Latter Prophets in Honor of Robert R. Wilson*, edited by John J. Ahn and Stephen L. Cook, 273–84. LHBOTS 502. New York: T&T Clark, 2009.

Tucker, J. Brian, and Coleman Baker, eds. *T&T Clark Handbook to Social Identity in the New Testament*. London: Bloomsbury, 2016.

Tulving, Endel. "Episodic and Semantic Memory." In *Organization of Memory*, edited by E. Tulving and W. Donaldson, 381–403. San Diego: Academic, 1972.

Turner, John C. "The Experimental Social Psychology of Intergroup Behaviour." In *Intergroup Behaviour*, edited by John C. Turner and H. Giles, 66–101. Oxford: Blackwell, 1981.

Turner, John C. "Henri Tajfel: An Introduction." In *Social Groups and Identities: Developing the Legacy of Henri Tajfel*, edited by W. Peter Robinson, 1–23. International Series in Social Psychology. Oxford: Butterworth-Heinemann, 1996.

Turner, John C. "Social Categorization and the Self-Concept: A Social Cognitive Theory of Group Behavior." In *Advances in Group Processes*, edited by E. J. Lawler, 2:77–122. Greenwich, CT: JAI, 1985.

Turner, John C. "Social Comparison and Social Identity: Some Prospects for Intergroup Behaviour." *EJSP* 5, no. 1 (1975): 5–34.

Turner, John C. "Towards a Cognitive Redefinition of the Social Group." In *Social Identity and Intergroup Relations*, edited by Henri Tajfel, 15–40. Cambridge: Cambridge University Press, 1982.

Turner, John C., Michael A. Hogg, Penelope Oakes, Stephen D. Reicher, and Margaret S. Wetherell. *Rediscovering the Social Group: A Self-Categorization Theory*. Oxford: Blackwell, 1987.

Turner, J. C., P. J. Oakes, S. A. Haslam, and C. McGarty. "Self and Collective: Cognition and Social Context." *Personality and Social Psychology Bulletin* 20 (1994): 454–63.

Turner, John C., and Rina S. Onorato. "Social Identity, Personality, and the Self-Concept: A Self-Categorization Perspective." In *The Psychology of the Social Self*, edited by T. R. Tyler, R. M. Kramer, and Oliver P. John, 11–46. New York: Psychology Press, 1999.

Turner, John C., and Katherine J. Reynolds. "The Story of Social Identity." In *Rediscovering Social Identity: Key Readings*, edited by Tom Postmes and Nyla R. Branscombe, 13–32. New York: Psychology Press, 2010.

Udoekpo, Michael Ufok. *Re-Thinking the Day of YHWH and Restoration of Fortunes in the Prophet Zephaniah: An Exegetical and Theological Study of 1:14-18; 3:14-20*. Bern, Switzerland: Peter Lang, 2010.

Udoekpo, Michael Ufok. *Rethinking the Prophetic Critique of Worship in Amos 5 for Contemporary Nigeria and the USA*. Eugene, OR: Pickwick, 2017.

Ullendorff, Edward. *Ethiopia and the Bible*. Oxford: Oxford University Press, 1968.

Ulrichsen, Jarl H. "Der Einschub Amos 4,7b–8a. Sprachliche Erwägungen Zu Einem Umstrittenen Text." *Orientalia Suecana* 41–42 (1992): 284–98.

Vallacher, Robin R., Peter T. Coleman, Andrzej Nowak, Lan Bui-Wrzosinska, Larry Liebovitch, Katharina Kugler, and Andrea Bartoli. *Attracted to Conflict: Dynamic Foundations of Destructive Social Relations*. London: Springer, 2014.

Van Leeuwen, Cornelius. "The Prophecy of the Yom Yahweh in Amos V 18-20." In *Language and Meaning, Studies in Hebrew Language and Biblical Exegesis*, edited by A. S. van der Woude, 113–34. OtSt 19. Leiden: Brill, 1974.

Voci, Alberto. "Perceived Group Variability and the Salience of Personal and Social Identity." *European Review of Social Psychology* 11, no. 1 (2000): 177–221.

Vogt, Ernest. "Waw Explicative in Amos 7." *ExpTim* 68 (1957): 301–2.

Volf, Miroslav. *Exclusion and Embrace: A Theological Exploration of Identity, Otherness, and Reconciliation*. Nashville: Abingdon, 1996.

Waard, Jan de. "Chiastic Structure of Amos 5:1-17." *VT* 27, no. 2 (1977): 170–7.
Waard, Jan de, and William A. Smalley. *A Translator's Handbook on the Book of Amos*. New York: United Bible Societies, 1979.
Wal, Adrian van der. *Amos: A Classified Bibliography*. 3rd ed. Amsterdam: Free University Press, 1986.
Waltke, B. K., and M. O'Connor. *An Introduction to Biblical Hebrew Syntax*. Winona Lake, IN: Eisenbrauns, 1990.
Wassen, Cecilia, and Jutta Jokiranta. "Groups in Tension: Sectarianism in the Damascus Document and the Community Rule." In *Sectarianism in Early Judaism: Sociological Advances*, edited by David J. Chalcraft, 205–45. London: Equinox, 2007.
Watts, James W. *Ritual and Rhetoric in Leviticus: From Sacrifice to Scripture*. Cambridge: Cambridge University Press, 2007.
Watts, John D. W. *Vision and Prophecy in Amos*. Grand Rapids: Eerdmans, 1958.
Weiss, Meir. "The Origin of the 'Day of the Lord' Reconsidered." *HUCA* 37 (1966): 29–60.
Weiss, Meir. "The Pattern of the 'Execration Texts' in the Prophetic Literature." *Israel Exploration Journal* 19, no. 3 (1969): 150–7.
Wellhausen, Julius. *Die kleinen Propheten übersetzt und erklärt*. Berlin: de Gruyter, 1963.
Wellhausen, Julius. *Prolegomena to the History of Ancient Israel: With a Reprint of the Article "Israel" from the Encyclopedia Britannica*. 1885. Reprint, Atlanta, GA: Scholars Press, 1994.
Wenham, G. J. "The Priority of P." *VT* 49, no. 2 (1999): 240–58.
Wetherell, Margaret S. "The Field of Identity Studies." In *The Sage Handbook of Identities*, edited by M. S. Wetherell and C. T. Mohanty, 326. London: Sage, 2010.
White, Hugh. "The Value of Speech Act Theory for Old Testament Hermeneutics." *Semeia* 41 (1988): 41–63.
Widengren, Geo. "Israelite-Jewish Religion." In *Historia Religionum: Handbook for the History of Religions*, edited by C. J. Bleeker and G. Widengren, Religions of the Past, 1:223–316. Leiden: Brill, 1969.
Williams, Donald L. "The Theology of Amos." *Review & Expositor* 63, no. 4 (1966): 393–403.
Williamson, H. G. M. "The Prophet and the Plumb-Line: A Redaction-Critical Study of Amos 7." In *In Quest of the Past: Studies on Israelite Religion, Literature, and Prophetism*, edited by A. S. van der Woude, 101–21. OTS 26. Leiden: Brill, 1990.
Wilson, Daniel J. "Copular Predication in Biblical Hebrew." MA thesis, University of the Free State, 2015.
Wilson, Robert R. *Prophecy and Society in Ancient Israel*. Philadelphia: Fortress, 1980.
Wilgus, Jason Blair. "Judgment on Israel: Amos 3–6 Read as a Unity." PhD diss., University of Edinburgh, 2012.
Wittenberg, G. H. "Amos 6:1-7: 'They Dismiss the Day of Disaster but You Bring Near the Rule of Violence.'" *Journal of Theology for Southern Africa* 58 (1987): 57–69.
Wodak, Ruth, Martin Reisigl, Karin Liebhart, and Rudolf de Cillia. *The Discursive Construction of National Identity*. Translated by Angelika Hirsch, Richard Mitten, and J. W. Unger. 2nd ed. Edinburgh: Edinburgh University Press, 2009.
Wöhrle, Jakob. *Die frühen Sammlungen des Zwölfprophetenbuches: Entstehung und Komposition*. BZAW 360. Berlin: de Gruyter, 2006.
Wolff, Hans Walter. *Joel and Amos*. Hermeneia. Philadelphia: Fortress, 1977.

Wolterstorff, Nicholas. "The Promise of Speech-Act Theory for Biblical Interpretation." In *After Pentecost: Language and Biblical Interpretation*, edited by C. Bartholomew, C. Greene, and K. Möller, 73–90. Scripture and Hermeneutics 2. Grand Rapids: Zondervan, 2001.

Wood, Joyce Rilett. *Amos in Song and Book Culture*. JSOTSup 337. London: Sheffield Academic, 2002.

Würthwein, Ernst. "Amos-Studien." *ZAW* 62 (1950): 10–52.

Yee, Gale A. "The Anatomy of Biblical Parody: The Dirge Form in 2 Samuel 1 and Isaiah 14." *CBQ* 50, no. 4 (1988): 565–86.

Zeijdner, H. "Bijdragen der Tekstkritiek Op Het O. T." *Theologische Studien* 4 (1886): 196–204.

Zerubavel, Eviatar. *Social Mindscapes: An Invitation to Cognitive Sociology*. Cambridge, MA: Harvard University Press, 2009.

Zerubavel, Eviatar. *Time Maps: Collective Memory and the Social Shape of the Past*. Chicago: University of Chicago Press, 2003.

Zevit, Ziony. "Expressing Denial in Biblical Hebrew and Mishnaic Hebrew, and in Amos." *VT* 29, no. 4 (1979): 505–9.

Zevit, Ziony. "A Misunderstanding at Bethel: Amos 7:12-17." *VT* 25, no. 4 (1975): 783–90.

Index of References

Hebrew Bible/Old Testament

Genesis
9	96
18:19	76, 77
19	85
19:19-20	85
45:6-8	82

Exodus
1:1–15:21	29
8:22	83
9:3-7	83
9:4	83
9:15	83
9:26	83
10:23	83
11:7	83
12:29	84
31:14	89
34:24	118

Leviticus
7:20-21	89
9:8-24	87
17:4	89
19:8	89
26:3-13	119

Numbers
9:13	89
13:19	87
14:26-35	88
21:35	118
31:26	83
32:13	89

Deuteronomy
2:12	118
6	70
6:20-21	70
26:5	55
28:1-14	119
28:10	118
28:11-12	118
28:22	82
29:8	54

Joshua
1:7	54
5:6	89

Judges
3:13	118

Ruth
1:8	80

1 Samuel
13:22	103

2 Samuel
1:17	111
8:13-14	119
21:1	82
24:11	49

1 Kings
8:37	82
12:31-32	50
13:33	50
17:1	82
22:1-28	50

2 Kings
13:7	36
14:25	72
18:15	54

2 Chronicles
6:28	82
9:29	49
33:1	55
35:25	111

Psalms
40:4 Eng.	91
40:5	91
95:8	89

Proverbs
17:10	81
21:31	103
27:22	81

Isaiah
13–23	35
14	111
16:5	117
29:6	103
56–66	28
63:1-6	27, 28
66:15	103

Jeremiah
1:5	76
5:12	81
7:22	88, 89
7:29	111
9:10	111
11:22	81

Jeremiah (cont.)

14:12-13	81	2:1	62	1:14	102, 103, 108
14:15-16	81	2:15 Eng.	79		
14:18	81	2:17	79	1:15	103, 108
15:2	81	2:20 Eng.	76	2–3	80
16:4	81	2:22	76	2:1-3	35
18:21	81	3:4	88	2:1	37, 44
21:7	81	10:14	103	2:2-3	103
21:9	81	11:1	79	2:4-5	35, 42
24:10	81	11:2	79	2:4	35, 36, 38, 44, 91
25–31 LXX	43	13:4	77		
26–32 LXX	35			2:5	103
27:8	81	*Joel*		2:6-16	42, 44, 45
27:13	81	1:4	83	2:6-12	104, 125
29:6	103	2:25	83	2:6-8	73, 74, 79
29:17-18	81	3:16	33	2:6	36, 45, 65, 73
30:6	82	3:17	33		
32:24	81	3:20-21	33	2:7	65
32:36	81			2:9-12	42, 58, 68, 73
34:17	81	*Amos*			
36:7	115	1–2	85	2:9-11	73
38:2	81	1:1-2	32, 45	2:9-10	72
38:9	81	1:1	32, 34, 40, 46	2:9-1	113
42:16-17	81			2:9	73, 74, 104
42:22	81	1:2	32-34, 36		
44:12-13	81	1:3–2:16	6, 31, 34, 35, 42	2:10-13	75
44:18	81			2:10-12	73
44:27	81	1:3–2:5	36, 97	2:10	72-75
46–51 LXX	43	1:3–2:4	124	2:11	73
46–51	35	1:3–2:3	78	2:12	53, 73, 79, 108
52:6	81	1:3-5	35, 97		
		1:3	43, 98	2:13-16	104
Ezekiel		1:4-5	103	2:14-16	74
19:1	111	1:5	41, 48	2:14-15	110
25–32	35	1:6-8	35, 97	2:16	97, 102, 104
26:17	111	1:6	35, 36, 43, 98		
27–28	111			3	74, 78, 95
27:2	111	1:7-8	103	3:1-2	58, 68, 74, 80, 84
28:12	111	1:8	41, 109		
32:2	111	1:9-10	35	3:1	45, 61, 62, 72, 75, 79
		1:9	36, 41, 43		
Daniel		1:10	103	3:2	61, 62, 75–9, 86, 94, 95, 99, 116
11:8	83	1:11-12	35, 41		
		1:11	41		
Hosea		1:12	103		
1:8-9	61	1:13-15	41	3:6	63
1:10 Eng.	62	1:13	36, 38, 44	3:7	32, 108
		1:14-15	103, 105	3:9–4:3	79

3:9-11	114	5:5	48, 112,	5:26	87, 90–2
3:9	98, 104		114	5:27	48, 90, 98
3:10	31, 79, 107	5:6	61, 104, 111, 112	6 6:1-17	107 106
3:11	64, 105, 110	5:7 5:8-9	111, 112 54, 107,	6:1-3 6:1	106 106, 116
3:12	79, 105, 106, 110, 115	5:8 5:10-13	111, 112 106, 112 111	6:2 6:3	98 102, 106, 107
3:13	74, 79	5:10-12	112	6:5	117
3:14-15	104	5:10-11	112	6:6	107
3:14	79, 102, 104, 109	5:10	53, 115, 119	6:7-9 6:7-8	114 107
4	79	5:11	65, 113, 119	6:7 6:9	48, 103 63, 110
4:1-3	79, 80		115		
4:1	62, 74, 79, 80, 105, 116	5:12-13 5:12 5:13	65, 113 53, 108, 112, 119	6:13 6:14 7–9	72 64 33, 45, 60, 94
4:2-3	48, 103				
4:2	102, 105	5:14-15	110–12, 115	7:1-3 7:1	45 45
4:4-5	80, 113, 116	5:14	61, 86, 106, 111,	7:2-3 7:3	114 46
4:4	58, 104		112	7:4-6	45, 104
4:6-11	58, 68, 72, 79–81, 113, 114	5:15	61, 109, 110, 112, 114, 115	7:4 7:5-6 7:6	45 114 46
4:6	81, 82	5:16-17	111, 115,	7:7-9	46
4:7-8	82		119	7:7	45
4:9	82	5:17	48	7:8	46, 48, 60,
4:10	83, 85	5:18-23	106		65, 81
4:11	72, 84	5:18-20	86, 102,	7:9	47, 48, 60
4:12	62, 81, 85		105, 106	7:10-17	6, 32, 45,
4:13–5:8	107	5:18	105, 106,		46, 124
4:13	107		109, 116	7:10-11	47
5:1-17	54, 110, 113	5:19	106, 107 86, 92	7:10 7:11	47, 63 47, 103
5:1-3	111	5:21-27 5:21-24	92	7:12-13	47, 49,
5:1	62, 74, 79, 105	5:21-23 5:21-22	106 86	7:12	108, 116 63
5:2	108, 111, 117	5:23 5:24	86 106	7:13	57, 104, 109
5:3	63, 109–11, 115	5:25-26	86, 87, 92, 93	7:14-17 7:14-16	47, 54 125
5:4-6	111, 115	5:25	72, 86–8,	7:14	54, 57
5:4-5	111		90, 91	7:15	55–61, 65,
5:4	61, 104	5:26-27	68		81, 86

Amos (cont.)		9:3	106	*Jonah*		
7:16-17	62	9:4	46, 48, 98, 115	3:9	115	
7:17	48, 63, 103	9:5-6	94, 108	*Micah*		
8	107, 108	9:5	108	4:1-5	119	
8:1-14	107	9:7-8	97			
8:1-3	46	9:7	45, 68, 78, 94, 96–9, 104, 116	*Zephaniah*		
8:1	45			2:3	115	
8:2	46, 60, 65, 81, 107, 114	9:8-10	110, 115-18	*Haggai* 2:17	82	
8:3	102, 107, 109	9:8	98, 116	*Zechariah*		
		9:9	116			
8:4-10	119	9:10	116	14:5	33	
8:4-6	107	9:11-15	60, 61, 90, 101, 102, 116, 117, 120, 121, 124	NEW TESTAMENT *John*		
8:4	74					
8:6	65					
8:7	108			2:16	61	
8:8-9	108					
8:8	108	9:11-12 LXX	126	*Acts*		
8:9	102, 107	9:11-12	62	7:42-43	92	
8:10	108, 111	9:11	93, 117, 119, 120	7:43	92	
8:11-12	108			15	126	
8:11	102	9:12	24, 62, 109, 118–20	15:16-18	126	
8:13	102, 107, 108			*Dead Sea Scrolls*		
8:14	91, 108	9:13-15	119	CD 7:14-15	92	
9:1-10	98	9:13	117			
9:1-4	46, 94, 98, 110, 114, 115	9:14	60, 61, 119			
		9:15	120			
9:1	110					

Index of Authors

Abrams, D. 9, 10, 14, 15, 17, 45, 126
Ackroyd, P. R. 57
Adamo, D. T. 94, 96, 97
Adams, J. W. 5
Alter, R. 39
Andersen, F. I. 34, 39, 51, 53, 59, 73, 80, 84, 85, 90, 91, 96, 106, 110, 111, 114
Andiñach, P. R. 64
Arnold, B. T. 101
Assmann, J. 70, 71, 99

Bach, R. 57
Baker, C. A. 4, 25, 59
Bamberg, M. 23, 27
Barentsen, J. 23
Barker, J. D. 102
Barsalou, L. W. 22
Barstad, H. M. 3, 70, 71, 80, 87, 90, 93, 102, 106, 108, 110, 115
Bartelmus, R. 55
Barton, J. 2, 3, 7, 36–8, 68, 77, 80, 88, 102
Bell, R. D. 3
Ben Zvi, E. 3, 71, 72
Bentzen, A. 37
Berger, P. L. 6
Berquist, J. L. 91, 92
Biddle, M. E. 116
Billig, M. 126
Bird, P. A. 2
Blanz, M. 20, 50
Blenkinsopp, J. 50, 52, 55, 56
Bliuc, A.-M. 19
Bongiorno, R. 19
Bons, E. 91
Bosman, J. P. 6, 25, 44
Botha, J. E. 5
Boyle, M. O'R. 76
Branscombe, N. R. 52
Brettler, M. Z. 2, 91

Briggs, R. S. 5
Brinthaupt, T. M. 9
Brown, R. 32
Brown, R. J. 12
Brueggemann, W. 62, 63, 77, 81, 96, 97, 99, 125
Buss, M. J. 3
Byrskog, S. 25, 69

Campos, M. E. 56
Carroll R., M. D. 2, 3, 34, 41, 42, 51, 54, 64, 65, 68, 81, 84, 85, 90, 104, 107–9, 112–15
Cathcart, K. J. 105
Cawasjee, S. D. 11
Childs, B. S. 5
Chisholm, R. B., Jr. 35
Christensen, D. L. 35, 36, 41
Cinnirella, M. 66, 120
Claassens, L. J. 64
Clements, R. E. 37, 75
Clifford, H. 87
Cohen, J. 121
Cohen, S. 43, 49
Coleman, J. 69
Collins, J. J. 68
Condor, S. 32, 66, 121
Coote, R. B. 90
Coser, L. 69
Cripps, R. S. 90, 118
Crouch, C. L. 36, 108

Davidson, B. 22
Davies, E. W. 7
Davis, A. R. 3, 49
De Fina, A. 23, 27
De Hulster, I. J. 28
Dearman, J. A. 2
Dell, K. J. 85
Dicou, B. 62

Dorsey, D. A. 110
Driver, G. R. 49, 55, 57
Driver, S. R. 90
Dunne, J. A. 118

Edelman, D. V. 61
Eidevall, G. 34, 36, 38, 39, 46, 48, 51, 56, 74, 80–2, 84, 88–91, 95, 97, 104, 110, 117
Ellemers, N. 15, 17, 50
Emerson, M. O. 5
Erikson, E. H. 9
Escobar, D. S. 2
Esler, P. F. 44, 59, 67
Everson, A. J. 105

Fensham, F. C. 37, 102
Ferguson, N. 1
Fields, W. 84
Filtvedt, O. J. 4, 7, 9, 23, 24, 67, 126
Fitzgerald, A. 82
Fleming, D. E. 102
Franke, C. 64
Freedman, D. N. 34, 39, 40, 51, 53, 59, 73, 80, 84, 85, 90, 91, 96, 106, 110, 111, 114
Fuligni, A. J. 16

García-Treto, F. O. 48
Garrett, D. A. 34, 47, 49, 80, 87, 90, 92, 93, 105, 110, 112, 119
Garton, R. E. 79
Gass, E. 55, 57
Geertz, C. 51
Gertz, J. C. 87
Gevirtz, S. 91, 92
Giffone, B. D. 4
Gillingham, S. 107
Glenny, W. E. 90, 91, 93
Goering, G. S. 111
Goffman, E. 8
Goldenberg, D. M 95
Goswell, G. 117, 118
Gottwald, N. K. 35
Gowan, D. E. 113
Greer, J. S. 3, 106

Hadjiev, T. S. 2, 35, 40, 73, 74, 81, 84, 90, 97, 106, 112, 114, 116
Hakola, R. 25

Halbwachs, M. 69
Hardie, E. A. 18
Harper, W. R. 40, 53, 74, 83, 91, 92, 95, 114, 118
Hasel, G. F. 2, 77, 101, 109, 114, 116, 121
Haslam, S. 10, 12, 14, 16, 18, 20–2, 45, 50, 67, 121
Hayes, J. H. 52, 73, 81, 82, 84, 89, 90, 92, 96, 106, 110, 112, 114, 117
Hays, J. D. 97
Hendel, R. S. 78
Hilton, D. J. 67
Hjelm, T. 6
Hoffmann, Y. 105
Hoffmeier, J. K. 52
Hogg, M. A. 9–11, 13–15, 17, 18, 22, 23, 45, 126
Holladay, W. L. 77
Holter, K. 97
Horrell, D. G. 9
Horton, R. F. 96
House, P. R. 102
Houston, W. J. 2, 5, 24, 33, 68, 107, 110, 114
Hubbard, D. A. 88, 90, 114
Hübenthal, S. 70
Huffmon, H. B. 75, 76
Hunter, A. V. 113, 114
Hutton, J. M. 38

Iggers, G. G. 68
Irudayaraj, D. S. 28
Irwin, B. 80
Isbell, C. 90

Jackson, J. J. 54
Jackson, L. A. 15
Jackson, R. L. 8
Jaruzelska, I. 2, 50
Jemielity, T. 85
Jenkins, R. 5, 8, 9
Jeremias, J. 34, 46, 51, 55, 84, 90, 91, 110, 112, 114
Jokiranta, J. 15, 25, 28
Jonker, L. C. 4, 26, 27, 126
Joyce, P. M. 3

Kakkanattu, J. P. 61
Kapelrud, A. S. 37, 55

Keener, C. S. 92
Keil, C. F. 96
Kelle, B. E. 68, 78
Kellermann, U. 62
Kessler, J. 80, 81
Kim, J.-W. 92
King, A. M. 44, 109
King, P. J. 82
Kleven, T. 80
Knippenberg, A. Van 50
Kraus, H.-J. 88
Kuecker, A. 10, 126

Lacoviello, V. 14
Lam, J. 79
Lanchester, H. C. O. 49, 90
Lau, P. H. 26, 75
Lehming, S. 56
Leininger, A. 16
Lemaine, G. 16
Lemos, T. M. 64
Lessing, R. R. 34, 84, 90, 110, 113
Levin, C. 33, 71
Levy, D. 69, 70
Lieu, J. M. 4, 5, 23, 24
Lim, K. Y. 66
Linville, J. R. 34, 40, 55, 56, 81, 90, 91, 103, 110, 126
Liu, J. H. 67
Lo, A. 110, 116
Lohfink, N. 75
Luckmann, T. 6
Luomanen, P. 6
Lust, J. 111

Marohl, M. J. 66, 67
Martin-Achard, R. 95
Mays, J. L. 1, 48, 50–2, 55, 61, 74, 90, 91, 110, 114
McConville, J. G. 60
McGarty, C. 19
McKeown, S. 1
McLaughlin, J. L. 106
McNally, R. J. 70
Meier, S. A. 91
Melugin, R. F. 2, 51, 52
Miller, C. L. 54
Miller, P. D. 47, 51, 61
Möller, K. 32, 34, 35, 39, 40, 73, 79, 81, 110, 114, 116

Moore, M. B. 68
Moughtin-Mumby, S. 106

Nägele, S. 118
Nam, R. S. 33
Nicholson, E. W. 77
Noble, P. 37, 39, 42, 43, 50, 51, 74, 78, 101, 103, 110, 113–16
Nogalski, J. D. 34, 116
Nwaoru, E. O. 80

O'Brien, J. M. 64
O'Connell, R. H. 41
O'Connor, M. 55
Oakes, P. J. 13, 19–22, 45, 49, 50
Ogden, D. K. 84
Olick, J. K. 69, 70
Onorato, R. S. 19

Park, A. W. 90, 93
Park, S. H. 101, 114
Parker, S. B. 75, 76
Paul, S. M. 33, 34, 36, 38, 40, 41, 46, 49, 52, 54, 55, 57, 64, 76, 81, 83, 84, 86, 87, 90, 96, 104–6, 110–13, 116–18
Peters, R. S. 11
Pfeifer, G. 3
Piper, R. A. 59
Platow, M. J. 12, 13, 16, 18, 20, 21, 67, 121
Polley, M. E. 37, 106
Pomykala, K. E. 117
Postmes, T. 19

Raabe, P. R. 38, 43
Rad, G. von 102, 105
Radine, J. 32, 36, 78, 91, 106, 118
Raitt, T. M. 113
Ranke, L. von 68
Reicher, S. D. 12, 13, 16, 18–21, 67, 121
Reimer, H. 2
Reventlow, H. G. 37
Reynolds, K. J. 14, 18
Rice, G. 95, 96
Richardson, H. N. 57, 117
Ridge, D. B. 54, 55, 57, 58
Rilett Wood, J. 91, 113
Rivera, G. J. 16
Roberts, H. C. 2
Roberts, J. J. M. 107

Index of Authors

Rosch, E. 22
Rottzoll, D. U. 2, 56
Routledge, R. 99
Rowley, H. H. 55, 79
Rudolph, W. 84, 88
Ryou, D. H. 40

Sadler, R. S. 94–7
Sandt, H. van de 92
Schart, A. 2
Schiffrin, D. 23, 27
Schmid, H. 118
Schmidt, W. H. 75, 89
Scholz, S. 64
Seibert, E. A. 64
Seitz, C. R. 66
Seleznev, M. 54
Sewell, D. R. 22
Sharp, C. J. 33, 46, 121
Shea, W. H. 82
Shepherd, M. B. 90, 92
Shirer, W. L. 67
Shulman, D. 8
Ska, J. L. 87
Smalley, W. A. 90, 112
Smend, R. 55
Smith, C. 5, 127
Smith, G. V. 53, 68, 74, 90, 96, 114
Smith, M. S. 106
Snodgrass, K. 4, 123
Soggin, J. A. 49, 51–3, 81, 84, 87–90
Sohn, S.-T. 76, 77
Spencer, S. 23
Stargel, L. M. 29, 66
Stavrakopoulou, A> E. 51
Steinmann, A. E. 35
Stets, J. E. 9
Steyn, G. J. 92
Stol, M. 91
Strawn, B. A. 95, 98
Stuart, D. K. 53, 87, 90, 117
Sweeney, M. A. 35, 88, 91, 117

Tajfel, H. 10–17, 32, 43, 44
Tal-Or, N. 43
Taylor, D. M. 12
Taylor, G. 23
Thang, R. K. H. 60, 63, 74, 117, 119
Thompson, H. O. 2, 45
Timmer, D. 2, 62, 118, 119

Triandis, H. C. 75
Tromp, N. J. 110
Tsevat, M. 56
Tucker, G. M. 33, 35, 51
Tucker, J. B. 25
Tulving, E. 70
Turner, J. C. 10–22, 32, 50

Udoekpo, M. U. 102, 114
Ullendorf, E. 95
Ulrichsen, J. H. 82

Vallacher, R. R. 32
Van Leeuwen, C. 105
Vinitzky-Seroussi, V. 69, 70
Voci, A. 45
Vogt, E. 56, 58
Volf, M. 5

Waard, J. de 90, 110, 112
Wal, A. van der 2
Waltke, B. K. 55
Wassen, C. 28
Watts, J. 51, 57, 89
Weiss, M. 37, 102
Welch, A. 84, 85
Wellhausen, J. 87, 96
Wenham, G. J. 87
Wetherell, M. S. 8
White, H. 5
Widengren, G. 77
Wilgus, J. B. 64, 80, 81, 86, 92, 93, 110
Williams, D. L. 3
Williamson, H. G. M. 46
Wilson, D. J. 54
Wilson, R. R. 52, 55
Wittenberg, G. H. 107
Wodak, R. 23, 24
Wöhrle, J. 35
Wolff, H. W. 34, 36, 37, 49, 52, 56–8, 60,
  62, 74, 80, 82–4, 87, 90, 91, 96, 107,
  110, 113, 115, 117
Wolterstorff, N. 5
Würthwein, E. 36, 52, 55

Yee, G. A. 111

Zeijdner, H. 83
Zerubavel, E. 67, 69, 70, 72, 93, 118
Zevit, Z. 56

www.ingramcontent.com/pod-product-compliance
Lightning Source LLC
Chambersburg PA
CBHW070642300426
44111CB00013B/2222